KENNETH NEWMAN

BIRDS

of the
Kruger
National Park

R50-70

1991 UPDATE

SOUTHERN
BOOK PUBLISHERS

ISBN 1 86812 377 4

Revised (second) edition, first impression 1991
Southern Book Publishers (Pty) Ltd
P O Box 3103, Halfway House 1685

Previously published by
Macmillan South Africa (Publishers) (Pty) Ltd

Cover design by Graphicor (Pty) Ltd
Set in $7\frac{1}{2}$ on 8 pt Univers
by Unifoto, Cape Town
Printed and bound by Marwin Productions Ltd., Hong Kong

FOREWORD

The major zoogeographical regions and wondrously varied ecosystems and habitats of the southern African subcontinent support an almost boundless diversity of vertebrate and invertebrate animal life. One of the outstanding glories of South Africa's wealthy animal life is its avifauna. Of the over 800 species listed for this region, many species are unfortunately dependent on specialised habitats, which are increasingly threatened today by the destructive by-products of human endeavour and unrestricted population growth. It is a sad fact that many species of birds in South Africa will eventually find complete protection, as elsewhere in the world, only in the larger national parks and wildlife reserves. Of these major conservation areas the Kruger National Park is the most important, as its 1 984 528 ha area of Transvaal Lowveld affords permanent or semi-permanent sanctuary to no less than 507 species of birds. This represents more than 58 per cent of the total number of species of birds in South Africa and a wider spectrum of protected species than for any other vertebrate class in the Park.

One could attribute this to the greater mobility of birds when compared with other vertebrates, which also explains the fact that only about half of the bird species in the Kruger Park can be considered as resident throughout the year. About 7,5 per cent are summer migrants to southern Africa, some 18 per cent are occasional vagrants to the area, while about 23 per cent are regular nomads to the area. A few species (1,5 per cent) are thought to visit the area only during winter.

The Kruger National Park, bordering the edge of the tropics and situated at the southern end of the Lowveld that commences in Zimbabwe, is an area of faunal transition. The affinities of the avifauna of the area are predominantly with the northern tropical fauna, but also include interesting elements of the South West Arid fauna, the Eastern Coastal fauna, the Southern Temperate fauna and even, on rare occasions, of the Marine fauna (seabirds are sometimes blown across the coast and the adjoining Lebombo mountains by cyclones along the Mozambique coast).

The general physiography and vegetational milieu of the Kruger Park include several subregions which constitute unique habitats from an ornithological point of view. These include the riparian forest along the Luvuvhu river at Pafuri, the *Androstachys* forests of the Bangu gorge area and the remote Nwambiya sandveld community along the eastern boundary, south of Pafuri. A number of bird species have been recorded here for the first time within the geographical boundaries of the Republic of South Africa, and they all represent major study areas for the professional or keen amateur ornithologist.

In view of the splendid opportunities offered by the Kruger Park for both the serious student of our rich array of avifauna and the casual birdwatcher, it has long been a major objective of the National Parks Board properly to introduce and interpret this important aspect of our animal life to visitors to this region.

As far back as 1961 Pienaar and Prozesky compiled a checklist of the birds of the Kruger National Park in *Koedoe*, with additions to this list in 1967. A pictorial guide to the birds of the Kruger Park was also published, in several volumes, by the National Parks Board in 1958-65. Subsequently, in 1974, A. Kemp produced an illustrated monograph on the distribution and status of the birds of the Kruger Park.

None of these publications, however, fulfilled the purpose of a complete and fully illustrated guide-book to the avifauna of this important conservation area.

We were fortunate indeed therefore when the renowned artist and ornithologist, Kenneth Newman, offered his services for this purpose. The result of his labours is this very detailed and magnificently illustrated fieldguide. All the bird species that have been recorded frequently in the Kruger Park to date are illustrated in full colour, and the interpretative value of the book is further enhanced by comprehensive notes on the natural history and identification characters of each species. The volume is fully cross-indexed and provided with complete lists of English and Afrikaans vernacular names, as well as scientific names.

This book will undoubtedly remain a standard work of reference for many years to come and will contribute immensely to the education and enjoyment of our visitors.

It therefore gives me great pleasure to introduce this valuable aid to our visiting public and it is my wish that they will use it to perceive and to appreciate the true splendour of our birdlife as well as the important role of birds in the ecology of this great National Park.

Dr U. de V. Pienaar
Chief Director, National Parks Board

CONTENTS

PREFACE

In 1950 two colleagues persuaded me to join them in what was to be my first visit to the Kruger National Park. We left Johannesburg on a Friday afternoon and eventually reached the entrance gate at Crocodile Bridge later that night, intending to have a few hours of well-earned rest in the car until the gate opened next morning. Perhaps I managed a few brief cat-naps just prior to dawn but much of that night was spent very wide-eyed while my friends slumbered peacefully.

Just ahead of the car was the firmly locked but flimsy entrance gate separating us, as I imagined, from the hordes of lurking big cats and other creatures which bite in the night. Behind us was the low causeway over the Crocodile River, its dark, slow-moving waters doubtlessly concealing countless numbers of those sinister reptiles after which it was named. On either side of the narrow dirt track on which we were parked tall, yellow 'elephant grass', just discernible in the pale light of a new moon, dwarfed us; beyond it was a black void only intensified by contrast if the car lights were switched on. I was highly apprehensive, terrified, to be truthful, of every rustle in the grass, each falling leaf; my imagination working overtime.

When the dawn finally dawned and our surroundings took shape, everything suddenly looked peacefully innocent. Just beyond that sinister wall of yellow grass was a small thatched hut from which a sleepy gate-keeper duly emerged. Across the water were agricultural fields, while the river itself, now bathed in warm sunshine, became alive. A kingfisher perched on a telephone wire and repeatedly dived or hovered for its breakfast, while dozens of other birds filled the air with mellow song. Darkest Africa had transformed itself.

I shall never forget the thrill of that first entry into the Park. It is a thrill I still experience when I go there, and I hope that I shall never lose it. Keyed-up with suppressed excitement and the promise of what lay ahead, we drove slowly towards Lower Sabie camp, three pairs of eyes scanning every bush and grass tuft. The soft roadside sand, smoothly settled from a recent rain shower, revealed numerous tantalising footprints left behind by the animals that had passed during the night. Most had melted into the bush long before our arrival but one group of impressions, different from the rest, intrigued us as they followed the road for some distance, sometimes on one side, sometimes on the other. They were an odd arrangement of mostly three points, occasionally four, and obviously left by more than one animal. We decided that claws were responsible and, confident of eventually catching up with the mysterious beasts, we pressed on with our eyes glued to the road and cameras at the ready. Alas, our first attempt at spooring ended in chaos and confusion. As we negotiated a sharp bend in the road we literally knocked our quarry flying. Five enormous black and white birds erupted into the air, seemingly from under the car wheels. They didn't fly far but resettled again just ahead and safely off the road. Both sides hastily adjusted ruffled feathers and took stock, the birds with indignant strides and backward glances over broad shoulders and we three all crowded at one window. Our first wild animals were the strangest birds I'd ever seen, enormous by normal bird standards, entirely black when walking, with bare red skin around their faces and vulgar balloon-like appendages at their throats. Their bills were massive and appeared not to close properly, their eyes swivelled about in a most unbirdlike and seductive fashion beneath long, sexy eyelashes and, to cap it all, they pranced along on tiptoe. Here at last was the explanation of those strange three- or four-pointed footprints, but one could not help thinking that a handbag slung over each wing would not have seemed out of place. We were still ogling these strange creatures when another car approached from the opposite direction. Passing us slowly, an apparently very knowledgeable gentleman leaned out of the driver's window and announced, in a rather superior manner, 'Turkey-buzzards!' Thus enlightened we pressed on in the comforting knowledge that, henceforth, we would know our turkey-buzzards when we saw them.

The more I thought of that name the more it worried me. My knowledge of birds was not extensive but I did know that a buzzard was a species of hawk, whereas those five beauties that we had encountered looked anything but hawk-like. As for turkeys the only likeness, it seemed to me, was the bladder-like appendages at their throats. I had seen buzzards and eaten turkeys, and the mind boggled at the possibility of the two interbreeding.

In fact this was the first of many bird identity problems which beset me on that first trip to the Park. It was not until our return home that I was able to consult Roberts' *Birds of South Africa* and establish what I had suspected, that turkey-buzzards did not exist in Africa. Our long-lashed birds were Ground Hornbills; those smaller black and white, rather comical birds with enormous yellow or red bills were not toucans but also hornbills, while the colourful azure-winged beauties frequently seen at roadsides were not Blue Jays but Lilacbreasted Rollers.

For some years following this first visit to the Kruger Park there was nothing available to help one identify bird species specific to the Park until the first of the late Mrs T. Campbell's multi-volume guides was published in 1958. These were a great help for many years and proved very popular, but they still fell short of providing a comprehensive coverage of all the bird species occurring in the Park. As the years passed and the annual number of people visiting the Kruger Park increased manyfold over what it had been in the early fifties, one heard with increasing frequency about the birds that visitors had seen there. With the worldwide wildlife awareness that blossomed in the 1960s, more and more people were taking an interest in the smaller creatures, especially the birds, and this trend continues to snowball. Bird-watching has become trendy and 'twitching' new species a competitive sport among its adherents. The Kruger Park, having as it does more than half of southern Africa's total bird species within its boundaries, caters handsomely for both local birders and the many thousands visiting each year from other countries. There was a clear need for a comprehensive guide, uncluttered by species that do not occur in the Park.

As the reader will have gleaned from Dr Pienaar's foreword to this book, a great deal of groundwork had already been covered prior to the 1960s by members of the Park's staff and other interested persons, although it remained unpublished. This work culminated in 1969 in the checklist produced by Dr A.C. Kemp, initially in cyclostyled form and, later, as a printed and partially illustrated checklist. Dr Kemp produced his checklist as a secondary work while engaged in a scientific study of the hornbills in the Satara region. While doing his daily routine of hornbill watching, he recorded other bird species and their relevant population densities, over a two-and-a-half year period, plotting their positions on a map. This resulted in the compilation of a thorough record of birds in the Satara or central region of the Park. Unfortunately Dr Kemp's studies did not necessitate more than an occasional visit to the northern and southern regions and so, understandably, the resultant checklist was somewhat biased in favour of the central region.

It happened that I had been keeping lists of the birds seen during infrequent visits to the Park for some years and when, in late 1972, I decided to start this present work, I used Dr Kemp's checklist as my springboard, expanding his known distribution data where possible, adding new information about each species as it came to hand and, of course, those cherry-on-the-pie sightings, a 'new' species for the Park. It is to the credit of Dr Kemp and others who produced earlier checklists that, although about thirty so-called new species have been discovered in subsequent years, only about two fall into the category of common, the rest being rare or very uncommon. From the start I have enjoyed the encouragement and friendship of Dr Alan Kemp and his charming wife Meg, and they have continued to add their more recent records to my own.

I have also enjoyed constant encouragement and cooperation from Dr U. de V. Pienaar, Chief Director of the National Parks Board and formerly Warden of the Kruger National Park, and all members of his staff that it was my pleasure to meet during the writing of this book. Every help and facility was at my disposal when needed and I am indeed grateful for it.

Finally, it is my hope that this fieldguide will encourage amateur and professional ornithologists alike to add new information about birds and their distribution in the Park, since I am fully aware that any work of this nature must be almost out of date by the time it is published. It is also my sincere hope that users of this little book will derive as much pleasure from the birds in the Kruger National Park as I have done.

K.N.

ACKNOWLEDGEMENTS

The fieldwork for this book would have produced very incomplete results had I not received help in various forms from friends interested in the project. I wish to especially acknowledge the hospitality and kindness extended within the Park to my wife and myself on numerous occasions by members of the staff, with whom it has been our pleasure to work and who have become lasting friends. Firstly, Mike and André English, who have so often made us welcome in their bushveld home and have taken a special interest in the work, while conveying us over many a rough track to remote corners of the Park with their sons Don and Ross (since grown to manhood and doing similar work to their father). To Don especially for his tireless enthusiasm and ability in finding birds' nests and supplying me with breeding records too numerous to count. Then to Ted and Sue Whitfield who have also put out the red carpet for us at their home in the Park, Ted having pursued moorhens and larks on my behalf and taken me on many a rewarding jaunt; to Flip Nel at his (then) lonely but paradisal home at Pafuri, who showed me seven Fishing Owls in less than three hours and shared with me the sighting of South Africa's first Redthroated Twinspot; to the late Harold Mockford, also at Pafuri, who supplied so many valuable bird records from his more than forty years' knowledge of the region; to Johan Kloppers, Tom Molentze, the late Thys Mostert and Johan van Graan, who have been our guides and companions on many interesting and rewarding trips; and to Ian Whyte who has been, and continues to be, most helpful in many ways.

Some of the fieldwork for the Skukuza area was undertaken at various times just over the fence, in the Sabie Sands Game Reserve, where it was possible to undertake some valuable work on foot along the Sabie and Sand Rivers without incurring the indignation of tourists who are confined to their cars. For these opportunities I wish to say a very special thanks to Irene Chalkley, her daughter Louise and son-in-law John for many an enjoyable stay at their farm Kingston (affectionately known as 'Warthog Wallow').

Then there are those many kind bird-watching friends, both in and outside the Park, most known to me but some unknown, and now too numerous to mention individually, who have sent me lists of the birds they have seen in the Park. In very many cases these lists and specific sightings have involved records of new species or fresh information about the distribution of listed species. It is this continual inflow of new data that has made this major revision possible, and I am extremely grateful to them all for their generous response. Indeed this latest edition of *Birds of the Kruger Park* is the result of a cooperative effort of all who are interested in the birds of the region. Long may it continue.

INTRODUCTION

It is important to realise that this little book is a fieldguide designed with the sole purpose of helping the user to locate and identify the many birds that occur in the Kruger National Park. It does not pretend to be a handbook, giving comprehensive information on any species. Those seeking further information on species, their distribution outside the Park, their breeding habits, etc. are recommended to consult *Roberts' Birds of Southern Africa.*

Within the Kruger National Park bird populations tend to fluctuate within any year and also from year to year. The main cause of annual fluctuations is the arrival in spring or early summer and departure in autumn, of large numbers of birds from elsewhere in Africa (the intra-Africa migrants) and from the northern hemisphere (the Palaearctic migrants). These annual visitors to southern Africa number many millions, and the Kruger Park gets its fair share of them. Some birds are called altitudinal migrants and their movements may be connected with better living conditions at lower levels in winter, that is, higher temperatures ensuring a more adequate food supply. Others, such as many frugivorous and granivorous birds, may move into the Park in response to seasonal fruit or grass-seed abundances, and may breed while there. Bird movements are still incompletely understood and the reasons behind the actions of many species are still in need of closer study.

Yet another factor influencing local bird movements is weather. In drought years, for example, many bird species may be entirely absent from the more stricken areas while others not normally present, such as some coursers, plovers and the Larklike Bunting (Plate 107) may abound temporarily, breeding and making the most of the optimum conditions. In years of good rains, when the foliage and grass cover are lush and the dams and pans full, many species that benefit from these conditions flourish and may temporarily extend their normal ranges within the Park. In these circumstances breeding will reach a peak and we will suddenly be aware of population increases in certain types of birds, especially those associated with water.

All these fluctuations are part of the normal picture. Species numbers may rise and fall, sometimes to surprisingly low levels, without having any lasting effect on the population's viability. A good example of this phenomenon is to be seen in the Openbilled Stork, a water-associated stork (Plate 8), which normally occurs near dams and pans in the north and east of the Park. Sometimes, for several years in succession, Openbills may be uncommon, appearing singly or in pairs only at scattered points. This usually happens because good rains have not fallen for several summers and conditions have not been suitable for their breeding. Then a good wet summer arrives, the Limpopo River spills over its banks and floodpans that may have stood empty for several years are filled. Immediately the Openbills move in, build their nests in the canopies of water-surrounded thorn trees and, by the end of summer, the Openbill population within the Park may rise from two dozen to five dozen. Should the following summer also be a wet one (and wet years frequently come in cycles), the birds will breed again and once more the numbers will leap. This trend may continue for four or five years and Openbills will be anything but uncommon in the Park.

Habitats

The type of habitat used by a bird is an all-important factor in its life. Many would disappear entirely if their preferred habitats were to go, since they would be unable to adapt to any other. Some species of birds are scarce or are strictly localised in the Park because their habitats are restricted. This state of affairs is particularly noticeable in wet-ground loving species, crakes, snipes and many other small wading birds, because a bush habitat does not boast many marshes. In many cases it is man's provision of dams that has created adjacent mini-marshes and increased both numbers and ranges of such species. Other uncommon habitat types are those preferred by rock-loving birds, rocky hills, cliffs and gorges, while yet another is well-developed riverine forest. True sandveld too is present only in the north-east, to the south of Pafuri, where the Nwambiya sandveld intrudes from Zimbabwe and Mozambique. It is here that one encounters a few species having affinities with the dry west.

Basically the Kruger National Park is a bushveld habitat divided into regions favouring certain dominant tree types, which in turn are dictated by soil types. The map on page 9 shows at a glance where the various veld types are to be found and will serve as a guide to the distribution of some birds. However, within this predominantly bushveld terrain three regions are worthy of special note. First, riverine forest or riverine bush, occurring as its name implies along river-banks, is a prime habitat for many varied species of birds. From the massive trees with their interlocking canopies that grow along the banks of the larger, permanent rivers to the isolated patches of dense bush that clothe the banks of the annual watercourses, bird numbers are usually greater than in the adjacent bushveld. These riverine habitats provide more shade and cover for the smaller birds, more food in the form of insect life and fruit-bearing trees and greater opportunities for nesting. Secondly, the open grassveld regions, most extensive north of Letaba and Shingwedzi, are attractive to many others such as bee-eaters, rollers, shrikes, cuckoos and storks and are good hunting grounds for the birder, especially after rains. Thirdly, also in the northern region, those great areas of stunted mopane bush *(Colophospermum mopane)* are of special interest, because they can be both rewarding and disappointing, according to the time of the year. For many months the mopane belt, as it is called, is dry and lifeless, an avian wilderness but for the presence of a few hardy species. In fact its extensive nature may act as a barrier to the spread of some species known to occur north of it. On the other hand, during good rains, and especially when the mopane bushes are in fresh leaf, these regions are well-frequented by birds.

Identifying birds

The best places to see birds in the Kruger Park are the camps themselves. They are frequently situated with good river views and are themselves highly attractive to numerous bird species. Trees, buildings, flowers, flowering shrubs, fruit-bearing trees and water all combine to provide birds with nesting places and food in greater abundance and with a higher degree of safety from predators than any similar area of bushveld. Add to this neat lawns on which to forage and an unending supply of scraps thrown to them by visitors and it is not difficult to see why camps have the most birds to the hectare.

The Park's rest camps are usually the best places to see swallows, swifts, thrushes, waxbills, sunbirds and many more. As already mentioned the rivers and their adjacent bush are excellent routes for the bird seeker. Dams and pans are in a similar category while they also provide the added opportunity of seeing some of the larger beasts coming to drink. Wherever one seeks birds the important rule is to drive slowly. There is little doubt that the number of birds identified in the Park decreases in direct proportion to the speed of travel. A good plan is to park at a river view, waterhole or other likely birding spot and to wait patiently with engine switched off. Many birds 'freeze' into immobility when a car approaches, only relaxing and continuing their normal activities when all foreign movement has ceased. So often, a few minutes after you have switched off the car engine, you become aware of birds close by that had previously been overlooked.

Binoculars are, of course, an essential part of the birder's equipment, and many of the smaller species cannot be properly studied without them. Many good makes are available and 7 x 30, 8 x 35 or 10 x 40 are to be recommended; the first figure refers to magnification and the second to the diameter of the front lenses. Generally speaking, the greater the diameter of the front, or objective, lenses the more light is gathered and transmitted and the brighter the image.

When looking at an unfamiliar bird, it is a good plan to adopt a simple system to help you remember its salient features once it has flown or hopped out of sight. First note its approximate size. This can be done by comparing it to a bird with which one is familiar; thus is it larger or smaller than a sparrow, a pigeon or a guineafowl? and so on. Next note its general colour scheme, e.g. black upperparts, white underparts and a bold white bar on its wing. Follow this with beak shape: a short conical beak like a sparrow, or longer and more finely proportioned, or is it long and curved? Next, what colour is the bill? What colour are the legs? These simple checks – size, general colour, bill shape, bill and leg colours, and anything else of particular importance such as a long tail – can be noted quickly and will save endless page-turning and frustration. These points, coupled with what the bird was doing at the time and the habitat in which it was seen, should take the observer a long way in establishing its identity.

Species descriptions

In this fieldguide 476 bird species have been illustrated and described, while a further 31 have been listed in the Appendix as having been reported in the Park, casual vagrants or species in need of further verification. If we include all the Appendix birds as 'certain', then the total list for the Kruger National Park will be about 507 bird species. So the answer to that frequently asked question 'How many birds are there in the Kruger National Park?' is, we don't know for certain. Obviously it is somewhere between 476 and 507 species, depending on whether or not you accept strays and stragglers.

The problem of species numbers is further dogged by the fact that leading authorities disagree on the specific status of some birds. As an example, the Black Kite and Yellowbilled Kite (Plate 27) are often lumped as a single species. Other examples are the resident Tawny Eagle and the migrant, non-breeding, Steppe Eagle (Plate 30) and the greybacked and greenbacked versions of the Bleating Warbler (Plate 82), to name but a few. In these cases I have been guided by local usage and personal preferences based on the known habits of the birds in question. Some of these decisions may turn out to be incorrect in time, but this method is probably as good as any in the light of present knowledge.

In the descriptive text for each illustrated species the bird's vernacular name is given first, in **bold** capital letters. These names are taken from the checklist of the Southern African Ornithological Society. The names used are considered to be the most appropriate common names for each species. Where alternative names are known to be in wide use they are also given. Present-day policy in regard to vernacular bird names is to use the one that is most descriptive of the bird, thus Olive Thrush is to be preferred to Cape Thrush. However, people will continue to use the bird names of their choice or those with which they have long been familiar, and there is no reason why we should not do this in discussion among ourselves. What is important is that when writing about birds we should try to adhere to the standard checklist names.

Immediately following the English vernacular name of each species is the Afrikaans name, if it differs from the English. This is placed between brackets and serves as a cross-check on species identity for those who may be more familiar with one name than the other. For instance, many people in South Africa of both official language groups refer to the 'Fret', and may not be aware that the Bronze Mannikin is one and the same species.

The third name given is the scientific name, by which the bird is known throughout the world regardless of language. This appears in *italic* type and refers to the bird's genus and species in that order.

These scientific names call for some explanation for the benefit of those unaccustomed to them. Birds, in common with all other forms of animal life, have all been placed in distinct groups for clarity of expression. It is all very well for the layman to refer to a 'Mossie' or a 'Willie Wagtail'; his friends may well understand what he means, but in other countries, even in other parts of the same country, these popular names may well refer to totally different species. Even the listed vernacular names tend to vary from country to country and are changed periodically on national lists as new information is gathered about birds' true affinities. Thus, based on an international system of scientific nomenclature originated in the eighteenth century by the Swedish naturalist, Carl Linnaeus, all animals (and this includes birds) have been placed in clear groups or taxa, using names based on Latin or in some cases ancient Greek, which obviates any risk of confusion. First, all animal life is placed in classes, and birds belong to the class Aves, mammals to the class Mammalia, insects to Insecta, and so on. These classes are divided into major groups known as orders. The orders are subdivided into families, the families into genera (genus in the singular) and the genera into one or more species. A species can be further divided into races or sub-species.

When the above system of scientific nomenclature is applied to the common 'Mossie' or House Sparrow, its credentials looks like this:

Class:	Aves
Order:	Passeriformes
Family:	Ploceidae
Genus:	*Passer*
Species:	*domesticus*

Thus, within the bird family PLOCEIDAE there is a genus known as *Passer,* and within that genus a specific bird known as *domesticus*. The name *Passer domesticus* can be regarded, in human terms, as given name and surname, although the order is reversed. The use of an animal's scientific name ensures that serious students throughout the world will at once know, without any possibility of confusion, which species is being referred to. Within the genus *Passer* there are several other species all closely related to *P. domesticus: P. diffusus,* the Grey-headed Sparrow, for instance, which is also found in the Kruger Park. The present form of our local House Sparrow is descended from a species introduced into Natal from India earlier this century. The Indian race differs in minor respects from the nominate European race and is given the sub-specific name of *Passer domesticus indicus* or, again in human terms, a second given name. In fact the nominate race of the House Sparrow, *Passer domesticus domesticus* (identical specific and sub-specific names denote that the bird is of the nominate race) was also introduced from Europe to various places in the Cape Province and elsewhere at about the same time. It interbred with the Indian race and seems to have been subjugated, very little trace of its specific plumage pattern being now discernible in the southern African bird. The third or trinominal name is used in this fieldguide only in rare instances, where it has been felt necessary to draw attention to the sub-specific status of a bird.

When writing scientific names it is customary to write them in *italic* characters, to use an initial capital letter for the generic name and small or lower-case letters only for the specific or sub-specific names.

Following the English, Afrikaans and scientific names is the section of text that explains the bird's relative abundancy in the Park, whether it is a resident breeding species and, if so, when it is known to breed, or whether it is a non-breeding summer migrant, a casual visitor, and so on. This information, based as it is on available data, is subject to eventual revision for many species about which we still know little. Those regions of the Park in which the bird is known to occur are described next and this too is subject to modification as new sightings, especially of the less common birds, are reported.

Following the foregoing information each species is briefly described. This is not a feather-by-feather description of its plumage (the illustrations make this unnecessary) but an attempt to highlight specific characters that are diagnostic and distinguish it from other, similar species. In cases where a bird closely resembles another attention is drawn to the fact, and the plate reference of the similar species given for purposes of comparison.

It is inevitable when describing birds that certain names be used for the parts of its anatomy and these may be unfamiliar to the reader. Familiarity with the 'Topography of a bird' drawing (below) is therefore recommended.

A bird's habits are a clue to its identity. Knowledge of whether it habitually climbs on tree-trunks in search of food, frequents marshy ground, treetops,

TOPOGRAPHY OF A BIRD

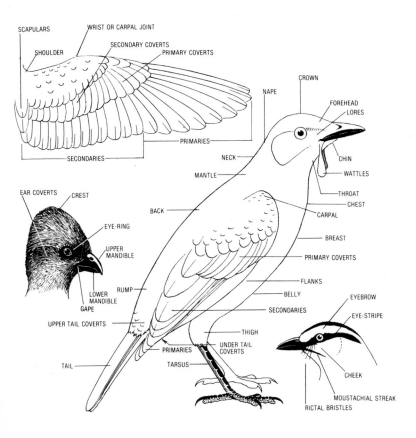

water or grassland, can save much time in fruitless searching. Where possible this information is supplied, as are its physical habits such as regular wing-flicking, tail-bobbing, head-jerking, etc.

The bird's voice is then described as a further aid to establishing its identity. Most birds have calls or songs, and many have both. In fact the division between the more elaborate calls and the more simple songs is a fine one. Bird vocalisations have various functions, among which the more important are contact between individuals or groups and territorial advertisement. At best any attempt at committing bird calls to paper in the form of the written word is an approximation, influenced by the writer's ability to interpret them. Calls, consisting mostly of single-syllable notes, are the easiest to express in words, and may suggest a similar-sounding language phrase. Bird songs, especially the more complicated (frequently the most beautiful), are notoriously difficult to express clearly and are all too often quite impossible. In such cases an attempt has been made to give the more frequently uttered notes in the song or to describe it as 'sweet', and so on. At this point it is appropriate to draw readers' attention to the tape by Len Gillard entitled 'BIRD CALLS OF KRUGER NATIONAL PARK'. The 168 bird calls on this tape have been specially selected to complement this fieldguide. The tape is strongly recommended to those seriously interested in the birds of the region.

Finally, at the end of each descriptive text, the bird's reference number is given. This number appears on the southern African checklist and coincides with the numbers used in other reputable books of the birds of our sub-region. Its presence is a further aid to cross-referencing.

The colour plates

The birds depicted on the 107 colour plates in this fieldguide have been drawn, so far as is possible, in such a way as to emphasise their characteristic shapes, colours, markings and stance. Where several species on a page closely resemble one another they are all drawn, at risk of monotony, in a similar stance to facilitate direct comparison. All the main figures on a plate are in approximate proportion to each other and, wherever possible, all birds in a family are drawn to the same proportions whether on the same plate or not. In a few cases it has been necessary to depict larger birds of a family to a smaller scale than others on the same plate, and in such cases they are clearly separated by a solid rule and an indication of the alternative scale; an example is Plate 63. Secondary figures, showing birds in flight or performing some other characteristic action, are not to the same proportions as the main figures.

It is customary in handbooks and fieldguides about birds to present the species in strict taxonomic order, that is to say in the order followed by the national checklist. This usually means that one begins with the Ostrich and the grebes, continues with seabirds, herons, ducks, etc. and finishes with canaries and buntings, if one is referring to the southern African list. In this fieldguide this convention has been used with elasticity. Because its basic purpose is to help with bird identification, and because many users may not be familiar with the various bird families and their characteristics, some species that have a visual resemblance to birds of another family have been illustrated with those they most closely resemble.

The scales used on each plate are convenient, easy-to-remember metric measurements: 10 cm, 15 cm, 45 cm, 60 cm. For the benefit of the many overseas visitors to the Kruger Park who may not be conversant with metric measures, the following comparisons may be useful:

10 cm = approximately 4 inches
15 cm = approximately 6 inches
30 cm = approximately 12 inches
45 cm = approximately 18 inches
60 cm = approximately 24 inches

Data collection

The information contained in this revised fieldguide includes all material received up to 31 January 1991. However, the status and distributions of many birds in the Kruger National Park are still not clear, therefore species accounts in the following pages will be further updated from time to time as new information becomes available. Reliable data concerning new bird species, and range extensions of known species within the Park, are always welcome. If you are positive of your identification please notify the author by post at: P.O. Box 667, Strathavon 2031.

Map of Place Names
of the Kruger National Park

Legend

— Main road

〜 Rivers

● Camps

0   50 km

N

1 Babalala
2 Balule/Ngotsamond Caravan Camp
3 Bangu region
4 Baobab Hill
5 Black Heron Dam
6 Boulders Private Camp
7 Boyela windmill
8 Engelhard Dam
9 Gorge
10 Gudzani Dam
11 Jock of the Bushveld Private Camp
12 Kanniedood Dam
13 Khandizwe Hill
14 Klopperfontein Dam
15 Kumana Dam
16 Leeupan
17 Lindanda
18 Makwadzi Pan
19 Malelane Private Camp
20 Malonga
21 Mangake Koppie
22 Mazanje
23 Maschicindzudzi
24 Mashikiripoort
25 Mavumbye
26 Mazithi Dam
27 Mbhatsi Picket
28 Middelvlei
29 Mlondozi Dam
30 Maqili Picket
31 Ntomeni Pan
32 Muzandzeni Picnic Place
33 Newu Dam
34 Ngotsamond Caravan Camp
35 Ngotso Dam
36 Ngwenyeni Dam
37 Nhlanganini Dam
38 Nhlanguleni
39 Nkovakulu Windmills
40 Nsemani Dam
41 Nshawu
42 Nshawu Dam
43 Nyandu Bush
44 Nyavadi Pan
45 Olifants Gorge
46 Orpen Dam
47 Pambana
48 Pionier Dam
49 Pumbe Pan
50 Reedbuck Vlei
51 Roodewal Private Camp
52 Salitje Picket
53 Satara Plots
54 Shabeni
55 Shilahlandonga
56 Siloweni Dam
57 Shimangwaneni Dam
58 Shimuwini Dam
59 Shigomane
60 Shipudza
61 Shitsalaleni Flats
62 Spokonyole Pan
63 Stolsnek Dam
64 Timbavati
65 Transport Dam
66 Tsende Picket

Map of Major Vegetation Areas of the Kruger National Park

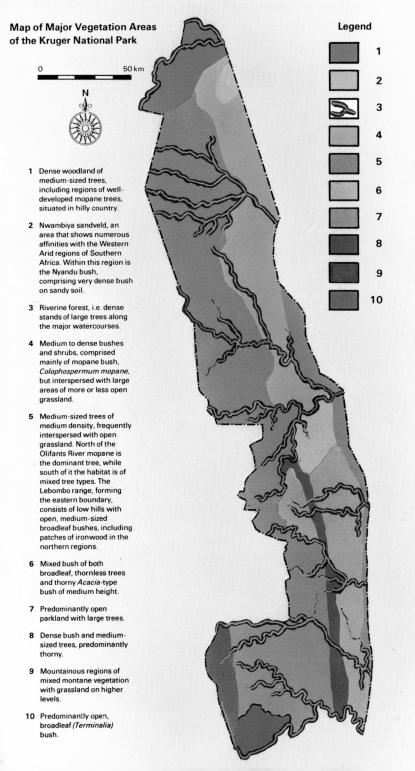

0   50 km

N

Legend

1
2
3
4
5
6
7
8
9
10

1 Dense woodland of medium-sized trees, including regions of well-developed mopane trees, situated in hilly country.

2 Nwambiya sandveld, an area that shows numerous affinities with the Western Arid regions of Southern Africa. Within this region is the Nyandu bush, comprising very dense bush on sandy soil.

3 Riverine forest, i.e. dense stands of large trees along the major watercourses.

4 Medium to dense bushes and shrubs, comprised mainly of mopane bush, *Colophospermum mopane*, but interspersed with large areas of more or less open grassland.

5 Medium-sized trees of medium density, frequently interspersed with open grassland. North of the Olifants River mopane is the dominant tree, while south of it the habitat is of mixed tree types. The Lebombo range, forming the eastern boundary, consists of low hills with open, medium-sized broadleaf bushes, including patches of ironwood in the northern regions.

6 Mixed bush of both broadleaf, thornless trees and thorny *Acacia*-type bush of medium height.

7 Predominantly open parkland with large trees.

8 Dense bush and medium-sized trees, predominantly thorny.

9 Mountainous regions of mixed montane vegetation with grassland on higher levels.

10 Predominantly open, broadleaf *(Terminalia)* bush.

Symbols used in the colour plates

♂ denotes MALE

♀ denotes FEMALE

J denotes an immature bird

Br denotes breeding plumage

N-Br denotes non-breeding plumage

Terms used to indicate bird status

Vagrant: a species not normally associated with the KNP

Rare: a species recorded 10 or less times a year in suitable habitat

Uncommon: a species recorded 30 or less times a month in suitable habitat

Fairly common: a species recorded 1-10 times a day in suitable habitat

Common: a species recorded 10-50 times a day in suitable habitat

Very common: a species recorded 50-100 times a day in suitable habitat

Abundant: a species recorded 100 or more times a day in suitable habitat

Seasonal: a species seen at certain times of the year only

Localised: a species seen only in restricted areas of suitable habitat

Resident: a species which occurs all year and is known to breed in the KNP

Passage migrant: a bird seen temporarily at a point that it passes through during migration; alternatively 'bird of passage'.

SPECIES ACCOUNTS

OSTRICH (Volstruis) *Struthio camelus.* Fairly common and widespread north of the Sabie River, but present in small numbers only in the south. Nests with eggs have been recorded July-September. An unmistakable and well-known species. The world's largest bird and entirely flightless. The few hundred birds within the Park are probably the last true members of the South African race that survive, others elsewhere in the country having been interbred with ostriches introduced from North Africa. Occurs mostly in the open and more lightly wooded regions, avoiding dense bush and hills. Males utter a dull 'roar' at night, like the distant roar of a lion. **1**

PLATE 1

Cormorants. Family PHALACROCORACIDAE. Webbed-footed, long-necked, hooked-billed fish- and frog-eating water birds, which hunt their prey beneath the surface, seizing it in their bills and surfacing to swallow it. Swim with body partially submerged and head held at an upward angle. Characteristically perch with wings outspread to dry.

1 REED CORMORANT (Rietduiker) *Phalacrocorax africanus*. A fairly common resident species occurring throughout the Park. Breeding has been recorded February-March. The female's non-breeding plumage shows more white on the underparts and resembles that of the immature; see illustrations. Usually occurs singly and may be seen at water points anywhere. Eats frogs and fish. **58**

2 WHITEBREASTED CORMORANT (Witborsduiker) *Phalacrocorax carbo*. Uncommon, breeding resident. Occurs mostly on large dams in the central region. A larger bird than (1). Adults are white to the lower breast only, the white thigh-patch often absent. Immatures entirely *pure white* on underparts; cf. immature of (1). Eats mostly fish. **55**

Darter. Family ANHINGIDAE. Aquatic birds similar to cormorants in habits and general appearance. Fish are speared on the bill under water, swallowed on the surface.

3 DARTER (Slanghalsvoël) *Anhinga melanogaster*. Fairly common and widespread. Breeding has been recorded February-April. More slender than a cormorant, the neck long, thin and with a distinct 'kink' in the middle, the bill spear-like, tail long. In non-breeding plumage more brown than black but long, lanceolate plumes remain on upperparts. Immature has chestnut underparts. On surface swims with body submerged, only neck protruding, hence the popular name 'Snake Bird'. Occurs on dams and rivers and dries its wings like a cormorant. **60**

Pelicans. Family PELECANIDAE. Very large, well-known, fish-eating birds with substantial bodies, longish necks, huge bills with spacious pouches beneath the lower mandible, short legs and webbed feet. Two species occur as vagrants in the Park.

4 WHITE PELICAN (Witpelikaan) *Pelecanus onocrotalus*. A rare, non-breeding visitor. Occurs in groups of up to approximately 20 birds, mostly in the northern regions. Adults are entirely white, the body with a pinkish tinge during the breeding season at which time the crest is longest. In flight the primary wing feathers are black. Immatures are brownish and can be confused with (5) but are larger and normally accompany adults. Usually fish in groups, driving the fish into the shallows. During the day may soar to great heights. **49**

5 PINKBACKED PELICAN (Kleinpelikaan) *Pelecanus rufescens*. An irregular non-breeding visitor occurring occasionally in large flocks. Smaller than (4), appearing grey at a distance. In flight the primary wing feathers are brown. Habits same as (4). **50**

PLATE 2

Herons. Family ARDEIDAE. Water-associated birds varying in size from small to very large. The four comparative silhouettes on this plate represent A: Dwarf Bittern (Plate 2), B: Squacco Heron (Plate 3), C: Little Egret (Plate 4), D: Grey Heron (Plate 5). Herons have long bills, necks and legs, and fly with the *neck tucked into the shoulders,* differing in this respect from storks, ibises and cranes. Herons seldom soar and are mostly solitary in habit except when breeding, when they sometimes form colonies of many hundreds. They perch readily in trees and feed on large insects, fish, frogs, small rodents and occasionally small birds. The adults of many species have long plumes on their heads and, in breeding plumage, may have filamentous plumes on their backs and lower breasts and may also change their bill and leg colouring temporarily. All have voices of a harsh, croaking nature, seldom heard unless alarmed. White herons are known as egrets.

1 DWARF BITTERN (Dwergrietreier) *Ixobrychus sturmii.* Rare and secretive. An intra-African migrant recorded at points all over the Park September-March, with attempted breeding recorded in the far north during February. Mostly nocturnal but less shy than (2) when seen by day. Frequents waterside trees and bushes, especially those standing in flood waters, and is less partial to reeds than some herons. Appears quite dark in the field but the orange-yellow legs and feet are conspicuous in flight and trail at an angle to the body. Flight action is slow and heavy for a small bird. May adopt an upright posture when disturbed; see illustration. **79**

2 LITTLE BITTERN (Woudapie) *Ixobrychus minutus.* Rare and secretive; probably a vagrant. Has been·seen throughout the Park in all seasons. A very small heron of reed-beds. When disturbed usually adopts an upright posture with the bill pointing skywards, the plumage stripes blending well with the reeds and making detection difficult. The immature is easily confused with those of other small herons (see 1 and 3) but is paler in colour and more streaky. **78**

3 GREENBACKED HERON (Groenrugreier) *Butorides striatus.* Common and widespread. A resident species and by far the most common heron in the Park. Breeding occurs October-April. Found at most tree-fringed waters. Is frequently flushed at river crossings when it flies into a tree and perches motionless. Easily confused with (1), especially in flight, but the black cap contrasting with the grey neck is diagnostic. It also frequently raises a crest which is absent in (1). The orange-yellow feet are also conspicuous in flight but the green back is not a field feature. The immature bird has distinctive whitish dots on the closed wings. **74**

4 RUFOUSBELLIED HERON (Rooipensreier) *Butorides rufiventris.* Rare. Recorded in small numbers at water points throughout the Park. The largest of the small herons, it appears blackish in the field, the dull rufous underparts and wings being apparent only at close range. The pale yellow legs and facial skin are good field characters. Only the female has the extended yellow throat line. A heron of secluded, well-vegetated waters. When disturbed it flies to a tree and perches until the intruder has departed. **75**

30cm

A B C D

J 1

♀ J ♂ 2

3 J

♂ 4 ♀

PLATE 3

1 SQUACCO HERON (Ralreier) *Ardeola ralloides.* Rare, but recorded at water points all over the Park September-May. An unobtrusive, small heron of cryptic colouration. In flight appears surprisingly white, and flaps its wings rapidly. Usually occurs singly, preferring well-vegetated waters, especially overgrown floodpans wih an abundance of water insects, small frogs, etc. **72**

2 BLACK EGRET (Swartreier) *Egretta ardesiaca.* Rare. Probably a non-breeding visitor. Has been recorded at water points over the length of the Park, occasionally in small flocks and usually during summer. Appears all black at a distance, with *yellow feet,* and has the unique habit of forming a canopy with its wings when fishing. May occur on any quiet river or dam. Flies with rapid wing-beats. **69**

3 WHITEBACKED NIGHT HERON (Witrugnagreier) *Gorsachius leuconotus.* Rare but widespread over the length of the Park. No evidence of breeding although it is assumed to be resident in the Park. Its nocturnal and secretive habits may conceal a more numerous presence. Not easily mistaken for any other heron, the distinct 'hangman's hood', yellow facial markings and legs plus general rufous colouring being diagnostic. The white back feathers are visible on both adults and immatures. Occurs on permanent rivers and well-wooded dams. Hides by day in dense water-side bushes or reed-beds, fishing only at night. **77**

4 BLACKCROWNED NIGHT HERON (Gewone Nagreier) *Nycticorax nycticorax.* Uncommon but widespread. Various nest-building activities have been recorded February-March but successful breeding records are lacking. Gregarious when breeding but otherwise of solitary habits. The adult is distinctly coloured as illus-trated, while in the immature (frequently mistaken for the next species) the upperparts are brown with pale tips to the feathers, giving a spotted effect; lower mandible, eye surround and legs yellow-green, eyes orange. This species hunts by night from some low branch close to the water where it may remain motionless for long periods, and roosts by day in trees or reeds. Feeds on freshwater crabs and other aquatic life. **76**

5

5 BITTERN (Grootreier) *Botaurus stellaris.* Rare but widespread throughout the Park. Larger than imma-ture of (4), differing in black crown, moustacial streak, paler underparts and warmer upperparts; in flight by greater wingspan, trailing feet. Solitary and secretive in vleis, marshes and grassy streams. When alarmed adopts a 'sky-pointing' posture as illustrated. In sum-mer utters a booming sound by day and night. **80**

30cm

N·Br

1

2

3

J

4

J

PLATE 4

1 CATTLE EGRET (Bosluisvoël) *Bubulcus ibis*. Uncommon but recorded throughout the Park at all times of the year, breeding occasionally when conditions are favourable. Otherwise occurs in groups of up to 20, sometimes more. In summer carries the buff breeding plumes on crown, lower neck and back, at which time the bill and legs are pinkish-orange. Outside the breeding season the plumage is pure white, the bill yellow with a dark tip, the legs and feet dull yellow, usually stained with mud. The immature has a black bill and legs; see illustrations. This is the common 'tickbird', seen with cattle in farming areas where it feeds on grasshoppers and other insects disturbed by the grazing animals. Does not normally frequent water when feeding but breeds and roosts near water. In the KNP often rests at dams and rivers. **71**

2 LITTLE EGRET (Kleinwitreier) *Egretta garzetta*. Uncommon non-breeding visitor. Occurs at rivers and dams at all times of the year throughout the Park. An entirely white, elegant egret having black bill and legs with *yellow feet*. Two long plumes are present on the head at all times (except in immatures) and, in the breeding season (October-March), filamentous plumes are present on the lower neck and back. A slender, long-necked egret, usually found singly at rivers and dams where it stalks fish, frogs and other small waterlife in the shallows. **67**

3 YELLOWBILLED EGRET (Geelbekwitreier) *Egretta intermedia*. A rare non-breeding visitor to water points throughout the Park all year. Is frequently confused with the larger Great White Egret (4) and the small Cattle Egret (1) because of the yellow bill in all three species. This egret is smaller than (4), the legs *dull yellow to orange on the upper half* (tibia) and black only on the lower half (tarsus) and feet at all times. It is more robust in appearance than (1) and has a proportionately longer neck with the characteristic 'kink' of the larger herons. Birds in breeding condition have filamentous plumes on the lower neck and back. Usually occurs singly or in pairs on quiet waters where it stalks frogs and other aquatic life. **68**

4 GREAT WHITE EGRET (Grootwitreier) *Egretta alba*. A widespread, common breeding resident. Is frequently misidentified as (3) because of its yellow bill when not breeding, the condition in which *it most commonly occurs in the KNP*. This species is much larger that (3) and has long, entirely black legs at all times. The black bill and filamentous plumes on lower neck and back are present for *only a brief period* while the bird is breeding. A tall, elegant, long-necked egret about the size of the Grey Heron (Plate 5), and usually seen standing motionless in shallow water or intently stalking its aquatic prey. The most frequently seen white heron at rivers and dams throughout the Park. Feeds on the usual assortment of fish, frogs and other waterlife. **66**

PLATE 5

1 **GREY HERON** (Bloureier) *Ardea cinerea*. Fairly common at dams and rivers throughout the Park. Breeds at several scattered localities. Normally a solitary bird which stealthily stalks fish and frogs in shallow waters, but may gather in small numbers to roost in trees at nightfall, sometimes with other large wading birds. The immature is a very much lighter grey, appearing almost white. Note the similarity to the Blackheaded Heron (4), especially the immature of that species. When flying, with typically slow wing-beats, the underwing is seen as a *uniform grey* colour. **62**

2 **PURPLE HERON** (Rooireier) *Ardea purpurea*. An uncommon non-breeding visitor recorded at water points throughout the Park. This heron has a liking for reeds and similar dense waterside vegetation where it may remain concealed for much of the day, emerging to feed in the late afternoon and evening. Its apparent scarcity within the Park may therefore be a reflection of its shy nature. Is often mistaken for (3) but note bill-size, head and neck colouring, much smaller overall size and slender stature of this species. **65**

3 **GOLIATH HERON** (Reuse Reier) *Ardea goliath*. A fairly common, very large resident heron which frequents large dams and permanent rivers throughout the Park; there are summer breeding records. This huge heron is similar in size to our largest storks but, because of its distinctive colouring, should not be confused with any other species except possibly (2), a much smaller bird. The Goliath Heron is usally seen poised motionless in shallow water where it feeds on fish, crabs and various reptiles. The flight is slow, with ponderous wing-beats, the wings being held bent downwards at the carpal joint and the legs trailing down at an angle to the body. **64**

4 **BLACKHEADED HERON** (Swartkopreier) *Ardea melanocephala*. An uncommon large heron, widespread at all times of the year. Occasionally breeds in the Park. Usually solitary or in pairs either close to water or away from it, its diet consisting of frogs, rodents, large insects and almost any other small creature it can seize. Is frequently mistaken for (1), especially in immature plumage. In flight the underwing shows distinct *black and grey* colouring; see illustration. **63**

20

PLATE 6

Cranes. Family GRUIDAE. Large, long-legged, terrestrial birds, differing from herons and storks in having shorter bills and being quite vocal. Unlike herons but in common with storks they fly with their necks extended. Of three species in Africa one occurs occasionally in the KNP.

CROWNED CRANE (Mahem) *Balearica regulorum.* Rare. Small flocks occur occasionally as non-breeding visitors. Likely to be seen anywhere. Unmistakable, the crest present in both sexes. Prefer grasslands, vleis and other marshy regions. The call is a trumpeting 'ma-hem'. **209**

Storks. Family CICONIIDAE. Large to very large long-legged and long-necked birds with straight, stout bills. Colouring mostly black and white or blackish. Storks walk with stately gait and frequently rest on the ground with the lower part of their legs stretched forward; see illustration of immature Marabou. In flight the neck is stretched out (unlike herons which fly with the neck retracted) and the legs usually trail down at a slight angle to the body. Most members of this family sometimes soar to great heights during the heat of the day, many are communal in habits and most frequent water or damp places to some extent. Food ranges from large insects, reptiles, frogs and other waterlife to carrion in one species. They have no voice except guttural sounds and hisses made at the nest, but bill-clapping is used as a greeting between pairs. The nests are large stick structures placed in trees, on rocks and cliffs or on the ground, according to species.

1 SADDLEBILLED STORK (Saalbekooievaar) *Ephippiorhynchus senegalensis.* A fairly common resident species found throughout the Park. This huge and striking stork normally occurs at pans, dams and rivers but, during periods of extensive rains, may move into flooded veld to feed. Breeding takes place during the winter months following summers of good rainfall and young birds, which are dull versions of the adults, are in evidence during September. Note that the male has a brown eye-ring and a small yellow wattle in contrast to the female's yellow eye-ring and lack of a wattle. The brightly coloured bill is visible at a distance and in flight. The Saddlebilled Stork feeds on fish, frogs and other waterlife in addition to small mammals caught in the veld. **88**

2 MARABOU STORK (Maraboe) *Leptoptilos crumeniferus.* Common to uncommon and unpredictable, numbers fluctuating within the Park from month to month. Flocks may suddenly appear in a district and remain there for days or weeks, these aggregations frequently being in response to animal culling operations where the Marabous vie with the vultures for the discarded remains. Is known to breed in the Park in small numbers but the population is augmented by sporadic arrivals from elsewhere. May often be seen at the remains of a lion kill where it towers above the squabbling vultures, driving them off with jabs of its powerful bill. Also feeds on fish, especially those trapped in drying pools. Has been known to gather at Redbilled Quelea colonies to devour the young after shaking them out of their nests. Locusts, termites, reptiles and rodents are also recorded in its diet. **89**

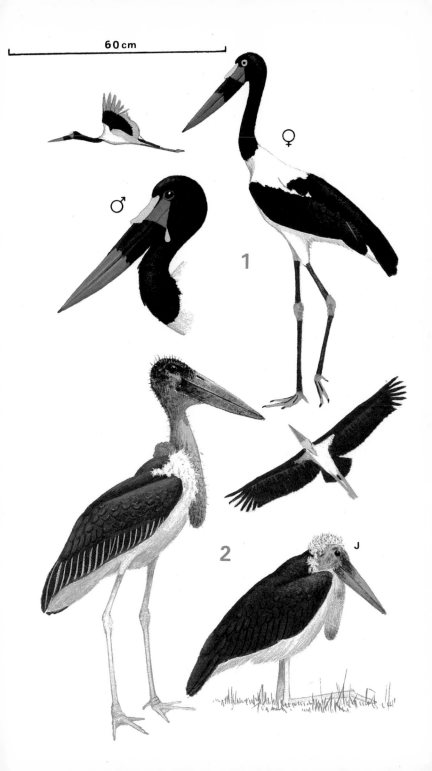

60 cm

♀

♂

1

2

J

PLATE 7

1 **WHITE STORK** (Witooievaar) *Ciconia ciconia.* An irregular non-breeding summer migrant from Europe. Its status within the Park varies from year to year, being locally abundant or rare. The reason for this annual fluctuation is obscure but is probably connected with rainfall and insect abundances, although years of excessive rain do not necessarily produce large numbers of this stork. When it occurs the White Stork usually arrives in late October and departs in March, but a few winter sightings have been recorded. In good years this species may be seen feeding in the veld in large numbers or, on hot days, soaring to great heights. It frequently associates with (3). The preferred habitat is the open grassland where locusts, army worms and other gregarious insect pests occur, but rodents, frogs, etc. are also eaten.   **83**

2 **BLACK STORK** (Grootswartooievaar) *Ciconia nigra.* A fairly common resident species occurring all over the Park. Breeding occurs April-August. Can be confused with (3), but is considerably larger and has diagnostic red bill and legs. An entirely aquatic feeder, the Black Stork occurs at pans, dams, and rivers within the Park, the principal food being large insects, fish and other waterlife. Normally a solitary species but non-breeding birds may gather in numbers to roost in trees where they sometimes mix with Woollynecked Storks (Plate 8).   **84**

3 **ABDIM'S STORK** or Whitebellied Stork (Kleinswartooievaar) *Ciconia abdimii.* In common with (1) this species is an irregular non-breeding summer migrant, and its numbers vary from year to year. In good years it may be locally very common and in other years entirely absent. When present in the Park this stork may be seen from late October when it arrives in large flocks from the Sudan and Ethiopia, until its departure in March. It may be confused with (2), especially in flight, but its *white back,* different proportions and usually communal behaviour should aid identification. Its habitat and food requirements are similar to those of (1) and the two species frequently associate.   **85**

1

2

3

60 cm

PLATE 8

1 YELLOWBILLED STORK (Nimmersat) *Mycteria ibis.* An uncommon water-associated stork. It may be seen throughout at pans, dams and rivers singly or, more usually, in groups of half a dozen. A flock of 170 has been recorded. Occasionally breeds in the Park; many immature birds may be seen at times which suggests that they have bred elsewhere. The distinctive colouring of the bill and head, and the slightly decurved shape of the bill should prevent confusion with other black and white storks. Will readily perch in trees and has the habit of standing with wings outspread on hot days. It catches aquatic life with vigorous sweeps of the bill under water, frequently submerging the head. **90**

2 WOOLLYNECKED STORK (Wolnekooievaar) *Ciconia episcopus.* An uncommon water-associated stork within the Park but a breeding resident. It may be found anywhere but is most common in the eastern half, usually near water but also in flooded lands and on airstrips after rains. Normally found in small groups and is known to roost communally with Black Storks (Plate 7) at times. The diet is fish, crabs, molluscs, small reptiles and insects. **86**

3 OPENBILLED STORK (Oopbekooievaar) *Anastomus lamelligerus.* A fairly common resident. May be seen in small flocks especially in the eastern regions. Appears black at a distance. In old, abraided plumage the back and breast plumes become faded to golden-brown. In years of good rains breeds colonially on floodpans of the Limpopo River where it builds nests in partially submerged trees; see illustration. During drought years may not breed for several years in succession and so the numbers fluctuate from a few dozen individuals to 300 or more within the Park. The name is derived from the gap in the bill, an aid to the manipulation of freshwater molluscs, but other water creatures have been recorded in the diet. **87**

Hamerkop. Family SCOPIDAE. Although the Hamerkop falls within the general order of birds known as CICONIIFORMES, which includes storks, ibises, spoonbills and flamigoes, it differs in so many respects from them that it has been placed in a separate family and is the only species within that family.

4 HAMERKOP *Scopus umbretta.* A fairly common resident species found throughout the Park, usually near water. The colossal nest, dome-shaped with an entrance below, may be seen at many dams and small rivers, while the bird itself can usually be seen fishing or flying nearby. Is frequently mobbed by the Forktailed Drongo (Plate 71) while flying, apparently being mistaken for a raptor. These peculiar brown birds are adept at seizing small fish in fast-running water below weirs and flooded causeways, but also catch frogs and water insects in still waters. When excited and in flight frequently utters a strangely squeaky call, 'kek-kek-kek . . .' at short intervals. **81**

PLATE 9

Ibises and spoonbills. Family PLATALEIDAE. A family of fairly large wading birds, most with long and decurved bills for mud-probing, or spoon-shaped as in the spoonbills, for water-feeding. All but one are silent in the field.

1 **SACRED IBIS** (Skoorsteenveër) *Threskiornis aethiopicus.* An uncommon non-breeding visitor recorded at various points within the Park, always in small numbers. An unmistakable bird which sometimes associates with Cattle Egrets (Plate 4). Will usually be found at water or on damp ground probing for insects, molluscs, etc. Silent in contrast to the next species (2). **91**

2 **HADEDA IBIS** (Hadeda) *Bostrychia hagedash.* A fairly common and widespread resident species occurring in small parties near rivers and dams. Breeding has been recorded in early summer. When flying, or when disturbed, is extremely noisy; the call is onomatopoeic, being a raucus and often-repeated 'Haa! Ha-de-daa'. **94**

GLOSSY IBIS (Glansibis) *Plegadis falcinellus.* An uncommon, non-breeding visitor to water points throughout the Park. Slender, lighter-bodied than other ibises, bronze-brown in colour with iridescent green patches on the wing when breeding. Usually seen near water or in damp areas. **93**

3 **AFRICAN SPOONBILL** (Lepelaar) *Platalea alba.* An uncommon species· which visits the Park in small numbers and occasionally breeds. At a distance may be mistaken for other white, water-associated birds but at close range the spatulate bill is diagnostic. Feeds mainly on water insects by moving the partially opened bill in the water with a sideways swinging action as illustrated, sometimes submerging the head. **95**

Flamingoes. Family PHOENICOPTERIDAE. Both the Greater and Lesser Flamingoes are highly gregarious birds and are similarly proportioned, being white to pink and having very long necks and legs with rather small bodies. They fly with both neck and legs fully extended and with fairly rapid wing-beats. Suitable brack waters for these birds are not found in the KNP and such individuals or flocks that occur from time to time seldom remain for long.

4 **GREATER FLAMINGO** (Grootflamink) *Phoenicopterus ruber.* An uncommon vagrant for which there are many records of individuals and flocks, mostly in the north of the Park. Appears all-white except when flying; the wing coverts are red, a feature lacking in immature birds. Larger and whiter than the next species, the bill *pink with a black tip.* **96**

5 **LESSER FLAMINGO** (Kleinflamink) *Phoenicopterus minor.* An uncommon vagrant which, however, sometimes occurs in the Park in large flocks, resting a short time on some pan or dam before departing again. The bill is *deep maroon red,* black at the tip. **97**

PLATE 10

Ducks and geese. Family ANATIDAE. Ducks as a group need little introduction but are, however, poorly represented in the Kruger National Park. Of the seventeen resident species in South Africa, only six occur regularly in the Park. A bushveld environment is not attractive to many duck species where the scarcity of permanent wetlands is probably a contributing factor.

1 WHITEFACED DUCK (Nonnetjie-eend) *Dendrocygna viduata*. A common nomadic species which occurs throughout the Park. Ducklings have been seen in February but breeding probably occurs throughout summer. May be seen at any time of the year in small groups or large flocks, the white face being diagnostic. Normally a quiet, retiring species. In flight individuals emit a clear whistling note 'whee-whee-wheeoo' which is repeated and taken up by others in the flock. **99**

2 FULVOUS DUCK (Fluiteend) *Dendrocygna bicolor*. An uncommon visitor. Has been seen at various dams and pans throughout the Park. The only fulvous coloured duck in the region. Has a marked preference for well-vegetated pans such as are found in the north-east of the Park and from where several of the records originate. In common with the previous species a whistling call is sometimes made in flight, a softer and less often repeated 'see-see'. **100**

3 EGYPTIAN GOOSE (Kolgans) *Alopochen aegyptiacus*. A common resident species widespread throughout the Park. Occurs at most water points and all rivers. Breeding probably takes place throughout the year, but most goslings are seen during the period August-January. Usually occurs in family groups, but rising flood waters on the larger rivers sometimes force many birds to gather on the last exposed sandbanks. A noisy species at times, females making loud 'honk-honk-haah-haah' sounds in addition to the male's wheezy hissing. **102**

4 SPURWINGED GOOSE (Wildemakou) *Plectropterus gambensis*. An uncommon nomadic species occurring in flocks at all times of the year and occasionally breeding. A large percentage of the birds seen are immature, and show little or no white on the plumage. Mature plumage is more glossy but the amount of white is variable. The adult male may be identified by the large caruncle on the forehead. Mostly seen on sandbanks on the larger rivers and on pans and dams elsewhere where they usually remain a few days only. This species is mostly silent but sometimes emits a high-pitched bubbling in flight. **116**

1

2

3

4

♀

♂

J

60cm

PLATE 11

1 PYGMY GOOSE (Dwerggans) *Nettapus auritus*. Uncommon resident. Occurs all over the Park in small numbers, breeding usually in winter. A very small but distinctive species found in pairs on secluded waters *with waterlilies and emergent grasses*. Difficult to see since it blends remarkably well with the vegetation. If alarmed, will either dive and swim underwater to denser cover or will take flight, making off with rapid wing-beats. Sometimes perches in trees. Feeds mostly on water lilies plus insects and small fish. Has a soft whistling call. **114**

2 WHITEBACKED DUCK (Witrugeend) *Thalassornis leuconotus*. Rare. Occurs mostly on floodpans in the far north, rarely further south. No breeding has been recorded. The distinctive profile with sloping forehead and wedge-shaped bill, the *white patch* at the base of the bill, plus the humped back and habit of sitting low in the water, are diagnostic. Like (1) is found on secluded pans with waterlilies and emergent grass, where it feeds on the seeds of each. Makes a soft whistle, 'cur-wee, cur-wee'. **101**

3 REDBILLED TEAL (Rooibekeend) *Anas erythrorhyncha*. An uncommon breeding visitor, chicks having been recorded in mid-summer. Occurs over the length of the Park, usually in small numbers and most commonly in summer. A fairly distinctive duck with its red bill and brown cap; cf. (4). Frequents large dams and pans feeding on a variety of plant and animal life by dabbling with head submerged. Normally a silent bird. **108**

4 HOTTENTOT TEAL (Gevlekte Eend) *Anas hottentota*. A rare visitor to dams and pans throughout the Park. Small size, brown cap and *slate-blue bill* distinctive; cf. (3) which has a *red* bill. In pairs or small groups on still waters; does not dive. **107**

5 MACCOA DUCK (Bloubekeend) *Oxyura maccoa*. Rare visitor to dams and pans throughout the Park. Blue bill, black head and rufous body of male distinctive; frequently swims with stiff tail erect. Female shows horizontal whitish streak below eyes; cf. female of next species. On still waters only; dives frequently and seldom leaves the water. **117**

6 SOUTHERN POCHARD (Bruineend) *Netta erythrophthalma*. A rare, non-breeding visitor recorded at pans and dams throughout the Park. An inconspicuous brown duck. The male has a bronzy sheen to the plumage, visible at close range; the eyes are red, the bill and legs slate-blue. The female is duller with a whitish 'C' mark running from behind the eye, over the ear coverts, to the throat. Feeds by diving and is generally silent. **113**

PLATE 12

1 AFRICAN BLACK DUCK (Swarteend) *Anas sparsa*. An uncommon resident duck, occurring on wooded rivers and dams throughout the Park. Breeds during winter. A brown duck with distinctive spotted-backed appearance. The slaty bill sometimes has a pinkish patch near its base. Frequents quiet waters with bush-lined banks, occasionally emerging to stand on rocks or semi-submerged branches when the orange legs are distinctive. Occurs in pairs or small family groups and frequently flies along rivers at dawn and dusk. Black Ducks feed on both aquatic insects and vegetation. In flight a loud 'quaak' is uttered at intervals by the female.   **105**

2 YELLOWBILLED DUCK (Geelbekeend) *Anas undulata*. Rare. A sporadic visitor reported from points throughout the Park with a single breeding record in winter. The yellow bill is both distinctive and diagnostic. May occur on any river or dam and is active at all times of the day. Feeds on aquatic vegetation by up-ending. A loud 'quaark, quaark' call is often made in flight.   **104**

3 KNOBBILLED DUCK (Knobbeleend) *Sarkidiornis melanotos*. A fairly common visitor throughout the Park. Ducklings have been seen in most of the summer months during seasons of high rainfall. The large male, with the conspicuous caruncle or comb on its bill, is unmistakable. The female, which is about half the size of the male and outnumbers it in most flocks, lacks the knob on the bill and is generally less glossy than the male. The immature is a dull version of the female while first-year young have pale buff underparts and dark brown upperparts with a distinct eye-stripe. A nomadic species occurring in flocks and remaining on favoured waters sometimes for months. In good rains will disperse to temporary pools and floodlands where they readily rest in trees. Feeds on vegetable matter by grazing, in addition to aquatic larvae. Generally silent.   **115**

Finfoots. Family HELIORNITHIDAE. Three species occur in the world, one in Africa. Between a cormorant and a duck in appearance, having lobed not webbed feet. Swim with much of the body submerged, the bill held high and the head jerking backwards and forwards. Of shy disposition and highly aquatic, flying only if pressed to do so.

4 AFRICAN FINFOOT (Watertrapper) *Podica senegalensis*. Fairly common resident on permanent rivers where the habitat is suitable. Breeding has been recorded August-May. A retiring species, spending much time swimming close to the river-banks beneath the overhang of trees. Often little more than the head and neck are visible, the body being almost completely submerged. Occasionally leaves the water to stand on rocks or low branches at which time the bright red feet are conspicuous. Feeds on aquatic animal life seized on the surface or by diving. Normally silent but sometimes makes a subdued clucking sound.   **229**

1

2

3

♀

♂ Br

♂ N-Br

♀

♀

♂

4

♂

60cm

PLATE 13

Grebes. Family PODICIPEDIDAE. Aquatic birds with no proper tail. Feed beneath the surface and can remain submerged for long periods. Seldom seen out of water. One species in the KNP.

1 **DABCHICK** or Little Grebe (Kleindobbertjie) *Tachybaptus ruficollis.* Common on dams and pans throughout the Park all year. Breeds at any time but nowhere permanently resident. A very small, compact swimming bird. The chestnut sides to the head and neck and the cream-coloured spot between eye and bill are diagnostic of the breeding plumage. Dives frequently and has a high-pitched chittering call. **8**

Gallinules, moorhens, coot, crakes and rails. Family RALLIDAE. Small to very small birds of the waterside and marshes, most having long toes for walking on floating vegetation; many are shy and secretive. Feed on vegetable matter, insects, crustacea, etc.

2 **LESSER GALLINULE** (Kleinkoningriethaan) *Porphyrula alleni.* Rare. Has been recorded at various water points in the Park. An irregular visitor, breeding December-April. An extremely shy species and difficult to observe. Spends much time clambering about in dense sedge or walking on floating vegetation. Makes a frog-like 'gurr' with a sharp clicking note. **224**

3 **LESSER MOORHEN** (Kleinwaterhoender) *Gallinula angulata.* An uncommon and irregular intra-Africa migrant. Nests with eggs have been found February-March. A small version of (4) but having orange or greenish legs and more yellow on the bill. Immature birds are olive-brown above, dove-grey below. Secretive, preferring small, secluded waters and temporarily flooded grass. Spends much time feeding in waterside vegetation. **227**

4 **MOORHEN** (Waterhoender) *Gallinula chloropus.* An uncommon, localised breeding resident. Occurs on seasonal floodpans and vleis in the north and east. Young birds have been seen September-October. A distinctive black and white waterbird with a red facial shield and greenish to yellow legs. Makes a fairly high-pitched 'krrrk'. **226**

5 **REDKNOBBED COOT** (Bleshoender) *Fulica cristata.* Rare. An irregular, non-breeding visitor. Reported from a few scattered localities only. A black bird with a conspicuous white facial shield and bill. The legs are grey, the eyes red and there are two red cherry-like knobs on the crown of the head. A bird of open waters, it spends more time swimming than out of the water. Makes a loud 'kowk'. **228**

6 **REDCHESTED FLUFFTAIL** (Rooiborsvleikuiken) *Sarothrura rufa.* Rare. Recorded in both the north and south of the Park. A very small, secretive crake of marshes and vleis. If flushed will fly a short distance before dropping back into cover. Makes a ventriloquial and much repeated 'ooo ooo ooo ooo dueh dueh dueh . . .' **217**

7 **BUFFSPOTTED FLUFFTAIL** (Gevlekte Vleikuiken) *Sarothrura elegans.* Rare. Recorded at three widely separated localities; moist, well-wooded regions. A very small, retiring species usually located by call, a softly ventriloquial and haunting 'ooooooooooooo-eeeeeeeeeee', like the sound of a tuning fork and rising at the end. **218**

8 **BAILLON'S CRAKE** (Kleinriethaan) *Porzana pusilla.* Rare. Seen once only near Nwanedzi, but may prove to be more widespread. A very small, secretive crake of dense waterside vegetation and marshy localities. The bold white streaking on the upperparts is diagnostic. Makes a series of hard, frog-like creaking sounds. **215**

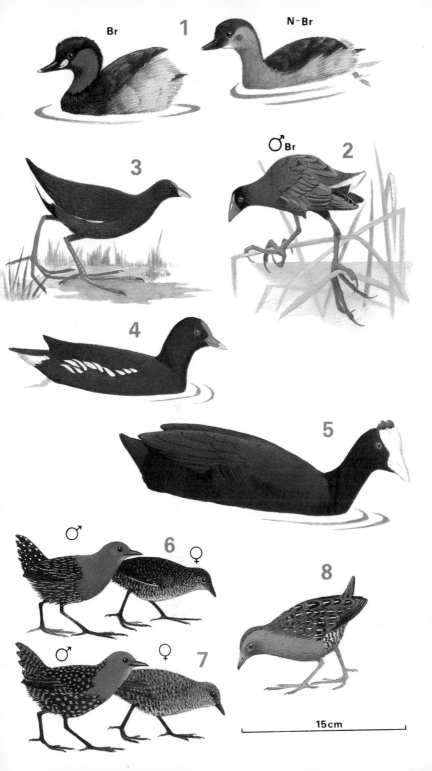

Br **1** **N-Br**

3

♂Br **2**

4

5

♂ **6** **♀**

8

♂ **7** **♀**

15 cm

PLATE 14

1 CORNCRAKE (Kwartelkoning) *Crex crex*. An uncommon but widespread summer visitor. Breeds in Europe. May be found near water but, more frequently, in rank grass away from water. Normally seen only if flushed, when it flutters off in a deceptively weak flight with legs dangling. **211**

2 AFRICAN CRAKE (Afrikaanse Riethaan) *Crex egregia*. Rare and secretive but widespread in the Park, especially in seasons of high rainfall. No breeding recorded. Larger than Baillon's Crake (Plate 13) and lacking the white streaking on the back. Is found at well-vegetated streams and pools, even rain puddles, but also away from water in well-grassed regions. Difficult to observe because of its shy nature. The call is a rapid series of high-pitched whistling notes 'ki-ki-ki-ki-ki . . .'. **212**

3 BLACK CRAKE (Swartriethaan) *Amaurornis flavirostris*. Fairly common resident at water points throughout the Park. Breeds in summer. This unmistakable little crake, unlike most of its relatives, is not shy and may be seen walking at the shoreline of many pans and dams. Yellow bill and red legs diagnostic. The voice is a growling 'churrr'. **213**

4 AFRICAN RAIL (Grootriethaan) *Rallus caerulescens*. Rare. Recorded occasionally in the north and east but its secretive habits may conceal a wider distribution. Larger than others on this plate, the long red bill diagnostic. Typically, keeps well hidden in waterside herbage, emerging occasionally to forage in the shallows. The normal call is a clear whistle 'preeeee' followed by a rapid, descending 'pi-pi-pi-pi . . .'. **210**

Jacanas. Family JACANIDAE. Wading birds with long legs and very long toes adapted to walking on floating vegetation.

5 AFRICAN JACANA (Grootlangtoon) *Actophilornis africanus*. Uncommon but widespread. Breeds throughout the year with a peak in summer. Distinctive and unmistakable. Inhabits well-vegetated pools and dams with water lilies. Young have entirely different head markings; see illustration and cf. (6). Flies low across the water and resettles with wings raised above its back. Feeds on insects found on water plants. Makes a strangely harsh 'kyowrrrr' call. **240**

6 LESSER JACANA (Dwerglangtoon) *Micorparra capensis*. Rare. One positive identification at Mlondozi Dam but probably occurs more frequently. Very small (sparrow size) jacana with distinctive rufous cap and eye-stripe, white eyebrow, yellow pectoral patches, entirely white underparts and yellowish legs; cf. immature of (5). Habits same as (5). **241**

Painted Snipes. Family ROSTRATULIDAE.

7 PAINTED SNIPE (Goudsnip) *Rostratula benghalensis*. Uncommon but widely distributed and probably resident within the Park. There are no breeding records. Seen regularly at certain dams, most often in the southern region. The female is more colourful than the male. An extremely shy and retiring bird, found on muddy shorelines where there is sufficient waterside vegetation for it to hide at the slightest disturbance. It bobs its hind quarters when alarmed. Feeds on small creatures found in mud, plus seeds. **242**

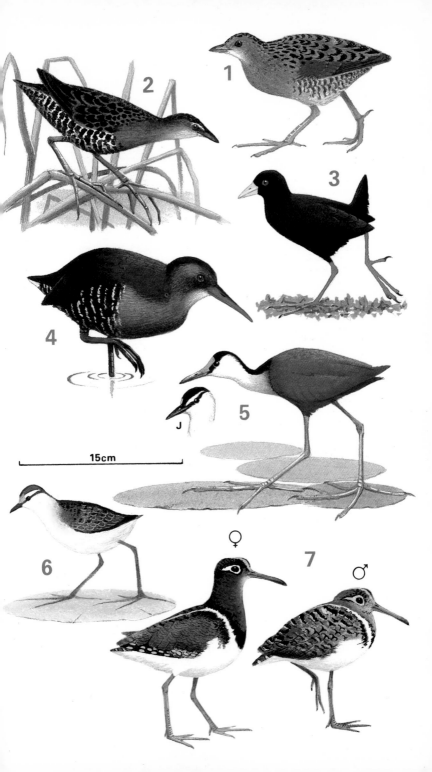

15cm

♀

♂

1

2

3

4

5

J

6

7

PLATE 15

Plovers. Family CHARADRIIDAE. Medium to small birds of shallow waters and shorelines, marshes or open veld. Most have shortish beaks (snipes are the exception) and long legs. Typically, move in short runs followed by a pause in which the head is jerked backwards. They feed on small insects, crustacea, etc. found on the ground or in mud. They lay their eggs in a simple ground scrape.

1 **AFRICAN SNIPE** (Afrikaanse Snip) *Gallinago nigripennis.* Rare. A summer vagrant to the Park recorded at isolated points throughout. A bird of marshy regions, seldom seen unless flushed when it calls 'chuck' and flies away in a zigzag path as illustrated. The very long bill, used for mud-probing, should prevent confusion with any other small wading bird. **286**

2 **CASPIAN PLOVER** (Asiatiese Strandkiewiet) *Charadrius asiaticus.* Rare visitor. Flocks, including immatures, have been seen both in the extreme south and far north. Males are usually seen in partial breeding plumage as illustrated; females may have incomplete rufous breast patch, the dark lower edge always absent. Non-breeding adults resemble immatures. Occurs on arid ground or airstrips with short or burnt grass, not always near water. Calls mostly at night, a shrill 'ku-wit' on take-off. **252**

3 **CHESTNUTBANDED PLOVER** (Rooibandstrandkiewiet) *Charadrius pallidus.* Rare, irregular visitor. Recorded only in the vicinity of the Letaba River. A very small, inconspicuous plover; females lack the black fore-crown and eye-stripe. Usually seen singly in gravel scrapes or on the stony shores of dams, pans and rivers. Makes a soft 'chuck' on take-off. **247**

4 **RINGED PLOVER** (Ringnekstrandkiewiet) *Charadrius hiaticula.* Rare vagrant. Occurs occasionally at dams and rivers throughout the Park. Broad black breast-band encircling neck plus orange bill and legs distinctive; cf. others on this plate. In flight shows a distinct white wing-bar. Singly or in small groups on shorelines of dams and rivers, often with (6). Has a two-syllabled call, a piping 'coo-eep' or 'too-li', and a raspy 'zik-zik-zik'. **245**

5 **KITTLITZ'S PLOVER** (Geelborsstrandkiewiet) *Charadrius pecuarius.* Uncommon resident, breeding mainly July-October. Scattered sightings throughout the Park indicate a sparse but wide distribution. A bird of dry flats near water, airstrips and similar expanses of open terrain. Usually occurs in small parties and will permit a fairly close approach. While running often calls 'trit-tritritritrit'. **248**

6 **THREEBANDED PLOVER** (Driebandstrandkiewiet) *Charadrius tricollaris.* Common resident, widespread throughout the Park at pans, dams and rivers, even on roads during rains. Breeds at all times of the year. The most common small plover, unmistakable in having two black bands across a white breast plus bright red colouring on the bill and around the eyes. Normally occurs in pairs or small groups. It stands and walks in a hunched posture with frequent bobbing of head and tail. Has a shrill call 'tiuu-it'. **249**

15 cm

PLATE 16

1 **LESSER BLACKWINGED PLOVER** (Kleinswartvlerkkiewiet) *Vanellus lugubris*. Uncommon. Resident some years and a visitor in others according to veld conditions. Recorded throughout the Park, breeding June-November. Inconspicuous and usually found in small parties (25 have been recorded in one group) in well-grazed or burnt veld. Stands still to avoid detection and is easily overlooked. The call is a melodious 'tee-uu'. **256**

2 **CROWNED PLOVER** (Kroonkiewiet) *Vanellus coronatus*. A common and widespread resident species found in pairs and small groups anywhere in the Park, preferring bare, overgrazed ground. Breeding has been recorded April-November. A distinctive plover with its red legs and bill, and white band surrounding a black cap. The normal call is 'kie-wieet'. When alarmed flies up calling noisily 'kree-kreep-kreep-dreep'. **255**

3 **BLACKSMITH PLOVER** (Bontkiewiet) *Vanellus armatus*. A common resident species widespread throughout the Park at large rivers, dams and pans. Breeds August-May. A distinctive and striking plover usually found in small parties and unlikely to be confused with any other. The immature has brown colouring where the adult is black. Active and noisy when disturbed, flying overhead and emitting a loud metallic 'klink, klink, klink' similar to the sound of a hammer on an anvil. **258**

4 **WATTLED PLOVER** (Lelkiewiet) *Vanellus senegallus*. Uncommon but probably resident in small numbers. Has been seen at scattered points all over the Park but breeding records are lacking. Can be confused with the next species but note *grey* not white underparts. Is usually seen in pairs or small family parties near water or damp localities. The call is a shrill 'peep-peep' uttered both on the ground and in flight. **260**

5 **WHITECROWNED PLOVER** (Witkopkiewiet) *Vanellus albiceps*. An uncommon resident species found regularly on the Luvuvhu and Olifants Rivers where it frequents sandbanks and sandy shores in pairs or small groups. Also occurs in small numbers on more southerly waters. Breeds during the summer. Easily confused with the previous species but has white top to entire head, white underparts and very long wattles. In flight the prominent white wings are distinctive. Is easily alarmed, flying off with loud cries of 'peep-peep'. **259**

6 **TURNSTONE** (Steenloper) *Arenaria interpres*. Rare Palaearctic passage migrant. Occurs in the Park occasionally September-April, staying a few days before moving on. A small, boldly marked wader with long body usually seen in non-breeding plumage. Feeds in a hunched, head-in-shoulders posture on the shoreline of dams, turning stones and pieces of caked mud with its bill. If flushed flies off revealing extensive white back and wing-bars. **262**

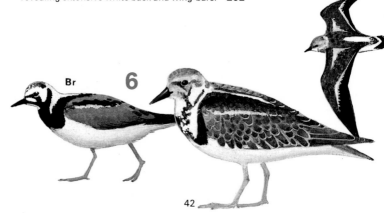

PLATE 17

1 WHITEFRONTED PLOVER (Vaalstrandkiewiet) *Charadrius marginatus.* Uncommon, but probably a breeding resident, especially on the Limpopo and Olifants Rivers. Has also been recorded at other scattered water points throughout the Park. Has a small, thick-set plover with pale buff upperparts and white, ochre-washed underparts and white forehead. Usually occurs in pairs which run about on sandbanks, feeding at the water's edge. On taking flight emits a soft 'twirit'. **246**

Waders. Family SCOLOPACIDAE. Grey, plover-like birds generally referred to as Palaearctic waders. They breed in the northern hemisphere April-June and, at this time, many assume rufous plumage, some ornate plumes in the Ruff. In the northern autumn they migrate south, millions arriving in southern Africa August-October, many still carrying traces of their breeding plumage, soon to be replaced by the drab, non-breeding colouring. Most occur in the Park as passage migrants, a few are present all year. Those which have been seen with partial breeding plumage are illustrated in both plumages. See Appendix for other, less frequent waders.

2 MARSH SANDPIPER (Moerasruiter) *Tringa stagnatilis.* Uncommon but recorded throughout the Park. The white underparts and forehead, long slender black bill and long greenish legs are diagnostic. Resembles a small version of the next species and, like it, shows a white back in flight, the feet trailing. Feeds quietly in shallow water with fairly slow, deliberate movements. The call is 'teeoo, chick'. **269**

3 GREENSHANK (Groenpootruiter) *Tringa nebularia.* Uncommon but present throughout the Park, a few all year. A large, long-legged and long-billed wader with very white underparts and, in flight, a white back and upper tail coverts showing as a conspicuous V-shape. Similar to the previous species but about twice its size, the bill very slightly upcurved. Usually occurs solitarily on rivers, dams, etc. On taking flight invariably utters a sharp 'chu-chu-chu'. **270**

4 RUFF (Kemphaan) *Philomachus pugnax.* Fairly common August-April, occasionally later. A moderately large wader with heavily marked upperparts, a fairly stout bill of medium length with a *pale patch at its base* and long legs of variable colouring; blackish, greenish or orange. The female is called a Reeve and is slightly smaller than the male. A thicknecked wader, usually occurring in flocks. In spring may be seen with white, black or rufous colouring about the neck and mantle, being vestiges of the very variable and ornate breeding plumage. In flight shows a broad white rump with a dark central line. **284**

5 SANDERLING (Drietoonstrandloper) *Calidris alba.* Rare Palaearctic passage migrant. Occurs occasionally on pans and dams during summer. A small shorebird of very white appearance and with a dark shoulder patch; bill short and thickish. Feeds along the shoreline in a hunched, head down posture, occasionally running for short distances. Flight low and direct, white wing-bars conspicuous. **281**

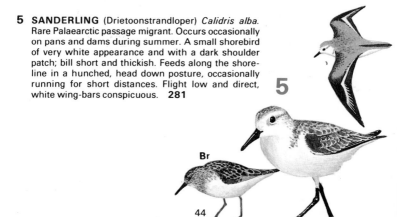

Br

44

PLATE 18

1 GREEN SANDPIPER (Witgatruiter) *Tringa ochropus*. Rare vagrant, may occur at any water point during summer. Larger, plumper than the next species, with longer bill. In flight shows bold white rump, barred tail and dark 'armpits'; cf. also (4). Solitary at edge of quiet streams and grassy ponds, often wading. On take-off towers upwards with a loud, shrill 'weet-a-weet' call. **265**

2 COMMON SANDPIPER (Gewone Ruiter) *Tringa hypoleucos*. Fairly common and widespread during August-April, a few all year, on small streams as well as large rivers and dams. Characterised by *white shoulder-patch* and the habit of *bobbing its rear end up and down*. Usually solitary. When alarmed flies off uttering a shrill 'twee-wee-wee', the flight low, interspersed with bouts of flapping and gliding on downward bowed wings. **264**

3 CURLEW SANDPIPER (Krombekstrandloper) *Calidris ferruginea*. A rare summer visitor recorded at various water points in the Park, sometimes in small flocks. The only small wader with a decurved bill. In flight shows a broad white rump. Feeds while wading, the head being lifted from the water between probes. In flight makes a soft 'chirrup'. **272**

4 WOOD SANDPIPER (Bosruiter) *Tringa glareola*. Fairly common in summer, a few all year. Distinguished by the heavily spotted upperparts, longish straight bill and yellowish legs. In flight differs from (1) in white underwings. Usually solitary, it feeds mostly at the water's edge or in damp grass. If flushed towers up to some height calling 'wee-wee-wee'. **266**

5 LITTLE STINT (Kleinstrandloper) *Calidris minuta*. Uncommon but may be seen at water points anywhere September-April. The smallest of the Palaearctic waders. Appears short-legged and hunched as it feeds in shallow waters, busily probing with quick movements of the head. Singly or in small groups. When disturbed flies off rapidly calling a repeated 'peep, peep'. **274**

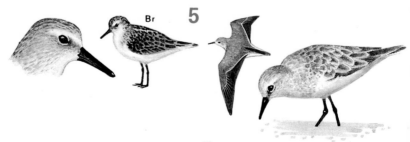

PLATE 19

Dikkops. Family BURHINIDAE. Plover-like birds, characterised by large heads and eyes, large 'knees' (tibiotarsal joint) and the absence of a hind toe. Nocturnal in habit, usually located by their strident calls. Two eggs are laid on the ground in spring and early summer. Dikkops feed on insects, crustacea and molluscs.

1 WATER DIKKOP (Waterdikkop) *Burhinus vermiculatus*. A fairly common resident, widely distributed at water points throughout the Park; breeds in summer. Differs from the next species in having a bar on the folded wing and by its preference for a waterside habitat. Inactive by day, but may be seen at waterside locations where it stands partially concealed in shoreline herbage. At night flies about calling a shrill, piping, 'we-we-whee-wheeoo-wheeoo . . .' fading at the end. **298**

2 SPOTTED DIKKOP (Dikkop) *Burhinus capensis*. Fairly common and resident throughout the Park, breeding in early summer. This very speckled species with its long, yellow legs and large, yellow eyes is seldom seen by day unless flushed from its roost among stones or under trees in dry terrain. It becomes active late in the day and may be seen on roads at this time and throughout the night. Very vocal in moonlight, it flies about restlessly and reveals its presence by a plaintive, eerie call 'chwee, chwee, chwee, tiu-tiu-tiu-tiu . . .' tailing off gradually and repeated frequently. **297**

Pratincoles and coursers. Family GLAREOLIDAE. Pratincoles are migratory and nomadic birds characterised by very short legs in relation to body-length. At rest or in their elegant, often erratic flight, they resemble terns. Feed mostly in the air in flocks. The related coursers are plover-like birds having bulbous heads, long legs and feet which lack a hind toe. They are entirely terrestrial, feeding on seeds and insects, especially harvester termites. Their eggs are laid on bare ground.

3 REDWINGED PRATINCOLE (Rooivlerksprinkaanvoël) *Glareola pratincola*. Uncommon nomadic resident, seen mostly July-February in flocks of up to 50 birds; breeding has been recorded in mid-summer at Engelhard Dam. In flight shows rufous underwing coverts ('armpits') and a white trailing edge to the inner wing or secondaries. Immatures have mottled breasts. Flocks frequent floodlands, marshes, dams and rivers where they may rise to great heights while feeding in graceful flight. When settling habitually stands briefly with wings raised. The in-flight call is 'kik, kik'. **304**

4 BRONZEWINGED COURSER (Bronsvlerkdrawwertjie) *Rhinoptilus chalcopterus*. Fairly common but nocturnal and secretive. Recorded all over the Park, breeding in early summer. A large courser with very distinctive head markings and clear white underparts; in flight the white rump is obvious. Is likely to be seen at nightfall when it sometimes ventures onto roads. When flying at night has a shrill call 'ji-ku-it' and also a plaintive, harsher call 'groraag'. **303**

5 TEMMINCK'S COURSER (Trekdrawwertjie) *Cursorius temminckii*. Uncommon, irregular nomad occurring at all times of the year and breeding in the Park during dry periods or after veld-burning, usually July-November. A small courser likely to be seen only in open regions of sparse grass. Runs quickly and then stops in an upright stance, occasionally bobbing its head and tail. Normally occurs in small parties. A quiet, inconspicuous bird, easily overlooked. **300**

6 BURCHELL'S COURSER (Bloukopdrawwertjie) *Cursorius rufus*. A rare, nomadic non-breeding visitor seen a few times in the north. Differs from (5) in having a grey back to the crown, more white on belly. Behaviour and habits similar to (5). **299**

7 THREEBANDED COURSER (Driebanddrawwertjie) *Rhinoptilus cinctus*. Rare. Seen twice only in the far north of the Park, the only records of this species in South Africa. The distinctive head and breast markings are unmistakable. Usually occurs in well-grassed woodland. **302**

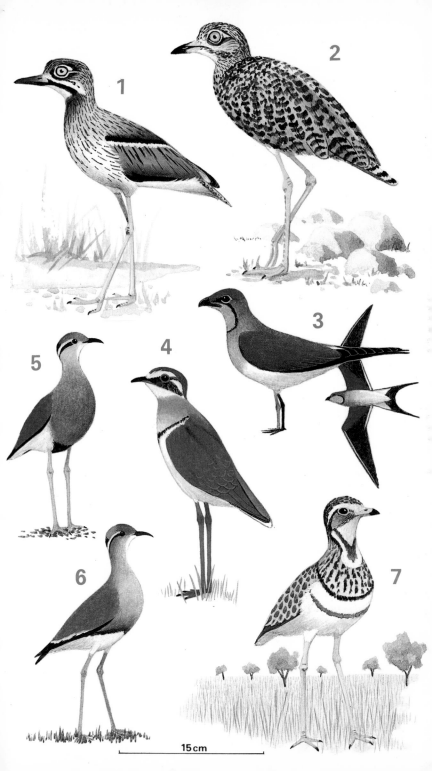

15 cm

PLATE 20

Gulls and terns. Family LARIDAE. Gulls are well known as coastal scavengers but the Greyheaded Gull is also found on inland waters. The related terns are more elegant, slender-winged, shorter-legged and feed by catching small fish and insects. Terns are normally silent.

1 GREYHEADED GULL (Gryskopmeeu) *Larus cirrocephalus*. An uncommon, non-breeding summer visitor. Adult has grey head, red bill and legs; immature lacks the grey head but has a dark smudge behind the eye, bill and legs dark. May occur at any water point. Single birds normally silent but feeding groups make loud, high-pitched 'kraaa' calls. **315**

2 WHISKERED TERN (Witbaardsterretjie) *Chlidonias hybridus*. Rare, non-breeding visitor. Grey body and black cap of breeding plumage distinctive; non-breeding birds differ from (3) mainly in pale grey (not white) rump and by black line from eye to nape. Occurs on any water, flying back and forth hawking insects or plucking them from the surface. Flight slower, more laboured and direct than (3). **338**

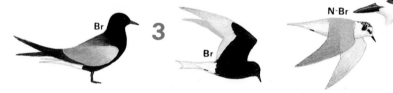

3 WHITEWINGED TERN (Witvlerksterretjie) *Chlidonias leucopterus*. Uncommon, non-breeding summer visitor. Normally seen in non-breeding plumage when it differs from (2) in a whiter rump and dark patch behind the eye extending to the crown. In March may occur with black or partially black breeding plumage. Feeds on insects caught in the air or on the water, and fish. Flight light and buoyant; cf. (2). **339**

Avocets and stilts. Family RECURVIROSTRIDAE. Black and white wading birds with very long legs and long, slender bills either straight or recurved. They feed on aquatic insects.

4 AVOCET (Bontelsie) *Recurvirostra avosetta*. Rare. An occasional vagrant, likely to be seen at water points anywhere in the Park. Quite unmistakable. Wades in shallow water sweeping its upturned bill from side to side as it feeds. The call is a liquid-sounding 'kluut'. **294**

5 BLACKWINGED STILT (Rooipootelsie) *Himantopus himantopus*. Uncommon but widespread resident. Unmistakable. Occurs singly or in small parties and is most regularly seen on the Olifants River. Picks its food from the water's surface and in mud. In flight may emit a high-pitched 'kik kik kik kik'. **295**

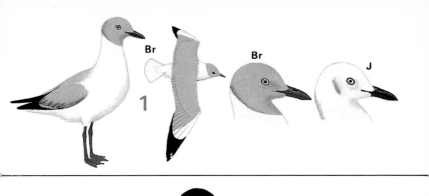

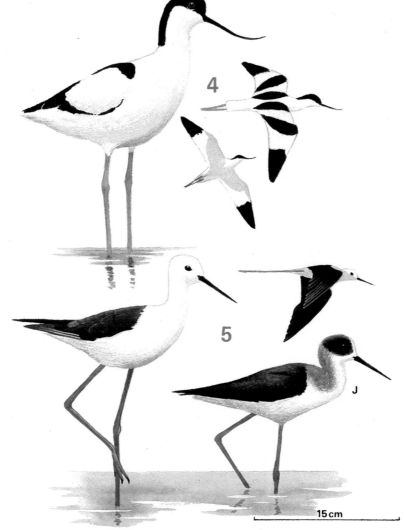

15 cm

PLATE 21

Bustards and korhaans. Family OTIDIDAE. Medium to large, long-legged, long-necked terrestrial birds, cryptically coloured, with bills and heads flattened, tails short and feet with three forward-facing toes. Most species have elaborate courtship or territorial displays involving plumage transformations, visual displays or unusual calls. They feed on vegetable matter, insects, small reptiles and rodents.

1 **BLACKBELLIED KORHAAN (LONGLEGGED KORHAAN)** (Langbeenkorhaan) *Eupodotis melanogaster*. Fairly common and widespread. Occurs all over the Park but only during summer in the south-west. Breeds October-February. Males may be distinguished from the next species by the fact that the black of the underparts extends in a thin line up the neck to the chin. The female has a *white* belly. Its long legs are a diagnostic feature. Occurs singly or in pairs in regions of open bush. The male has a distinctive territorial call delivered in three different postures, starting and ending with the neck withdrawn into its shoulders and wings drooped. Next, the head and neck are stretched fully upwards with bill held high and the sound 'waak' (or 'phwoe') is made; then the head is lowered about half-way to the body and it utters a throaty grunt followed by a five-second pause, and finally a sharp whip-like sound 'ooor . . . whip!'; see illustrations. It also performs a courtship flight, descending from about 50 metres above the ground with wings raised and plumage fluffed. **238**

2 **REDCRESTED KORHAAN** (Boskorhaan) *Eupodotis ruficrista*. A common resident all over the Park; breeds September-February. Smaller than (1) and found at times in quite dense bush. The distinct cream-coloured V-marks on the upperparts are diagnostic. The male's rufous crest is seldom visible and is not a recognition feature. The female has a broad white band across the lower breast; in the male this is reduced to a small patch on either side of the breast. Both sexes have black bellies. The male's territorial call commences with a series of throat-clicks, slowly at first, then increasing in speed and suddenly changing to a series of shrill, piercing whistles 'phee-phee-phee . . .' repeated many times. In courtship the pair perform a duet, a rapidly repeated 'wuk-wuk-wuk-wuk . . .' by both sexes, rising in volume and increasing in frequency to 'wuka-wuka-wuka-wuka . . .'; then the male switches to the whistling call while the female either continues as before or makes a series of rapid clicks. At the onset of the breeding season the male flies up almost vertically to about 30 metres and then tumbles headlong as though shot. **237**

3 **KORI BUSTARD** (Gompou) *Ardeotis kori*. A common resident in the north, less common in the south. Breeds in summer. The largest flying land bird, second in size only to the Ostrich. Usually seen in pairs when the males' greater size can be appreciated. The male has a curious courtship display; the throat pouch is inflated, the neck feathers splayed outwards, revealing their white bases; the head, with crest raised, is drawn back and the breast thrown out; the wings are drooped and the tail deflected upwards and forwards over the back to expose the white undertail coverts. In addition to vegetable matter and small animal life, it also has a liking for the gum that exudes from the bark of certain *Acacia* trees, hence the Afrikaans name. Normally a quiet species, although the male calls 'wum-wum-wum-wumum' in the mating season. **230**

60cm

PLATE 22

Sandgrouse. Family PTEROCLIDAE. Pigeon-like, cryptically coloured inhabitants of sandy regions, the males more boldly patterned than the females. Their eyes protrude from the head, which affords the birds a 360 degree field of vision and enables them to keep a potential source of danger in view while facing in the opposite direction. Their flight is rapid, the birds often covering long distances morning and evening to reach water where, at certain favoured pools, they may be seen arriving to drink in their hundreds or even thousands. Short legs cause sandgrouse to walk in a shuffling, dove-like manner. Three or four eggs are laid in a simple ground depression. One species occurs in the KNP.

1 DOUBLEBANDED SANDGROUSE (Dubbelbandsandpatrys) *Pterocles bicinctus.* Common and widespread throughout the Park with numbers greatest in the north. A resident species, breeding in the dry months. An inconspicuous bird easily overlooked but for its tendency to flush suddenly and without warning at the approach of a vehicle. Occurs in pairs in sandy regions with sparse grass cover and is often found searching for seeds at roadsides. Makes a soft 'weep-weeu, chuck-chukkie, weep-weeu' and a sharp 'chuck-chuck' when flushed. **347**

Guineafowls. Family NUMIDIDAE. Large, partridge-like birds, having mostly un-feathered necks and heads with horny excrescences or crests, unspurred legs and blackish plumage covered with small white spots. Highly gregarious in habits except when breeding, at which time pairs leave the flock temporarily, laying 6-8 eggs in a well-concealed ground scrape.

2 HELMETED GUINEAFOWL (Gewone Tarentaal) *Numida meleagris.* A common and widespread resident, breeding November-May. A well-known and unmis-takable species, the blue neck and wattles, red cap and horny casque being diagnostic. The chick, illustration (a), is buffy-brown striped dark brown over head and body. Half-grown chicks (b) are predominantly brown, darker on the upperparts, and the head stripes remain until the casque starts to grow. Immatures (c) have the neck feathered and are less strikingly coloured about the head than the adults, with a rudimentary casque. Frequents well-grazed regions and river banks for preference, and occurs in flocks numbering sometimes many dozens, which come regularly to water in the evenings. Feeds on seeds, tubers and various other vegetable matter plus insects, being particularly attracted to termites. The normal call is a much repeated 'kerbek-kerbek-kerbek . . .', the alarm note a rasping 'kek-kek-kek-kek-krrrrr-kek-kek-kek . . .'. Females also utter a fairly shrill, piping, 'pittoo, pittoo . . .'. **203**

3 CRESTED GUINEAFOWL (Kuifkoptarentaal) *Guttera pucherani.* Fairly common locally within its restricted range, occurring in numbers only in the regions of Pafuri, Punda Maria and the Nwambiya flats, more sparsely on the Lebombo Hills (especially in stands of ironwood trees *Androstachys johnsonii*) as far south as Nwanedzi. Breeds throughout the summer. More secretive than (2), frequenting thick bush with a dense understratum. Occurs in flocks of about 20-30, and feeds on tubers, seeds, fruits and various other vegetable matter obtained, together with insects, by scratching in the soil. Has a rattling alarm note and a 'tick-tack, tick-tack, tirr, tirr, tirr' call. **204**

PLATE 23

Buttonquails or hemipodes. Family TURNICIDAE. Diminutive, ground-dwelling, quail-like birds, closely allied to sandgrouse and pigeons. They are peculiar in lacking a hind toe, while the females are larger than the males and more richly coloured. Cock buttonquails do most of the egg-incubation and are entirely responsible for the care of the young. The sexes are more likely to be seen singly than are true quails, but adults with chicks are sometimes seen at roadsides. Two species occur in the KNP, both nomadic by nature.

1 KURRICHANE BUTTONQUAIL (Bosveldkwarteltjie) *Turnix sylvatica.* Common and widespread in summer only, breeding throughout the season in years of good rainfall. Difficult to distinguish from the next species but has *yellow eyes,* is less rufous about the head and underparts and has dark, heart-shaped spots on the flanks; the male is a faded version of the female. Occurs in dry grassland and woodland. Has the habit of flushing almost at one's feet or in front of an approaching vehicle, to fly a short distance and then drop to the ground, running off at a tangent. The flight is less vigorous than that of true quails. Females make a ventriloquial 'dooo . . . dooo . . .' at about 2-second intervals. **205**

2 BLACKRUMPED BUTTONQUAIL (HOTTENTOT BUTTONQUAIL) (Kaapse Kwarteltjie) *Turnix hottentotta.* Uncommon. Present all year but no breeding records exist. More rufous than the previous species, apparent when the bird flies and a definite aid to identification; the male is less richly coloured. In the KNP occurs in well-developed grassveld and at the edges of vleis. Habits otherwise as those of (1), the voice similar but of lower pitch. **206**

Francolins and quails. Family PHASIANIDAE. Francolins fall into two groups: those which run off when approached, only taking flight if hard pressed, and those which crouch in the face of danger, flushing suddenly only when about to be stepped on; in this respect resembling the action of partridges. All are notoriously difficult to identify from plumage alone but their calls are distinctive, loud and frequently heard. Six francolins and two quails, which are much smaller relatives, occur in the Park.

3 COMMON QUAIL (Afrikaanse Kwartel) *Coturnix coturnix.* Irregular, recorded August-April throughout the Park. Sometimes abundant in seasons of good rain. Chicks have been recorded in April. The male differs from the male of the next species in being less richly coloured, but otherwise the head patterns are similar. The female has paler underparts and more white about the head than the female of (4) but, unless seen on a road, is usually encountered only when flushed when the two species are almost indistinguishable; the pair fly off with whirring wings and resettle at some distance. Normal call 'whit-*whit*it, whit-*whit*it'; when flushed calls 'pree-pree-pree', a useful recognition feature. **200**

4 HARLEQUIN QUAIL (Bontkwartel) *Coturnix delegorguei.* Irregular but very common throughout the Park in summers of good rain. Breeding has been recorded January-March but varies with rainfall. The rich rufous colouring of the male is diagnostic when visible, the female almost indistinguishable from the female of (3). When flushed can best be identified by call. When present occurs in numbers in grassy regions. The male has a loud, ringing call 'wit, wit-wit, wit, wit-wit-it'. On being flushed calls 'kree'. **201**

15cm

PLATE 24

1 COQUI FRANCOLIN (Swempie) *Francolinus coqui.* Fairly common throughout the Park. Has been seen with small chicks November-May. A small, rather secretive francolin normally seen only when crossing roads. Occurs in pairs and family parties. When alarmed either crouches or walks stealthily in a crouched attitude, neck outstretched. Prefers regions of long grass. May be located by its calls, the usual one heard being a high-pitched 'bee-kwik bee-kwik . . .' or 'co-qui co-qui . . .' (from which the name is derived) repeated at any time of the day. The male also has a territorial crowing call, a shrill, descending 'kek, KEK, kek-kek-kek-kek-kek-kek' often repeated at dawn and dusk.   **188**

2 CRESTED FRANCOLIN (Bospatrys) *Francolinus sephaena.* A common resident all over the Park; breeding has been recorded December-July. The characteristic dark crown, the feathers of which are often raised in a short crest, and its habit of cocking its tail like a bantam chicken, are features which readily identify this francolin. Usually occurs in family groups and frequents roads to forage in elephant droppings. Eats many bulbs, seeds and berries in addition to insects. The call is said to resemble the words 'beer and cognac' but is perhaps better described as a shrill 'kwirri kwerri' often repeated at dawn and dusk.   **189**

3 SHELLEY'S FRANCOLIN (Laeveldpatrys) *Francolinus shelleyi.* Uncommon but thinly distributed throughout the Park. Chicks have been seen in June. A secretive species, it favours lightly wooded, stony ground on hillsides. The white throat, the reddish breast and flanks surrounding a patch of speckled black and white on the belly are all diagnostic. When disturbed lies close, flushing only at the last moment. The shrill call, usually heard at sunset, resembles the words 'I'll drink yer beer' and is repeated several times.   **191**

4 NATAL FRANCOLIN (Natalse Fisant) *Francolinus natalensis.* Common and widespread. Occurs throughout the Park in suitable habitat with chicks recorded May-August. Has red or orange legs *and* bill plus an erect stance with tail held low. Common along rivers and on koppies. Very noisy at sunrise and sunset, or if disturbed; the call is a loud, descending 'kwali, KWALI, kwali'; when alarmed makes a raucous cackling.   **196**

5 SWAINSON'S FRANCOLIN (Bosveldfisant) *Francolinus swainsonii.* Very common throughout the Park, even abundant in the central region. Chicks have been recorded February-August, with a peak March-May. The only dark brown francolin in the Park with red face and neck and *black legs*; cf. next species. Prefers regions of short, overgrazed grass and spends much time on roads, especially after rain if the grass is long. The male has the habit of standing on fallen logs, anthills, etc. from where it makes its harsh crowing call which starts loudly and then descends and fades 'krrraaak-krrraaak-krrraaak . . .'.   **199**

6 REDNECKED FRANCOLIN (Rooikeelfisant) *Francolinus afer.* Rare. Has been positively identified in the Satara-Nwanedzi region only. A vagrant from Mozambique which should be watched for in the eastern regions. Has the same red face and neck as the previous species but the *legs are red,* the underparts black with white streaks. Has a harsh, crowing call 'kwoor, kwoor, kwoor, kwirr . . .' fading at the end.   **198**

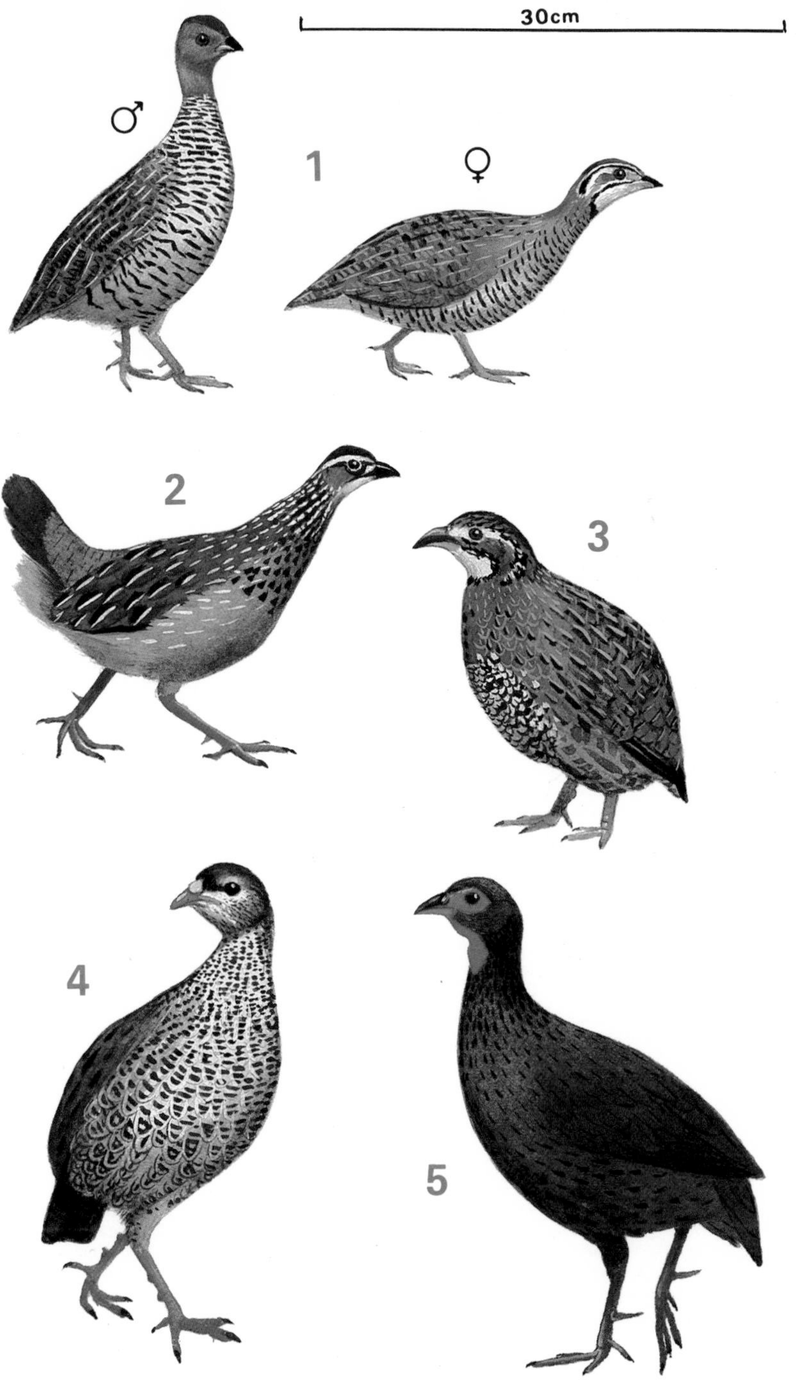
30cm
♂
1
♀
2
3
4
5

PLATE 25

Vultures, kites, eagles, buzzards, hawks, harriers and Gymnogene. Family ACCIPITRIDAE. A large, distinctive group of diurnal flesh-eating birds, commonly referred to as raptors and characterised by hooked bills, talons adapted for grasping (with the exception of vultures) and nostrils placed in a fleshy cere at the base of the bill. Females are usually larger than males, immatures usually with different plumage to adults. All are capable of powerful flight and sustained soaring. Most members of the family are silent birds except when excited or in display. Their voices are high-pitched and their calls of a 'kek-kek-kek . . .' nature, distinguishable only with difficulty. Voices are therefore described only in those few species which call habitually. The term 'hawk', often used erroneously for any member of the family, is applicable only to goshawks and sparrowhawks.

Vultures. Large scavenging birds with heads more or less devoid of feathers, heavy, hooked bills and feet not adapted for grasping as in other birds of prey. Vultures feed on dead animals which are sought while soaring at a great height, the descent of the first bird causing others to converge on the spot. Of the six vulture species recorded in the Park four are resident and two are visitors, one of them rare.

1 WHITEBACKED VULTURE (Witrugaasvoël) *Gyps africanus.* A common resident and by far the most numerous vulture in the Park. Breeding is usually in small, loose colonies, the nests placed in large trees on riverbanks and the eggs laid in June. With age becomes very pale and is thus easily confused with the larger Cape Vulture (2) but can be separated by eye colour at close range: dark brown as against golden brown or straw-colour in the latter. Almost impossible to distinguish from the Cape Vulture in flight unless the white rump is visible. On overcast days may be seen sitting in trees, reluctant to fly without thermal assistance. Congregate at water to bathe. **123**

2 CAPE VULTURE (Kransaasvoël) *Gyps coprotheres.* An uncommon non-breeding visitor. Occurs all over the Park but is most common in the south and during the summer. A large vulture, the adult is very pale, almost white. Eye colour is golden-brown to straw in contrast to the dark brown eye of the Whitebacked Vulture (1) with which it can be confused. Occurs at kills in small numbers only, usually being greatly outnumbered by Whitebacks, which, however, it dominates. **122**

3 SECRETARY BIRD. Family SAGITTARIIDAE. (Sekretarisvoël) *Sagittarius serpentarius.* This bird is not a vulture but a terrestrial bird of prey, and placed in a family of its own. A fairly common resident species found throughout the Park. Breeding has been recorded in October and midsummer, the nest placed in the crown of an *Acacia* thorn. A fairly well known and distinctive bird, normally seen striding through the veld in pairs. Will feed on almost any small creature, including snakes, and also devours the eggs of terrestrial birds in addition to their young. Frequently takes to the air and soars to a great height. **118**

60 cm

PLATE 26

1 **HOODED VULTURE** (Monnikaasvoël) *Necrosyrtes monachus*. A fairly common resident species throughout the Park. Breeding takes place July-October. A small vulture having a relatively weak bill, feeding on offal and the softer parts of carcasses. The adult illustrated is in breeding plumage. Within the Park many immatures are seen, some having a combination of brown down on the head, and white pants. In flight appears square-winged and dark, differing from the much larger Lappetfaced Vulture (3) in having less white visible on the legs and lacking the diamond-shaped tail of that species. **121**

2 **WHITEHEADED VULTURE** (Witkopaasvoël) *Trigonoceps occipitalis*. Uncommon but resident. Nests with eggs have been recorded July-August, in one case the nest of a Tawny Eagle (Plate 30) being used. A very handsome vulture, striking both at rest and in flight; almost entirely white on underparts and head, female only with white secondary flight feathers, face and legs pink, the bill red with blue at base. Immature much browner on head and underparts. Flight pattern also distinctive, female showing more white on wings than male. Frequently seen in pairs and less common at kills than others of the family. Has been known to kill small animals itself. **125**

EGYPTIAN VULTURE (Egiptiese Aasvoël) *Neophron percnopterus*. Very rare vagrant. There exist a handful of reported sightings only. Is generally very scarce in southern Africa, although formerly common. An unmistakable small white vulture with yellow face and bill; in flight the wedge-shaped white tail and pied wing pattern are diagnostic. Immatures are brown and resemble the immature of (1) but have the head and neck fully feathered. Could occur anywhere in the Park. **120**

3 **LAPPETFACED VULTURE** (Swartaasvoël) *Torgos tracheliotus*. A fairly common resident species throughout the Park. Breeding starts June-July. This is the largest of the vultures and, though similar in colouring to the very much smaller Hooded Vulture (1), note that the head is a deep purple-red with much loose skin around the ears and neck, the bill massive. Immature plumage is similar to the adult but white down may be present on the head, the underparts are entirely brown, and white feathers may be present on the back. When this vulture arrives at a kill it dominates the scene until satiated, bouncing into the fray with an upright gait and its huge wings spread, and will peck at any smaller vulture slow to give way. **124**

1

J

J

J

2

3

60 cm

PLATE 27

1 **CUCKOO HAWK** (Koekoekvalk) *Aviceda cuculoides*. An uncommon resident species found throughout the Park. The banded underparts of adult resemble the marking of certain cuckoos, and its name stems from this. The head has loose feathers on the crown which form a crest at all ages; a characteristic feature when the bird is at rest. In flight the wing shape is reminiscent of a large falcon but the movements are slow and heavy-winged. Usually occurs in well-developed riverine forest. Feeds on small reptiles such as lizards and chameleons, and on insects. **128**

2 **YELLOWBILLED KITE** (Geelbekwou) *Milvus migrans parasitus*. A common intra-Africa migrant and common in the Park August-March with breeding recorded in early summer. A fairly large, all brown kite with a distinctly forked tail, yellow bill and legs. On the upper wing a crescent shape of paler feathers is noticeable in flight; see illustration. In addition to eating small rodents, obtains much of its food by scavenging along roads and around camps, and is then seen flying at low altitude in search of food scraps, the long tail being continually twisted from side to side as the bird manoeuvres. An extremely bold bird at camps, snatching food from tables or from the hand when offered. Also forms flocks when many birds are attracted to a food source such as carrion or when flying termites are emerging, and stays in the vicinity for days. At times calls repeatedly in flight, a high-pitched 'kleeeuw'. (This and the Black Kite (3) are races of the same species.) **126**

3 **BLACK KITE** (Swartwou) *Milvus migrans migrans*. A fairly common non-breeding intra-Africa migrant, present throughout the Park in summer, but in smaller numbers than (2). Differs from the Yellowbilled Kite in having a less deeply forked tail, a grey head and mantle and a black bill, only the cere being yellow. Apart from the pale head, is generally darker than (2) but, in flight, has the same upperwing pattern made by paler wing coverts. When the tail is spread it appears square-cut, not forked. The immature has pale underparts, streaked and blotched darker. Its habits are identical to those of (2) with, perhaps, a greater tendency to flock. (This and the Yellowbilled Kite are races of the same species.) **126**

PLATE 28

Snake eagles can be separated from true eagles by their unfeathered legs and large owl-like eyes set in square, loosely feathered heads. Their feet are small for eagles but powerful and adapted to gripping and crippling snakes. These are then killed by twisting pecks on their spines and devoured directly into the stomach, not the crop. When carrying snakes to their young, snake eagles partially ingest them and leave only short lengths hanging freely from their bills. At the nest the young pull at this protruding section and thus retrieve the entire snake. The Bateleur is considered to be an aberrant snake eagle.

1 **BATELEUR** (Berghaan) *Terathopius ecaudatus*. A common and widespread resident eagle, breeding January-April. The adult with its heavy, apparently tailless body and bright red face and legs is unmistakable. In flight the flying-wing appearance, the very short tail, and the distinctive black and white underwing colouring are diagnostic. A further field character is its habit of tilting from side to side in flight. Note differences in wing pattern between male and female both while at rest and in flight, and the normal rufous-backed form (a) as opposed to the less common cream-backed form (b). The immature carries plumage (c) for about five years, passing to plumage (d) prior to attaining the adult colouring after seven years. Compare Brown Snake Eagle (3). At all stages the immature has a longer tail than the adult. The Bateleur is normally seen flying at no great height and covers great distances daily without apparent effort. Will eat carrion and may be seen at kills. Also eats birds and small mammals, catching them by a rapid flying approach while they are feeding on the ground. **146**

2 **BLACKBREASTED SNAKE EAGLE** (Swartborsslangarend) *Circaetus gallicus*. Uncommon but resident. Breeding has been recorded June-August. The adult is frequently mistaken for the Martial Eagle (Plate 32) but, at rest, the smaller size, unfeathered legs and large eyes can be noted. In flight the underwing at all stages is *light* in colour, not dark as in the Martial. The immature in its first plumage (a) can be confused with many other brown raptors, especially (1) and (3) on this plate, but is lighter in build than (1) and paler in colour than (3). This species hunts its prey by repeatedly hovering at some height, and is unique among eagles in this respect. Snakes are usually seized, carried off alive and killed in the air. **143**

3 **BROWN SNAKE EAGLE** (Bruinslangarend) *Circaetus cinereus*. Fairly common and resident throughout the Park, breeding January-February. A rather conspicuous brown eagle through its habit of still-hunting: perching in an exposed situation to watch the surrounding veld for snakes. When perched the stance is erect, as illustrated. The adult is plain brown with large eyes and whitish legs. In flight the dark body and underwing coverts contrast with silvery-white flight feathers while the bands on the spread tail are clearly discernible. The immature (a) leaves the nest closely resembling the adult. Later it adopts heavily mottled underparts with much white feathering in evidence (b) prior to its adult plumage. Snakes are more frequently killed on the ground than in the previous species, with larger snakes being caught. **142**

60 cm

♂ ♀ Jc

♀ Jd Jd

1 a Jc

b ♂

2 Jb Jb Ja

Jb 3 Ja

PLATE 29

1 BOOTED EAGLE (Dwergarend) *Hieraaetus pennatus*. Rare and non-resident, is seen mostly in summer and autumn. A very small eagle which could be mistaken for a Black Kite (Plate 27) or Wahlberg's Eagle (3), especially in flight. Occurs in two colour forms, totally dark brown (a) or white or pale buff (b), the buff form probably representing immature plumage of the white. Pale birds are more common than dark ones. Small white shoulder patches are diagnostic and may be seen in flight. Note distinctive pattern on upper wing caused by pale coverts, seen as a crescent shape in flight; cf. Black Kite (Plate 27). In soaring flight the tail is fanned, rounded and often flexed from side to side, wings held slightly forward. Flapping flight is rapid with four or five wing-beats followed by a glide. Captures small mammals and birds on the ground.   **136**

2 LESSER SPOTTED EAGLE (Gevlekte Arend) *Aquila pomarina*. A common non-breeding visitor from Europe recorded throughout the Park October-March. When perched, a very nondescript brown eagle of small size with *closely feathered legs* resembling stovepipe-trousers. Only the immature is spotted on the wings. In flight appears heavy-winged, the wings having almost parallel leading and trailing edges, tail short and rounded, head protruding little. The distinctive white rump and wing markings of the immature diminish with age and are vestigial in the adult. Is most often seen feeding at termite emergences and Quelea colonies (Plate 97), where it eats the chicks, with other raptors, especially Steppe Eagles (Plate 30).   **134**

3 WAHLBERG'S EAGLE (Bruinarend) *Aquila wahlbergi*. A common intra-Africa breeding migrant, arriving in August and departing March-April. Occurs all over the Park and starts to breed almost immediately after arrival. A few birds over-winter in the Park. Very variable in plumage colouring as illustrated (a), (b) and (c). Combinations of these occur, pale birds having dark heads and dark birds with pale heads, while some pale individuals are light brown, not pure white. In the Park the most common form is (b). A feature common to all but the darkest colour form is a darkening around the eyes. The legs are fully feathered but do not appear as slender as those of (2). The underwing pattern is merely a lightening of colour towards the base of the primaries. The flight shape shows narrow, parallel wings and *square tail held closed* except when manoeuvring; thus the impression is of two planks of wood in the form of a cross. The majority of small brown eagles seen in summer are this species. The diet is small mammals, birds, reptiles, etc. plus termites.   **135**

60 cm

PLATE 30

1 **LONGCRESTED EAGLE** (Langkuifarend) *Lophaetus occipitalis.* Uncommon. Assumed to be a non-breeding visitor. Sightings have been made all over the Park at all times of the year. An unmistakable dark brown eagle, the long crest being obvious at all times. There is a variable amount of white on the legs, sometimes none. The flight pattern is distinctive as illustrated. Feeds mostly on vlei rats.   **139**

2 **STEPPE EAGLE** (Steppe-arend) *Aquila nipalensis.* Fairly common seasonally and locally. A non-breeding migrant from Asia, occurring in the KNP November-February. A gregarious, large brown eagle considered by some to be a migrant race of the Tawny Eagle (3) to which, in any case, it is closely related. The adult is very dark brown on the body (darker and plainer than the darkest Tawny), wings and legs, sometimes with a pale patch on the crown or nape. Sub-adult is similar but may still have light patches on the wings. Feet, cere and gape are rich chrome-yellow, the gape being large, prominent and extending to a point *level with the back of the eye.* Heavily feathered legs give a baggy, trousered appearance. Immature has much paler, faded plumage, almost white at times, thus closely resembling pale Tawny Eagle (3d). Bold white emarginations on wing feathers, especially in flight, are diagnostic. Feeds on the ground at termite emergences, sometimes in great numbers. Also known to gather at Quelea (Plate 97) breeding colonies and eat young birds from the nests.   **133**

3 **TAWNY EAGLE** (Roofarend) *Aquila rapax.* A fairly common and widespread resident eagle; breeds during winter, the eggs being laid in June. Variable in colour from blond, almost white young birds (d) to the more tawny or dark brown adults (a), (b) and (c). Dark adults have warm brown plumage overlaid with black blotches, *not* plain brown as adult Steppe Eagle (2). Immature may be almost indistinguishable from immature Steppe but white emarginations on wings are less obvious. At all ages the gape is paler yellow, smaller and less obvious, extending backwards to a point *beneath the centre* of the eye. The legs are also less baggy in appearance than in (2). Will sometimes mingle with the migrant Steppes, especially when feeding on termites, otherwise not gregarious in the KNP. Normal diet small mammals, game birds and carrion, habitually visiting kills made by carnivores. **132**

PLATE 31

1 **AYRES' EAGLE** (Kleinjagarend) *Hieraaetus ayresii.* Rare. A non-breeding summer visitor. There have been a number of recorded sightings of this small eagle, mostly in the northern region, all adult birds. Ayres' Eagle superficially resembles the next species but is smaller and more agile. Some individuals, probably females, are so heavily blotched on the underside as to appear quite dark (b) while others are only lightly spotted (a). The leading edge of the wing is frequently unspotted and then shows as a white patch on the folded wing. The forehead may be white or dark; in the latter case the effect is of a dark cap over the eyes. The underwing is heavily barred and the undertail shows a broad, dark terminal band and three narrow bands in flight. The immature is very much lighter, as illustrated. A swift, rapacious little eagle which catches birds in rapid pursuit. Prefers well-wooded regions and spends much of the day concealed in a leafy tree. **138**

2 **AFRICAN HAWK EAGLE** (Grootjagarend) *Hieraaetus fasciatus.* A fairly common, widespread resident species which breeds in winter. A medium-sized eagle, secretive at rest, preferring large, well-foliated trees, but pairs may be seen soaring on most days if searched for. The sexes are similar though female is generally more heavily marked on the underparts. Flight pattern very distinctive, the 'windows' in the wings being diagnostic. Immatures, as illustrated, are quite different, this plumage gradually becoming whiter and more spotted on the underparts, the spots increasing in density from the sides of the body and the buff colouring fading to white from the centre outwards. Sub-adults may therefore be seen with buff only on the sides of the chest, flanks and legs. The upperparts also darken gradually but white feather-tips remain until maturity. The diet is mainly francolins and guineafowls but small mammals are also taken. **137**

3 **CROWNED EAGLE** (Kroonarend) *Stephanoaetus coronatus.* Uncommon and localised. Is most often seen at Pafuri but also occurs occasionally further south. Breeds in summer. A large, very powerful eagle, heavy in stature, comparatively short-winged and long-tailed. The dark upperparts and richly barred underparts of the adult give the impression of an overall dark bird. The immature passes from stage (a) to stage (b) over a period of about three years, perhaps more. At all stages the crown is raised only when the bird is excited, but the loose feathers are raised by the wind. Occurs in indigenous forests and well-developed riverine forests. A territorial display is performed in the air in the vicinity of the home range, the male executing a series of steep dives and ascents with a few flaps at the top of each climb when the high-pitched call 'kewee-kewee-kewee . . .' is heard. The Crowned Eagle kills mammals up to the size of a bushbuck, while monkeys, dassies (rock hyrax) and guineafowls are often taken. **141**

PLATE 32

1 **AFRICAN FISH EAGLE** (Visarend) *Haliaeetus vocifer.* A fairly common resident species found at permanent rivers and dams throughout the Park. Breeding occurs in winter. This handsome and well-known eagle is unmistakable in adult plumage. Newly fledged immatures are very different (a), but on close examination the emergent white demarcation lines of the breast and back can usually be detected beneath the heavy brown blotches. This gradually clears with age until, at one year, the plumage pattern (b) resembles that of the adult. The loud ringing call is heard frequently in the KNP: 'weeah-hya-hya'. The diet is mainly fish but this species has piratical tendencies and mammal remains found in nests have probably been robbed from other eagles or taken from carnivore kills. **148**

2 **MARTIAL EAGLE** (Breëkoparend) *Polemaetus bellicosus.* A fairly common and widespread resident species. Breeds in winter. This powerful and striking eagle may be confused with the smaller Blackbreasted Snake Eagle (Plate 28). Note that the Martial has *fully feathered legs,* spots on the white underparts and, in flight, shows a *dark underwing.* The immature is much paler all over, lacking the dark throat and upper breast of the adult, but is similar in size. This species feeds on small mammals (including antelopes up to the size of young impalas), gamebirds, monitor lizards, etc. Frequently hunts by concealing itself in a well-foliated tree near open ground ahead of approaching flocks of guineafowls or mongooses in order to surprise the prey as it emerges from cover. **140**

3 **BLACK EAGLE** (Witkruisarend) *Aquila verreauxii.* An uncommon and very localised resident. Found regularly only in the far north where it breeds; rare elsewhere in the Park. Nests on cliffs during winter. An unmistakable large, black eagle with a white V on its back. In flight the wings appear to be nipped-in at their junction with the body. The immature can be confused with the Tawny Eagle (Plate 30), but has a distinctive rufous crown contrasting against dark upperparts and pale legs heavily marked with dark brown. The distribution pattern of this species in the KNP follows that of its principal prey, the dassie (rock hyrax). Although suitable cliffs and rocky koppies occur throughout the Park, the hyrax is unaccountably absent south of the Olifants River and so, too, is the Black Eagle, with the exception of occasional wandering immatures. **131**

PLATE 33

Buzzards. Medium-sized raptors, not unlike small eagles in size and colouring, but with unfeathered legs. The Lizard Buzzard (Plate 34), a somewhat aberrant species, differs from others in our region in being smaller and resembling an Accipiter hawk in both colouring and general behaviour. Buzzards feed on small creatures, such as rodents, lizards, frogs, small birds and insects.

1 **STEPPE BUZZARD** (Bruinjakkalsvoël) *Buteo buteo vulpinus*. An uncommon, non-breeding Palaearctic migrant, present throughout the Park October-March. Plumage variable. The most common colouring is as illustrated (a) but the dark form (b) and the russet form (c) are frequently met with, and there are variations in all plumages. A diagnostic feature common to all except, perhaps, the very dark form, is a distinctly pale zone across the breast immediately beneath the darker chest colouring. In flight the fanned tail shows as pale pink or cinnamon. Immatures of all adult forms have the underparts streaked or blotched as illustrated, the eye honey-coloured. This species is usually encountered while perched on a tree branch from where it watches the ground for prey, and could be mistaken for a Brown Snake Eagle (Plate 28) but is much smaller and lacks the large yellow eyes of that species. Also spends much time soaring. This is the raptor commonly seen in summer perched on telegraph poles on main roads. It is never common in the Park. In flight calls 'kreeeee' when excited. **149**

2 **HONEY BUZZARD** (Wespedief) *Pernis apivorus*. Rare. A Palaearctic summer visitor, recorded occasionally. Could occur anywhere in the Park. Rather larger than the previous species but could easily be mistaken for it. Adult plumage is variable, (a) probably being the most common form, while a dark form (b) and one with entirely white underparts are known. The eye is *yellow* (not brown as in the Steppe Buzzard). The flight pattern is fairly distinctive in that the long tail has two dark bars across its centre and one terminal bar, while the underwing shows a heavily barred pattern with dark carpal joints. The wings are rather longer than those of other buzzards and the small head protrudes well forward of the wings. When perched in trees is usually under the leaf canopy and not in an exposed position. Is sometimes found on the ground investigating wasps' nests, termite burrows and seeking other insects, its principal diet. Prefers well-wooded country. **130**

PLATE 34

1 LIZARD BUZZARD (Akkedisvalk) *Kaupifalco monogrammicus.* Uncommon but widespread throughout the Park. A resident species, which has been recorded with young in the nest during August and early November. A small, Accipiter-like buzzard, at rest identified by the *black line on a white throat,* bright red legs and cere plus a distinctive white bar across the tail (occasionally two white bars). In flight could be mistaken for the Gabar Goshawk (Plate 35) but for the characteristic white tail-bar. The body appears more bulky than that of the Gabar and the flight has a less urgent quality about it, since it is direct, low and with alternate flapping and gliding. Spends much time perched in a tree, often partially concealed by the foliage, and thus is frequently overlooked. May be more common than is indicated by reported sightings. Feeds on lizards, snakes, rodents and insects. The call is 'pheeeo-wot-wot-wot-wot . . .' uttered while perched or flying.   **154**

2 JACKAL BUZZARD (Rooiborsjakkalsvoël) *Buteo rufofuscus.* Rare visitor. There have been several reports of this species over the years, but it has not been seen since 1974. The adult, with its chestnut breast and tail, is distinctive both at rest and in flight; in the latter case the boldly contrasting pattern on rounded wings, and a reddish tail, are diagnostic. The immature may be even paler on the underparts than illustrated, darkening progressively to assume adult plumage. Both at rest and in flight could be mistaken for an immature Hawk-Eagle (Plate 31) but is smaller and has bare legs as against the eagle's fully-feathered legs; in flight the tail is shorter, the wings more rounded. Differs from the immature Black Sparrowhawk (Plate 36) in larger, more bulky proportions, shorter, less distinctly barred tail and less agile behaviour. A rather heavy-looking buzzard, similar in size to a small eagle. Frequents mountainous regions, often in pairs, but also hunts away from hills.   **152**

3 BLACKSHOULDERED KITE (Blouvalk) *Elanus caeruleus.* A fairly common species, present all year but numbers greatly augmented by visiting birds during summer. Occurs all over the Park, with breeding recorded in winter. A small, distinctive raptor having pure white underparts and grey upperparts with black shoulders. The immature is brownish on the upperparts, the feathers tipped pale, while the underparts are washed rusty; the eyes yellowish against the deep red of the adult. Spends much time perched in an exposed position from where it watches the ground beneath for small prey. When concentrating has the habit of raising and lowering its tail continually. In flight hovers frequently while examining the ground. A very elegant little raptor and a great rodent-catcher.   **127**

1

2

J

3

30cm

PLATE 35

Accipiter hawks. Small to medium-sized raptors having short, rounded wings, fairly long tails and slender legs and toes. Generally known under the vernacular names of sparrowhawk and goshawk, they specialise in catching small birds by means of a fast pursuit from a well-foliated tree in wooded country. The smaller species resemble one another closely and can best be separated by the presence or absence of white on the rump or tail. Secretive by day but inclined to hunt at dawn and dusk.

1 LITTLE SPARROWHAWK (Kleinsperwer) *Accipiter minullus.* Uncommon but resident throughout the Park with a greater density in the far north. Breeding has been recorded in September. A very small hawk, the adult best identified by the small white rump and the two white spots on the closed tail which appear as two broken bands when the tail is fanned. The immature has a profusion of blackish drop-shaped spots on the underparts. The eye is yellow. This little bird favours dense bush, preferably near water. Extremely bold and dashing in flight but easily overlooked at rest. **157**

2 LITTLE BANDED GOSHAWK (Gebande Sperwer) *Accipiter badius.* A fairly common resident throughout the Park and the most common of the Accipiter hawks. Breeds in summer. In this small hawk the rump and upper side of the closed tail are entirely plain grey (compare with others on this plate). In some individuals there is a variable amount of white spotting visible on the mantle and upperwing coverts. The eye is deep red. The immature has a yellowish eye, yellow legs and the plain rump of the adult but is otherwise similar to the immature of the next species. A bold and dashing little hawk which regularly hunts at dusk. In addition to birds it is also known to catch lizards, bats and other small mammals. **159**

3 GABAR GOSHAWK (Witkruissperwer) *Micronisus gabar.* Fairly common and widespread throughout the Park; a resident species which breeds in summer. Two colour forms occur, the normal (a) and the melanistic form (b). In both adult forms the cere and eyes are red and the legs orange-red (coral). The important identifying feature of the normal adult is its *broad white rump* which is easily seen in flight; see illustration and compare with the larger, heavier Lizard Buzzard (Plate 34). In the melanistic form the white rump is absent and the underwing is whiter than in (a) while the bird itself is slightly larger. The immature can be confused with the immature of (2) but it has the broad white rump of the adult (a); the eye is yellow, the legs flesh-pink. This is a common hawk of the open country, and is more frequently seen hunting by day than are other small Accipiters. The melanistic form is frequently seen in the Park. This hawk has been recorded as killing birds up to the size of a Redbilled Hornbill (Plate 62), but also eats insects and small mammals. **161**

4 OVAMBO SPARROWHAWK (Ovambosperwer) *Accipiter ovampensis.* Uncommon. Has been recorded at scattered localities in the Park. Immatures have been seen but no firm breeding records exist. The adult has a dark eye, orange, yellow or red cere and orange-yellow legs. A narrow white rump is usually visible in flight, but on the upper tail there are three fairly clear bands of off-white through which run two parallel white feather-shafts. The immature occurs in a pale form (a) and a rufous form (b). In both forms the eye is hazel, the legs creamy-yellow in (a) and dull orange-yellow in (b). Both immature forms have a characteristic dark ear-patch. In the KNP occurs in woodland. **156**

30 cm

PLATE 36

1 AFRICAN GOSHAWK (Afrikaanse Sperwer) *Accipiter tachiro*. A fairly common species for which there are widespread records. This Accipiter favours heavily wooded conditions where it is usually resident. There are no breeding records. A larger species than those shown on the previous plate but otherwise similar to that group in respect of colouring. At all stages the upper surfaces are dark brown with no other distinguishing features, while the eyes are hazel-brown to yellow, legs and feet yellow. The immature could be mistaken for the young of the Little Sparrowhawk (Plate 35) but is very much larger than that species. Though generally secretive the African Goshawk reveals itself in a daily morning territorial display flight. It flies a few hundred metres up, continually emitting a characteristic sharp 'krit' at two- or three-second intervals. Usually heard before 09h00. In addition to birds it is recorded as eating insects, reptiles and crabs. **160**

2 BLACK SPARROWHAWK (Swartsperwer). *Accipiter melanoleucus*. Rare, but probably resident in regions of suitable habitat. Scattered sightings have been made over the length of the Park with the greatest concentrations in the far north. There are no breeding records. This large Accipiter favours a forest habitat and is therefore most likely to be found in association with large riverine trees. In this respect its distribution within the Park is similar to that of the previous species. In the adult two colour forms occur: the normal or white-breasted form (a) and the melanistic form (b). The white-breasted form and the immature could be mistaken for the African Hawk-Eagle (Plate 31), but note that this species has *bare* legs whereas those of the eagle are fully feathered. A very secretive bird which spends much of its time concealed in well-foliated trees, and is therefore mostly overlooked. Bold and swift when hunting, its chief prey being gamebirds and doves. **158**

3 DARK CHANTING GOSHAWK (Donkersingvalk) *Melierax metabates*. A fairly common resident species. Occurs throughout the Park but shows a marked preference for regions of dense bush, especially mopane and the impenetrable bush of the Nwambiya sandveld. Breeds in summer. The most common grey hawk of the lowveld, it perches on the tops of bushes or other exposed vantage points in a very erect attitude, its red cere and long red legs being characteristic. The immature could be confused with others of this group but its size and exposed perching behaviour should aid identification. Feeds on a variety of small mammals, reptiles and large insects, and has been seen to rob a Brown Snake Eagle (Plate 28) of its prey. The characteristic call may be made for long periods, 'phaleeoo-phwe-phwe-phwe-phwe . . .' the last sound being repeated up to 30 times. **163**

30 cm

PLATE 37

Harriers. Medium-sized birds of prey of marshlands and open grassland. Slim of body and long-winged, the females are larger than the males and usually show marked differences in plumage. Harriers typically hunt by quartering the ground methodically in low, leisurely flight with much gliding, the wings being held in a slightly raised attitude. Four species have been recorded in the Kruger National Park, but all are very scarce.

EUROPEAN MARSH HARRIER (Europese Vleivalk) *Circus aeruginosus.* Not illustrated. Rare summer visitor. Male differs from African Marsh Harrier (1) in paler underparts and more streaky breast; in flight by paler underwings. Female much darker, almost black, with pale crown and leading edges to wings. Behaviour and habitat as (1). **164**

1 AFRICAN MARSH HARRIER (Afrikaanse Vleivalk) *Circus ranivorus.* A rare casual visitor. Has been recorded a few times at widely separated points in the Park, but always in times of heavy rains. Wider winged than the other harriers on this plate, the adult displays marked white edges to the forewings in flight. Sexes are similar. The immature has a broad whitish band across the breast and a variable amount of white on the nape. Usually occurs in damp localities, vleis, marshes, flooded lands, etc., where it glides low on spread wings, the head lowered as it scans the ground for rodents, frogs and small waterbirds on which it preys. Rests on the ground, seldom in trees. **165**

2 PALLID HARRIER (Witborsvleivalk) *Circus macrourus.* Uncommon Palaearctic visitor during the summer months. The male is very pale, resembling a large gull in flight, with the five black primary feathers forming only a narrow wedge at the wingtips. The female is entirely different, as illustrated, and is virtually inseparable from the female of the next species except for the white ruff-collar behind the dark ear coverts, visible at close range. A diagnostic feature common to both females is the white upper tail coverts. Occurs over open grasslands and sparsely bushed regions where it quarters the ground in typical harrier fashion. The wing-beats are slow and methodical, interspersed with glides, and the body does not move up and down with each wing movement as is the case with the next species. Perches readily on bushes and low trees, in addition to settling on the ground. **167**

3 MONTAGU'S HARRIER (Blouvleivalk) *Circus pygargus.* An uncommon Palaearctic summer visitor. Occurs in the central and northern regions during summer. The male is very similar to that of the previous species, though slightly smaller, and differs in having slightly darker grey upperparts, rufous streaking on the lower breast and belly, and a blackish bar across the folded wing. In flight is distinguished by *a black bar on the secondaries* of each upperwing, plus a greater number of black primary feathers which show as a larger black wedge shape at the wingtips when compared with the Pallid Harrier. As stated under Pallid Harrier, the females of both harriers are almost indistinguishable in the field, but this species lacks the white ruff-collar; differs from the African Marsh Harrier in lighter build and pronounced banding on the tail, in addition to white upper tail coverts. Habits as for the Pallid Harrier. **166**

50 cm

PLATE 38

1 BAT HAWK (Vlermuisvalk) *Macheiramphus alcinus.* Uncommon and localised, but resident. Recorded throughout the Park in suitable riverine habitat. No definite breeding records but a bird has been seen carrying prey, apparently to a nest, near Pafuri in February. At rest looks like a dark brown buzzard with large head, prominent whitish eyes (the upper eyelid showing white when the eye is closed) and unfeathered legs of the same colour. Plumage shows some variation in individuals. The throat may be whitish with a dark central stripe visible at close range, the flanks or belly may be whitish while, normally, white under-feathering is visible beneath the loose feathers of the nape. Perches in a forward-leaning, hunched attitude, the folded wings protruding beyond the tail. In flight appears falcon-like, reminiscent of a Hobby (Plate 39), the flight rapid and purposeful and the wing-action silent as in owls. Hunts at dawn and dusk mostly, but may be seen flying during the late afternoon and dull, heavily overcast mornings. Preys on bats and small birds such as swallows, eating them whole while on the wing. Roosts by day within the leaf canopy of a large tree. A secretive species at all times. The call is a falcon-like 'kwik-kwik-kwik-kwik'. **129**

2 OSPREY. Family PANDIONIDAE. (Visvalk) *Pandion haliaetus.* An uncommon but widespread non-breeding Palaearctic migrant. Occurs mostly in summer with some winter records. A medium-large, fish-eating brown and white raptor. At rest the crested head and masked appearance, orange-yellow eye and white underparts are diagnostic. The breast band is vestigial in some individuals, strongest in immatures. In flight the long wings are usually held in an angled position, the flight rather slow and flapping. Is usually seen perched on a tree or post near large waters or hunting over the water, hovering occasionally. Seizes fish by a direct plunge from some height, wings partially folded. **170**

3 GYMNOGENE (Kaalwangvalk) *Polyboroides typus.* A fairly common and wide-spread resident species. A nest with young has been found in November. A medium-large raptor with a bare face, loose feathers on the nape, long slender legs and a long tail with a distinct white bar. Basically grey with black flight feathers, sometimes with dark carpal patches on the upperwing, the banded underparts being visible only at close range. The immature progresses from dark brown to pale, mottled brown as illustrated, and at these stages identification is difficult, only the bare face, ruff and presence of white under-feathering being diagnostic. In flight the adult is distinctive but the immature is again confusing, resembling a heavy-winged Steppe Buzzard (Plate 33) in pattern. In habits a peculiar bird, feeding on small reptiles and the young of other birds obtained by probing into tree or rock crevices or birds' nests (especially hole-nesters), the long legs having specially adapted joints that enable the bird to reach into otherwise inaccessible places. Also feeds on frogs, insects and vegetable matter. Is frequently harassed by smaller birds. **169**

30cm

1

2

3

J

J

30cm

PLATE 39

Falcons. Family FALCONIDAE. Small birds of prey characterised by their long and pointed scythe-like wings. Females are generally larger than males. True falcons attack birds in flight by a fast dive or 'stoop' from above, killing or stunning the victim on impact. Characteristic calls are high-pitched 'kek-kek-kek-kek' sounds, usually made to express agitation. Kestrels are small falcons, which eat insects caught in the air with their feet and small mammals hunted from a perch.

1 **PEREGRINE FALCON** (Swerfvalk) *Falco peregrinus*. A rare, sparsely distributed resident (race a) and a non-breeding summer visitor (race b). Race (a) has been found breeding October-November in the north of the Park. Normally occurs in association with cliffs. In flight characterised by fairly pointed wings, the tail shortish and held closed unless in soaring flight. The normal flight is a series of rapid but shallow wing-beats followed by a short glide. When attacking flying birds it employs a very fast dive on semi-closed wings. At rest the plumage of the upperparts appears slate-grey to dark brown, the black moustachial streak contrasting with the pale face. Note that the top of the head is dark; compare with the Lanner (2). The Peregrine is seen solitarily unless breeding, and spends much of its day perched, making only brief sorties for hunting. The food is mostly birds. **171**

2 **LANNER FALCON** (Edelvalk) *Falco biarmicus*. Uncommon but thought to be resident within the Park. Breeding, although unconfirmed, is believed to occur at several known sites. The resident population is probably augmented by visiting nomadic individuals during summer. Sightings have been made in early August with pairs seen in courtship display, and in late February. May be distinguished from the smaller but similar Peregrine and Hobby by the presence of a *rufous crown* at all ages, and by more rounded wings in flight. The Lanner is active during the day and frequently soars, at which time the tail is fanned; see illustration. While favouring the vicinity of rocky cliffs, this species may also be found over open ground and hills. Preys on birds to a large extent, surprising its victims by a fast, shallow dash and grabbing them on the ground. **172**

3 **HOBBY FALCON** (Europese Boomvalk) *Falco subbuteo*. A fairly common non-breeding Palaearctic migrant, present November-March. Recorded over the length of the Park but appears to favour the Punda Maria, Olifants and Stolznek regions to which individuals probably return each year. This small falcon is characterised by heavy markings on body and underwing, so that it appears darker than the Peregrine and Lanner, while the rufous thighs and undertail coverts are diagnostic in the adult. The immature lacks the rufous colouring. Flies rapidly and with agility on very long, pointed wings like a large swift. Fast wing-beats are interrupted by brief glides when hunting. Preys on small birds, plus bats. Is most active at dusk and on overcast mornings. May form small flocks when feeding on emerging termite alates, the birds catching the insects with their feet and transferring them to their bills in flight; at these times the flight is slower, with much graceful twisting and turning. **173**

15 cm

PLATE 40

1 AFRICAN HOBBY FALCON (Afrikaanse Boomvalk) *Falco cuvierii.* Rare. Exact status unknown. Has been seen in the far north and near Satara. Completely rufous underparts distinguish this falcon. In flight its shape and actions are similar to those of (3) of which it is merely an African form. Little is known about the behaviour of this falcon apart from the fact that in the Eastern Cape it tends to haunt forest edges. **174**

2 REDNECKED FALCON (Rooinekvalk) *Falco chicquera.* Rare visitor. Birds seen occasionally in the far north are thought to move in from Mozambique where they are known to occur. There are no breeding records for the KNP. Identified by rusty crown and nape plus well-barred appearance; the immature has a dark crown, underparts less heavily barred. Usually seen in association with Borassus palms or baobab trees from where it hunts small birds in short, swift sallies. **178**

3 PYGMY FALCON (Dwergvalk) *Polihierax semitorquatus.* Status uncertain. Numerous sightings of this species in the northern regions suggest a small resident population but breeding records are lacking. It is known to occur in Mozambique in small numbers. Very small size, white underparts, grey upperparts (plus rufous mantle in female) diagnostic; in flight shows heavily spotted wings and tail. Usually in pairs. Often in association with Buffalo Weaver nests in baobab trees (see p.214). Feeds on small birds, lizards and large insects. **186**

4 SOOTY FALCON (Roetvalk) *Falco concolor.* Uncommon summer visitor. Occurs throughout the Park with most sightings in the east and north. Adults entirely dark grey; folded wings *extending beyond the tail;* cf. next species. The immature has creamy underparts heavily blotched grey. Usually solitary. Perches by day in large trees, often near water. Hunts mostly at dusk, pursuing small birds. **175**

5 DICKINSON'S KESTREL (Dickinsonse Grysvalk) *Falco dickinsoni.* A fairly common but localised resident species. Breeding has been recorded October-December. May be seen regularly only in the far north, occurring as a vagrant further south. A slenderly built, elegant grey kestrel which perches on dead trees in an erect posture. The very pale grey head and rump are clearly seen at all times. In flight the movements are swift and graceful on slender wings. In the KNP Dickinson's Kestrel frequently breeds in holes in baobab trees. The food is small birds, reptiles and insects. **185**

1

2

♂

3

♀

J

4

5

15 cm

PLATE 41

GREATER KESTREL (Grootrooivalk) *Falco rupicoloides.* Rare but is seen in small numbers in the far north; there are no breeding records. Larger than (1) and (2) and lacking a grey head; at rest appears entirely rufous with a profusion of black spots and bars on both under- and upperparts. The eyes are whitish. In flight reveals white underwings with a dark trailing edge and barred tail. Usually occurs in grassland where it perches for long periods on a tree or powerline. A nomadic species. **182**

1 ROCK KESTREL (Rooivalk) *Falco tinnunculus.* Uncommon but resident in small numbers. Is seen most regularly in the Hlamalala grass flats east of Punda Maria but also occurs in the hills adjacent to the Crocodile River. Breeds in early summer. Differs from the previous species in having a grey head and, in flight, well marked underwing and broad subterminal bar on tail; from (2) in rich rufous underparts and non-gregarious habits. This small, rufous kestrel is usually seen perched on a dead tree, post or on power lines. When hunting on the wing it may *hover* for quite long periods. Feeds on small birds, small mammals, reptiles and insects. **181**

2 LESSER KESTREL (Kleinrooivalk) *Falco naumanni.* A seasonally common Palaearctic migrant occurring in the grass flats of the northern half of the Park during summer. Can be confused with (1) but in both sexes the underparts are pale in contrast to rufous upperparts. Usually occurs in flocks. Flies in a leisurely fashion, wheeling and turning at no great height over open ground. Catches insects, especially flying termite alates, in its feet and passes them to its bill to be eaten on the wing. **183**

3 EASTERN REDFOOTED KESTREL (Oostelike Rooipootvalk) *Falco amurensis.* An occasionally common but irregular summer visitor from Eastern Asia. A small kestrel, usually occurring in flocks. Habitually perches on telephone wires or dead trees making occasional sallies to catch flying insects. Compare with (2) and (4) with which it often associates. **180**

4 WESTERN REDFOOTED KESTREL (Westelike Rooipootvalk) *Falco vespertinus.* Status and habits much as for the previous species although rather less frequent. **179**

15 cm

PLATE 42

Pigeons and doves. Family COLUMBIDAE. Within this family large species tend to be called pigeons and small ones doves, otherwise there is no apparent distinction. With a few exceptions all have grey or brown plumage. The so-called wood doves are characterised by having brown primary feathers in their wings and two bold black bars across their backs. Most are ground feeders, eating grain and seeds, while a few are frugivorous. Their calls are of a 'cooing' or 'hooting' nature with the exception of the Green Pigeon (Plate 43).

1 **MOURNING DOVE** (Rooioogtortelduif) *Streptopelia decipiens*. Fairly common in its restricted range. A resident species which has been recorded over the length of the Park but is seen regularly only at Pafuri, Letaba, Pumbe, Gudzani Dam, Satara, Salitji Picket and Lower Sabie. It is common only at Letaba Camp where breeding has been recorded in August. The general appearance of this species is very similar to other collared doves on this plate but the head is completely grey except for a white throat, and the underparts are white. At close range the pale yellow eye with red surround is visible. Makes a soft 'kuk-kurr' repeated once or twice; also a soft 'kur-r-r-r'. **353**

2 **REDEYED DOVE** (Grootringduif) *Streptopelia semitorquata*. A common and wide-spread resident species. Occurs all over the Park but shows a distinct preference for the more wooded regions. Breeds throughout the summer months. Similar to (1) but more generally pink in colour and has only the cap grey. This is a fairly large and plump dove which spends much time perched, often calling. The red eye is not a field feature. The call is one of the characteristic sounds of the bushveld 'coo-coo, coo-KUK-coo-coo' or 'Cuckoo, why DON'T you work?' **352**

3 **CAPE TURTLE DOVE** (Gewone Tortelduif) *Streptopelia capicola*. A very common and widespread resident species. Breeding probably occurs throughout the year. Can be confused with (1) and (2) but is smaller than either and shows very little pink about the neck and breast, since it is more uniform grey in colour, although lighter and darker individuals occur. Has a characteristic display flight in which males climb steeply and then spiral down on stiffened wings, often calling. Has a harshly repeated call resembling the words 'work HARDER'. **354**

4 **LAUGHING DOVE** (Rooiborsduifie) *Streptopelia senegalensis*. Common, but less so than (3). Occurs throughout the Park and yet may be found to be unaccountably absent from some regions occasionally. Breeding takes place throughout the year with a peak in January. This little dove is familiar to most people since it is widespread and common throughout the country. Within the KNP it may be seen in all rest camps and on roads, walking about in characteristic hunched posture in search of seeds and scraps. The pinkish head and cinnamon breast with black spots, plus the rusty-coloured back, are diagnostic. The call is a soft 'coo, coo, CUK-coo-coo'. **355**

5 **NAMAQUA DOVE** (Namakwaduifie) *Oena capensis*. Fairly common resident but numbers fluctuate markedly. A bird of the more open country and not likely to be seen about camps. Feeds on the ground and flies off low and at great speed when flushed, the long tail, brown wings and double bars on the back being diagnostic. Makes an explosive, low-pitched 'twoo-hoo', the accent on the first note, the second note much quieter. **356**

15 cm

1

2

3

4

♂

5   J

♀

PLATE 43

BLUESPOTTED DOVE (Blouvlekduifie) *Turtur afer*. Rare, but possibly resident in the far north. Differs from the next species in having blue (not green) wing spots, red bill with yellow tip and a generally browner appearance. Is seen occasionally in the Punda Maria region, even in camp. The voice is similar to that of numbers (1) and (2) but ends abruptly after *six to nine* quick final notes 'hoo, hoo, hoo, huwoo, huwoo, hu-hu-hu-hu-hu-hu-hu', not as prolonged as in (2), softer and more abruptly ending than in (1). **357**

1 EMERALDSPOTTED (GREENSPOTTED) DOVE (Groenvlekduifie) *Turtur chalcospilos*. A common and widespread resident species. Breeding probably occurs throughout the warmer months. This conspicuous dove is frequently flushed from the roadside by vehicles, at which time its brown wings and barred back are easily seen. A fairly tame species which will allow a close approach, the green wingspots showing clearly in good light. The call is a familiar sound in the KNP 'du, du . . . du-du . . . du . . . du . . . du, du, du-du-du-du-du-du . . .' descending and fading at the end, and differing in this respect from the otherwise similar calls of the Bluespotted and Tambourine Doves. **358**

2 CINNAMON DOVE (Kaneelduifie) *Aplopelia larvata*. Rare and very localised. Has been recorded only in the extreme north of the Park at Punda Maria and Pafuri. An inhabitant of forest and dense bush. Tends to stay in thick cover and is very difficult to see even where it is known to occur regularly, since it feeds on the ground in poor light conditions. Is most often detected by its soft, low call 'hoo-oo'. **360**

3 TAMBOURINE DOVE (Witborsduifie) *Turtur tympanistria*. An uncommon and localised resident species. The white underparts are diagnostic. Seen along heavily wooded rivers but shy and elusive. Usually perches in a low position in dense bush or feeds on the ground, making off at speed when approached. Best located by call, very similar to those of the two previous species but *ends abruptly after a long series* of quick notes 'du, dudu, du, du, dudu, du-du-du-du-du-du-du-du . . .'. **359**

4 RAMERON PIGEON (Geelbekbosduif) *Columba arquatrix*. Rare. An irregular visitor to the far north. An unmistakable large greyish pigeon wth distinctive yellow bill, eyering and feet. Occurs in flocks which range widely in fast, direct flight in search of fruiting trees where they feed in the canopies. Shy and wary. The voice is a harsh 'crrooo' or 'crrooo-*coo*'. **350**

5 GREEN PIGEON (Papegaaiduif) *Treron calva*. A common and widespread resident species which breeds in summer. Feeds on wild fruits, especially figs, and is therefore most abundant in riparian forest and on koppies where these trees occur. This beautiful pigeon is unmistakable but often avoids detection by remaining motionless in trees where its green plumage blends well with the leaves. If approached closely a feeding flock will explode from a tree and make off at great speed. The voice is quite unlike that of other pigeons but is very difficult to describe: a fairly high-pitched but melodious bubbling and descending trill. **361**

6 ROCK PIGEON (Kransduif) *Columba guinea*. Rare, exact status uncertain. Has been seen at scattered points all over the Park. A rock-loving pigeon normally associated with cliffs on which it roosts and breeds, while it flies daily to feed and to water. A large pigeon with distinctive reddish colouring and white spots on the wings. Usually seen in flocks flying at some height. The voice is a deep, harsh series of 'coos'. **349**

PLATE 44

Parrots. Family PSITTACIDAE. As a family of birds which has been popular as caged birds for years, parrots need little introduction. They have very stout bills adapted to cracking hard seeds and nut kernels, and feed by clambering about the branches of the food tree. They are usually seen in pairs or groups and fly in a fast and purposeful manner. Two species are found within the Kruger National Park. They nest in holes in trees.

1 BROWNHEADED PARROT (Bruinkoppapegaai) *Poicephalus cryptoxanthus*. A common and widespread resident. Occurs in all regions of the Park and has been found breeding in April and May. A small parrot, distinguished from the next species by the all-brown head and, in flight, by the yellow underwing coverts. Is easily detected when feeding by its shrill, shrieking call, a sound not unlike that made by a rusty hinge. **363**

2 CAPE PARROT (Grootpapegaai) *Poicephalus robustus*. Fairly common in its restricted range, which is the northern end of the Park. During the rainy season is numerous all over the northern districts, especially around Punda Maria, but during the dry season is found mostly in the Pafuri region. Has been found breeding from March to August. A large parrot, the red forehead, shoulders and thighs being distinctive in the adult. Young birds do not have these markings. In flight the bright green back is very obvious. Its habits are very similar to those of the previous species and the call is almost indistinguishable. **362**

Louries or touracos. Family MUSOPHAGIDAE. Fruit-eating birds peculiar to Africa. Either forest or savanna dwellers, the first group are beautifully coloured and the second drab. All have crests on their heads and move through trees with an agile, springing action. They build simple, dove-like nests of sticks. One of each group is found in the Kruger National Park.

3 PURPLECRESTED LOURIE (Bloukuifloerie) *Tauraco porphyreolophus*. Fairly common and widespread. A resident species found in riverine forests and koppies where fruiting trees occur. A very colourful bird and quite unmistakable. Prefers large trees where it moves along the branches in springing hops and leaps. In flight, displays brilliant scarlet wings. The call is a series of 'krok, krok' sounds. **371**

4 GREY LOURIE or Go-away Bird (Kwêvoël) *Corythaixoides concolor*. A common and widespread resident species. Breeds in all seasons. A well-known and unmistakable bird found all over the Park in open bush country; its plain grey colouring and distinctive head crest are diagnostic. Flies in a clumsy, heavy manner alternately flapping and gliding in undulating flight. Grey Louries feed on fruits and flowers, and are especially attracted to the blossoms of *Acacia robusta*. The call, from which is derived its alternative name, is 'kwehhh' or 'ker-wehhh' translated to 'Go-away'. **373**

PLATE 45

Cuckoos and coucals. Family CUCULIDAE. Cuckoos are brood parasites, laying their eggs in the nest of a host species. Ten cuckoos occur in the KNP, all except one being summer visitors. Glossy cuckoos are small, iridescent green birds, while the others are larger and more soberly coloured, with long and tapering tails, and flying with deep wing-beats. Cuckoos feed on insects, and are partial to hairy caterpillars. Coucals are related but build nests and raise young in the normal manner. They feed on a variety of insects, reptiles, small mammals and young birds.

1 KLAAS'S CUCKOO (Meitjie) *Chrysococcyx klaas.* Fairly common throughout and present all year. Calls mostly between July and February. The male is similar to the next species but lacks green bars on the flanks, having instead a few indistinct dusky bars. Also lacks a distinct white eyebrow. The tail is white, with the exception of three green central feathers. The female resembles the male or has much more bronze about the head and shoulders as illustrated, plus fine brown bars on the underside. The immature resembles the female and has a *black beak;* cf. immature of next species. Shy and unobtrusive. The voice is a mournful 'hueet-jie' or 'Meitjie' as in the Afrikaans name. Parasitises batis flycatchers, sunbirds, the apalis group and the Longbilled Crombek (Plate 82). **385**

2 DIEDERIK CUCKOO (Diederikkie) *Chrysococcyx caprius.* Common and widespread September-March, occasionally later. Differs from the male of the preceding species in having a white eyebrow, distinct green barring on the flanks and white spots on the wings. Female resembles male but is usually more coppery above. The immature has a *coral pink* bill. Conspicuous in the breeding season: the male calls loudly in its chosen territory and chases other males. Parasitises birds with ball-type nests: weavers, bishop birds, sparrows, etc. The call is onomatopoeic, resembling the bird's name 'dee-dee-deederik', a plaintive sound frequently repeated. **386**

3 REDCHESTED CUCKOO (Piet-my-vrou) *Cuculus solitarius.* Common seasonally all over the Park in wooded habitats. Arrives early October and calls continually until late December, seldom later. Prefers dense woodland and is therefore somewhat localised. The only cuckoo with a russet upper breast. Flies with deep wing-beats and is easily confused with the next species. Parasitises robins. May be located by the well-known call 'Piet-my-vrou', sometimes repeated all day and even at night. **377**

4 AFRICAN CUCKOO (Afrikaanse Koekoek) *Cuculus gularis.* Fairly common and widespread from September-March. A very grey cuckoo, paler on the upperparts than the previous species and lacking a russet breast; cf. the next species from which it differs only in more yellow bill, black only at tip. Occurs in both woodland and open scrub country. Is known to parasitise the Forktailed Drongo. Calls 'KooKUK'. **375**

EUROPEAN CUCKOO (Europese Koekoek) *Cuculus canorus.* Only the bill illustrated. Uncommon summer visitor. Exactly like the previous species except for darker bill, greenish only at the base. Does not breed nor call in Africa. **374**

5 STRIPED CUCKOO (Gestreepte Nuwejaarsvoël) *Clamator levaillantii.* Fairly common and widespread October-April. Occurs in a variety of habitats, at times common in the northern mopane scrub. Can be confused with the white form of the next species but the spotted throat and breast are diagnostic. Is known to parasitise the Arrowmarked Babbler. The call is 'kur kur kur', followed by a rapid series of 'kwi kwi kwi . . .' notes repeated about twenty times. **381**

6 JACOBIN CUCKOO (Bontnuwejaarsvoël) *Clamator jacobinus.* Fairly common throughout from October-March. Occurs in two colour forms as illustrated (a and b). Both have crests and conspicuous white spots on the folded wing. A restless, noisy species, parasitic on bulbuls, shrikes and the Paradise Flycatcher. The call is a very loud, ringing 'kleeuw-wee-wip, kleeuw, kleeuw, pewp, pewp'. **382**

1 ♂ ♀

J

2

3 J

R.chested

European

African

4

5

6 a b

30 cm

PLATE 46

J

1 **GREAT SPOTTED CUCKOO** (Gevlekte Koekoek) *Clamator glandarius*. Uncommon but widespread October-March in open woodland. A large, crested cuckoo with heavily spotted upperparts and long wedge-shaped tail. Young birds, which may be seen in late summer, have reddish-brown primary feathers and are darker about the head; see illustration above. In the KNP it parasitises starlings, especially Burchell's and Longtailed Glossy Starlings. The call is a harsh 'keeow-keeow-keeow'; at times is very noisy. **380**

2 **THICKBILLED CUCKOO** (Dikbekkoekoek) *Pachycoccyx audeberti*. Uncommon but occurs throughout the Park all year in well-wooded regions. A large cuckoo without a crest. Has dark grey to dark brown upperparts, white underparts and a long, graduated tail with white tips to the feathers. The thick bill is yellow and black or pink and black. Young birds have large white spots and patches on the upperparts, larger than the spots of the last species, and may be seen in late summer. A restless, hawk-like cuckoo with slow, deliberate movements. Is known to parasitise Redbilled Helmet-Shrikes. The call is a loud, querulous cry, expressed as 'chwee-cher-cher' or 'oui-yesyes'. **383**

3 **BLACK CUCKOO** (Swartkoekoek) *Cuculus clamosus*. Fairly common only in the extreme north and south-west of the Park. Has been recorded from October and, where it occurs, is most vociferous in November. Probably remains in the Park until about March but records are lacking. A wholly black or slaty cuckoo of open woodland. Parasitises the Boubou and Crimsonbreasted Shrikes. Has a very monotonous, frequently repeated call 'whoo-whoo-whee' which can be expressed as 'I'm so-sick'. Calls all day and often at night. Also has an excitable 'wind-up' call 'yowyowyowyowyowyow' which reaches a crescendo and then dies away. **378**

4 **BLACK COUCAL** (Swartvleiloerie) *Centropus bengalensis*. Rare, but scattered records exist over the length of the Park during wet seasons. Probably an occasional visitor. Quite unmistakable. A bird of moist vleis and swampy regions. The call is a low 'oom, oom, oom' given with the bird in a hunched posture, then a double-noted 'pop-pop' with the head raised. When excited calls 'kwik kwik kwik'. **388**

5 **BURCHELL'S COUCAL** (Gewone Vleiloerie) *Centropus superciliosus*. Common, widespread and resident. Breeds in summer. A large, clumsy bird of vleis, riverbanks and thick bush, seldom far from water. An unmistakable and striking species, seen mostly in low bushes or on the ground. Frequently suns itself in an exposed position in the early mornings and after rain. The South African race (a) normally lacks a white eyebrow but individuals of race (b) do occasionally occur. Feeds on large insects, small mammals, frogs, lizards and nestling birds. The call is a series of descending notes 'doo, doo, doo-doo-doo-doo-doo . . .' and resembles the sound of liquid pouring from a bottle. **391**

PLATE 47

Owls. Families TYTONIDAE and STRIGIDAE. Nocturnal birds of prey, divided into two families on anatomical grounds. The Barn Owl and Grass Owl belong to the family Tytonidae and are visually distinct from other owls in having heart-shaped facial discs. They also lay their eggs at intervals yet incubate from the date of the first-laid, so that the young in a clutch may vary in age from newly hatched to fully feathered. Owls of the family Strigidae do not do this. Owls gulp their prey whole when size permits, and later regurgitate bones, feathers and other hard matter in the form of a cast or pellet. They are possessed of acute sight and hearing and, in some species, a modification of their wing feathers renders their wing-movements silent enabling them to hear while flying. Many owls have ear-like tufts on their heads which in fact are not ears but plumage adornments. Owls construct no nest but use any convenient hole or ledge and, in the larger species, take over the disused nest of a diurnal raptor or other large bird.

1 MARSH OWL (Vlei-uil) *Asio capensis.* Uncommon and localised, but resident. Usually breeds during the period March-May. An inhabitant of vleis and marshy areas. Occurs regularly in the Hlamalala flats east of Punda Maria and may prove to be more widely distributed than is presently known. Is active during the late afternoon and early morning, often sunning itself on a post. Otherwise is seen only at night when it may appear on roads. A medium-sized brown owl with very small 'ear-tufts' and dark eyes. When flushed from grass during the day is inclined to *fly up and circle*, observing the intruder from above before resettling; it differs in this behaviour from the Grass Owl (4) which shares the same habitat (see illustrations). Feeds on frogs, small rodents, birds and insects. This is generally a silent owl but will emit strange squeals to distract intruders near the nest, which is placed in grass. **395**

2 WOOD OWL (Bosuil) *Strix woodfordii.* An uncommon and localised resident species, recorded in the riparian forests of the Limpopo, Luvuvhu and Sabie Rivers. May occur in forested regions elsewhere. Strictly nocturnal and arboreal in habits. The diet is insects, mice, frogs and other small creatures. The male's call is a rapid 'HU-hu, hu-HU-hu-hu, hu-hu'. The female replies with a higher pitched single note 'hoo' or may repeat the male's call in a higher pitch. **394**

3 BARN OWL (Nonnetjie-uil) *Tyto alba.* Fairly common throughout the Park. Breeding appears to reach a peak in the period May-July, and nests with ten and twelve eggs have been recorded. Seldom seen by day but its call is frequently heard at night. A very pale, slimly built owl with a distinctly heart-shaped facial disc; cf. the closely related Grass Owl (4). When breeding sometimes uses the nest of the Hamerkop (Plate 8). Preys mainly on rodents. The call is an eerie, shrill cry. **392**

4 GRASS OWL (Grasuil) *Tyto capensis.* Rare but probably a resident in grassy localities. Has been reported from many scattered points in both summer and winter but frequent confusion with the Marsh Owl (1) makes estimation of its exact status difficult. Very similar to (3) but upperparts browner. Inhabits grasslands and breeds on the ground in vleis like (1) but is seldom seen during the day unless disturbed, in which case it *flies away* and resettles; see illustration. At the nest it may stand its ground and menace the intruder, hissing loudly and spreading its wings. Its diet consists of rodents. **393**

15 cm

PLATE 48

1 SCOPS OWL (Skopsuil) *Otus senegalensis.* Common throughout the Park. A secretive resident species seldom seen by day but is in fact widespread. Breeds June-November. This diminutive owl, measuring a mere 15 cm, has plumage patterns resembling the bark of a tree. When perched close to a tree trunk during the day this camouflage renders the bird almost invisible. The effect is further enhanced by its habit of depressing its feathers to appear long and thin, and of raising its 'ear' tufts and closing its eyes, which creates the illusion of a short branch stump. The most common colouring is grey as shown in illustration (a), but some individuals tend to be brownish as (b). Irrespective of colour the illustrations show (a) in cryptic, erect posture and (b) in relaxed mood. The diet is mostly moths and other insects. Its call, sometimes heard by day, is a soft 'prrrp' repeated at intervals of about 8 seconds, especially on moonlit nights. **396**

2 WHITEFACED OWL (Witwanguil) *Otus leucotis.* Uncommon but widely distributed and resident. Breeds June-November. This is the largest of the small owls, its pale colouring and black-rimmed white face with orange eyes being diagnostic. A species of open woodland, often found along dry water courses and usually in pairs. Feeds on small rodents and insects. The call is an explosive, bubbling hoot 'w-h-h-h-oo-oo'. **397**

3 PEARLSPOTTED OWL (Witkoluil) *Glaucidium perlatum.* A common resident species found throughout the Park, breeding August-November. This small owl is best identified by its earless, rounded appearance and brown-streaked underparts with pearl-like spots on them. The brown upperparts are also well spotted while, in contrast to the yellow eyes, there are two black marks behind the neck. When the bird is seen from behind these marks have the appearance of eyes; see illustration. A woodland species often active by day and frequently mobbed by other small birds. The diet is rodents, birds (as large as a Laughing Dove) and insects. The call, occasionally heard by day, is a long series of ascending whistling notes followed by a series of descending notes 'tee, tee, te, te, te, te, te, te, te ... teew, teew, tew, tew, tew, tew, tew ...' **398**

4 BARRED OWL (Gebande Uil) *Glaucidium capense.* Uncommon but widespread and resident. Breeds August-November. This is another earless, roundish owl somewhat larger than (1) and (3) and identified by the bold white wing-spots and the barred arrangement of all other spots both above and below. Usually roosts in pairs in fairly thick bush but does emerge to perch openly late in the afternoon. Feeds on small rodents and large insects. Makes a low 'krroo-krroo'; also strange bubbling and whistling has been recorded. **399**

15 cm

PLATE 49

1 **PEL'S FISHING OWL** (Visuil) *Scotopelia peli.* Uncommon and very localised. A resident in its restricted habitat of riparian forest on the permanent rivers. Occurs regularly along the Limpopo, Luvuvhu and Olifants Rivers and has also been seen at scattered points elsewhere. Nests with eggs have been found in April at Pafuri. The largest owl in South Africa characterised by its rufous colouring. When relaxed the facial disc creates a squarish head but when excited the feathers are puffed, giving the head a round appearance. This owl is not seen by day unless flushed from the large trees in which it roosts. At night it frequents floodpans where fish have been isolated by receding waters or quiet pools in rivers, to hunt from a low branch, at times several may gather at the same pool. The calls are varied and numerous, comprising hoots and screeches.   **403**

2 **GIANT EAGLE OWL** (Reuse Ooruil) *Bubo lacteus.* A fairly common and wide-spread resident owl. Occurs in all regions and has been found breeding June-October. Pale greyish colouring on the underparts is produced by very fine transverse barring on a white background; the upperparts are darker. The eyes are dark brown with *pink eyelids.* This species is usually found in association with large trees along rivers and watercourses and frequently perches openly in the early evening. Preys on mammals such as hares and galagos, and birds including other owls. The call is a series of grunts 'hu-hu-hu, hu-hu'. Immatures emit a long, drawn-out whistle which may be repeated for long periods.   **402**

3 **SPOTTED EAGLE OWL** (Gevlekte Ooruil) *Bubo africanus.* Fairly common and widespread over the whole Park, breeding July-November. Not usually seen by day but road counts at night reveal its presence in fair numbers. A fairly large owl with yellow eyes, 'ear' tufts, and underparts which are finely banded with an overlay of buff and dark blotches. When walking the tail is held clear of the ground and the legs appear long, an attitude in which this owl is commonly seen on roads at night. Is dazzled by vehicle lights and is a frequent road casualty. Feeds on a variety of rodents, beetles, scorpions, birds, etc. The eggs are laid in any convenient place, on bare ground, among rocks, on cliff ledges, in hollow trees or other birds' nests. The call, commonly heard at night at rest camps, is usually in the form of a duet by both sexes, the male's deep 'hooo whooo' being answered by the female's softer 'hu'.
401

15 cm

PLATE 50 (see also following two pages)

Nightjars. Family CAPRIMULGIDAE. Nocturnal, insectivorous birds having soft, cryptically coloured plumage, short beaks, wide gapes surrounded by stiff bristles, large eyes and short, weak legs. They hawk insects at night, lying up by day. If approached may not flush until nearly trodden on; instead they close their eyes to narrow slits, thereby reducing the sun's reflection and so enhancing their camouflage. All so alike as to be nearly indistinguishable but can be identified by characteristic calls. In the hand can be identified by wing and tail formulae, illustrated both on this plate and on the following two pages as an aid to the identification of road kills.

1 PENNANTWINGED NIGHTJAR (Wimpelvlerknaguil) *Macrodipteryx vexillaria.* Fairly common but localised. A summer-visiting intra-Africa migrant which probably breeds in the Park. Occurs in the far north and south-west, being numerous south of Pretoriuskop. The male in nuptial plumage is unmistakable, but the wing pennants drop after breeding. The female wing lacks white spots. The voice is a soft, high-pitched cricket-like twittering. **410**

2 RUFOUSCHEEKED NIGHTJAR (Rooiwangnaguil) *Caprimulgus rufigena.* Uncommon resident. Recorded mostly in the north and south of the Park and breeding September-November. Pale in colour with a pale buff collar and no rufous colouring below the white throat spots. The female has buff wing-spots. The male only has a white patch at the tips of the two outer tail feathers. Makes a sustained churring sound resembling a motorcycle engine, plus a repeated 'dug-dug-dug . . .' in flight and 'keeuw, keeuw, keeuwoo-keeuwoo' from the ground or perch. Also claps its wings in flight. **406**

3 EUROPEAN NIGHTJAR (Europese Naguil) *Caprimulgus europaeus.* Fairly common and widespread during summer. A non-breeding Palaearctic migrant. A large, dark nightjar which roosts lengthwise along branches during the day. Has no rufous collar and the male has white patches only at the tips of the two outermost tail feathers. The female lacks white wing-spots and has small buff tail-tips. Mostly silent in Africa but 'coo-ic' may be uttered in flight. **404**

4 FIERYNECKED NIGHTJAR (Afrikaanse Naguil) *Caprimulgus pectoralis.* A common and widespread resident. Breeds September-November. A fairly rufous nightjar, especially about the head, with large white patches at the tips of the outer two tail feathers. The female has smaller wing and tail spots than the male. Roosts lengthwise on branches or on the ground. At night hawks from a stump or post to which it returns frequently. The characteristic call is a wavering 'wheeo, whee-wheeoo-wheeoo' interpreted as 'Good Lord, deliver us', and heard throughout the night. **405**

5 MOZAMBIQUE NIGHTJAR (Laeveldnaguil) *Caprimulgus fossii.* Fairly common and widespread resident throughout the Park, breeding in early summer. The entire edge of the male's outer tail feathers is white, whereas in the female they and the wing-spots are buffy. Roosts in shade on the ground. Utters a sustained frog-like gurgling from the ground, *alternating in pitch* like a small engine; cf. the call of (2). **409**

6 FRECKLED NIGHTJAR (Donkernaguil) *Caprimulgus tristigma.* Fairly common and widespread in hilly regions throughout the Park. A resident species, breeding September-November. A dark, heavily speckled nightjar, cryptically coloured to match the rocks on which it roosts and nests. The male's outer tail feathers have sub-terminal spots, lacking in the female. The call is a double note 'wheeoo-whoo', sounding like 'Poor *Will*'. **408**

15cm

♀

♂

1

♀

♂

2

♂

3

♂

4

♂

5

♂

6

These illustrations show the major wing-feathers and outer tail-feathers with the outer webs of each blackened for clarity. The position of the wing emargination or 'kink' in relation to the wing-spots, the format and colouring of the wing-spots, if present, plus the presence or absence of bold tail markings are diagnostic for each species. The normal, irregular buff patterning present on nightjar feathers has been omitted. This diagram is intended to aid identification of nightjar road kills.

♀ 1

PENNANTWINGED NIGHTJAR
No spots on wing or tail.
Emarginations subtle.

2 ♂

RUFOUSCHEEKED NIGHTJAR
White spot on four main wing-feathers within the emarginations.
Large white tips to two outer tail-feathers.

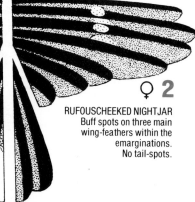

♀ 2

RUFOUSCHEEKED NIGHTJAR
Buff spots on three main wing-feathers within the emarginations.
No tail-spots.

3 ♂

EUROPEAN NIGHTJAR
White spots on three main wing-feathers within the emarginations.
White tips to two outer tail-feathers.

♀ 3

EUROPEAN NIGHTJAR
Wing-spots entirely absent.
Emarginations subtle.
Small buff tips to two outer tail-feathers.

OF NIGHTJAR WINGS AND TAILS

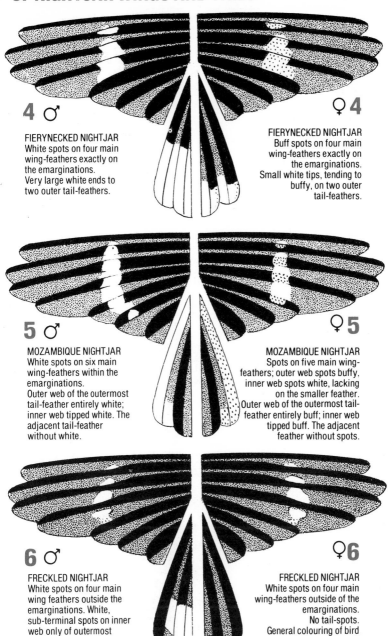

4 ♂

FIERYNECKED NIGHTJAR
White spots on four main
wing-feathers exactly on
the emarginations.
Very large white ends to
two outer tail-feathers.

♀ 4

FIERYNECKED NIGHTJAR
Buff spots on four main
wing-feathers exactly on
the emarginations.
Small white tips, tending to
buffy, on two outer
tail-feathers.

5 ♂

MOZAMBIQUE NIGHTJAR
White spots on six main
wing-feathers within the
emarginations.
Outer web of the outermost
tail-feather entirely white;
inner web tipped white. The
adjacent tail-feather
without white.

♀ 5

MOZAMBIQUE NIGHTJAR
Spots on five main wing-
feathers; outer web spots buffy,
inner web spots white, lacking
on the smaller feather.
Outer web of the outermost tail-
feather entirely buff; inner web
tipped buff. The adjacent
feather without spots.

6 ♂

FRECKLED NIGHTJAR
White spots on four main
wing feathers outside the
emarginations. White,
sub-terminal spots on inner
web only of outermost
tail-feather and on both
webs of adjacent feather.

♀ 6

FRECKLED NIGHTJAR
White spots on four main
wing-feathers outside of the
emarginations.
No tail-spots.
General colouring of bird
very dark speckling all
over.

PLATE 51

Swallows and martins. Family HIRUNDINIDAE. Small aerial-feeding birds with long wings, forked tails (in swallows), short beaks and wide gapes. Swallows are generally blue above and pale or reddish below, sometimes with streaks, spots or bars of a darker colour, and many have tail-streamers. The closely related martins are generally brown above, white or brownish below and have square tails. Swallows and martins either make nest-burrows in earth or construct various forms of nests with mud pellets. Their food is insects caught on the wing. Some species are resident in Africa while others are non-breeding migrants from the Palaearctic region, arriving here in early summer. Swifts are unrelated to swallows and martins.

1 REDBREASTED SWALLOW (Rooiborsswael) *Hirundo semirufa.* A fairly common intra-Africa migrant found throughout the Park August-April, breeding in summer. This is the largest swallow in the KNP and may usually be seen in pairs in the vicinity of road culverts under which it builds its mud nest. Its flight is slow, gliding and leisurely, affording ample opportunity to see the red underparts. It has a soft warbling call. **524**

2 MOSQUE SWALLOW (Moskeeswael) *Hirundo senegalensis.* A fairly common resident species in the north, ranging south to the Satara region. Builds its mud nest in a hole in a tree, especially baobabs, and has been found breeding all summer. Closely related and similar to (1) but has a white throat and upper breast and *white underwing coverts.* May be seen at any time of the year in the north, particularly near Punda Maria and Pafuri. Frequently drinks from dams and pans by skimming the water. Flies slowly, with much gliding. The voice is a nasal, tin-trumpet-like 'hrrrp'. **525**

3 GREATER STRIPED SWALLOW (Grootstreepswael) *Hirundo cucullata.* An uncommon resident species, reported only infrequently north of Shingwedzi, being seen more often in the south. Breeds all summer. A fairly large swallow that glides a great deal. The markings on the breast are not apparent in flight (in contrast with the next species) and the rump is so pale as to appear almost white. Builds a mud chamber with a tubular entrance against the underside of rocks and the eaves of buildings. The voice is a soft 'chissik' uttered frequently in flight. **526**

4 LESSER STRIPED SWALLOW (Kleinstreepswael) *Hirundo abyssinica.* A common and widespread resident species. Breeds all summer. More heavily striped than (3), the underparts appearing grey in flight, the orange cap comes over the ears and the rump is distinctly orange. Flies more actively than (3) and glides for briefer periods; also builds a similar nest. The voice is a distinct series of four descending squeaks that suggest their being squeezed out 'eh-eh-eh-eh'. **527**

15 cm

PLATE 52

1 EUROPEAN SWALLOW (Europese Swael) *Hirundo rustica.* Abundant seasonally. A non-breeding Palaearctic migrant arriving in the KNP in September and departing in April. The most common swallow during summer in all regions. On arrival and prior to departure carries long tail-streamers, but these are moulted soon after arrival and are *entirely absent* during much of its stay here. In flight the dark neck and throat are diagnostic. Has the habit of sitting on road surfaces, often in large numbers, and of skimming the roads in flight. **518**

WHITETHROATED SWALLOW (Witkeelswael) *Hirundo albigularis.* Rare. Has been seen at scattered points in the southern half of the Park. No evidence of breeding. Distinguished by white underparts with black breast-band. Occurs mostly near water; if breeding builds mud nest beneath bridges and culverts. Associates freely with other swallows. The call is a soft twittering; it also has a warbling song. **520**

2 WIRETAILED SWALLOW (Draadstertswael) *Hirundo smithii.* A resident species fairly common at large rivers, dams and camps. Breeds mainly August-April, sometimes later. The only swallow with complete orange cap and very fine, wire-like tail-streamers. The immature has a brown cap and lacks tail-streamers. Builds a cup-shaped mud nest under bridges, stone and concrete structures and eaves. Within the Park is usually found near rest camps and bridges, frequently perching on bridge rails. **522**

3 PEARLBREASTED SWALLOW (Pêrelborsswael) *Hirundo dimidiata.* Rare but resident. Has been recorded at points over the entire Park with breeding in summer. A small swallow having plain blue upperparts, plain white underparts and no tail-streamers. The nest is a small mud cup normally placed under rocks and in burrows. **523**

SOUTH AFRICAN CLIFF SWALLOW (Familieswael) *Hirundo spilodera.* Rare in the Park; probably a non-breeding visitor. Resembles (1) in having a dark throat but has an orange breast, vent and rump plus more square tail. Usually occurs in flocks but single birds mix with other swallows. Has a four-syllabic call 'chor, chor, chor, chor'. **528**

4 GREYRUMPED SWALLOW (Gryskruisswael) *Pseudhirundo griseopyga.* A fairly common resident species. Is regularly seen on the Letaba and Olifants Rivers. The only swallow with a grey cap and rump. Not easily identified in flight as the grey cap is not evident at a distance and the grey rump may be so pale as to appear almost white, thus causing confusion with the House Martin (Plate 53). Best identified by behaviour. The only swallow in the Park to nest in ground burrows, frequently close to a river. **531**

1

J

2

3

4

15cm

PLATE 53

1 HOUSE MARTIN (Huisswael) *Delichon urbica.* A fairly common non-breeding Palaearctic migrant. Annual influxes are irregular and unpredictable but the species has been recorded November-March. A blue and white martin with a distinct white rump and slightly forked tail. Is usually seen in flocks and frequently associates with the European Swallow (Plate 52). Can be confused with the Grey-rumped Swallow (Plate 52), but has a pure *white* rump, not greyish, a blue cap and a shallow fork in its tail.   **530**

2 BROWNTHROATED MARTIN (Afrikaanse Oewerswael) *Riparia paludicola.* An uncommon winter visitor. Has been recorded April-August only from Nwanedzi northwards. Breeding occurs during the winter months. A small, inconspicuous martin, completely brown except for some white on the underparts. Usually seen near rivers and mixes freely with other swallows. Sometimes perches on partially submerged branches in rivers. The nest is a tunnel burrowed into a sandy riverbank, several usually occurring in close proximity.   **533**

3 BANDED MARTIN (Gebande Oewerswael) *Riparia cincta.* Rare, precise status unknown. Has been recorded only in winter on the Olifants and Letaba Rivers, with no evidence of breeding. This is an intra-Africa migrant normally regarded as a summer visitor to South Africa. A fairly large and distinctive martin usually seen in pairs. The flight is slow and leisurely, the birds alighting on a perch to rest frequently. **534**

4 ROCK MARTIN (Kransswael) *Hirundo fuligula.* Uncommon and very localised but a resident species. Found regularly only in the vicinity of Lanner Gorge, Pafuri, where a colony is known to be resident. Has also been recorded on the Letaba River occasionally and may breed in Olifants Gorge. An all-brown martin which frequents cliffs. Normally seen in small flocks flying slowly with much twisting and turning. Appears wider-winged than other swallows. Builds a bowl-shaped mud nest under a rock overhang during summer.   **529**

5 (EUROPEAN) SAND MARTIN (Europese Oewerswael) *Riparia riparia.* Rare, non-breeding summer visitor; may occur anywhere in the Park. Smaller than (3) and lacking white eyebrows; underwings dark not white, tail slightly forked. Flocks frequent open waters and grasslands, mixing freely with other martins and swallows.   **532**

1

2

3

4

15 cm

Swallows and martins have wider, comparatively more rounded wings than swifts.

Swallows are blue on their upperparts, white or orange, sometimes spotted on their underparts.

Swallows may have orange caps, foreheads or throats, and buff or orange-coloured rumps.

Martins are brown, the underparts usually paler. The House Martin is the exception, since it has the appearance of a swallow.

Martins have squarish tails with white 'windows' in them, visible when the tail is fanned.

Swallows have forked tails, often with long streamers on the outer feathers, and frequently have 'windows' in the tail.

Swallows glide frequently between bouts of flapping flight.

Swallows and martins can perch.

COMPARED WITH SWIFTS

The wings of a swift are slender, scimitar-like and appear to sweep straight back from the body with little bend at the carpal joint.

Swifts are dark grey-brown, blackish or ash-brown, and mostly appear all dark in flight.

Swifts may have whitish throats and white rumps, but no bright colours.

Swifts may have square or forked tails;

in our region only the Palm Swift has tail streamers.

Only the large Alpine Swift and the small Batlike Spinetail have white on the belly.

Swifts sometimes fly with their wings steeply angled upwards.

Most swifts fly very rapidly with only brief gliding spells.

Swifts cannot perch.

PLATE 54

Swifts. Family APODIDAE. The most aerial of birds, settling only for roosting and breeding purposes. Swifts cannot perch on branches or wires, and do not settle on the ground. They are able to cling to rough, vertical surfaces such as rocks, but more usually enter their nests, under the eaves of buildings or in rock crevices, by flying in directly. Though superficially similar to swallows they are quite unrelated, and lack the swallows' attractive colouring, being usually blackish-brown, sometimes with white patches. See previous two pages for comparisons.

1 PALM SWIFT (Palmwindswael) *Cypsiurus parvus.* Fairly common but localised resident throughout the Park. Breeds during summer. A fast-flying, slender, greyish coloured swift, the tail appearing needle-like when closed. Usually occurs in small flocks, especially near well-developed palms in which they breed, and may be seen wheeling about these trees at high speed at Pafuri and most rest camps and rangers' houses where palms occur. The voice is a thin, high-pitched scream. **421**

2 BLACK SWIFT (Swartwindswael) *Apus barbatus.* A resident and casual visitor, common only at Pafuri where it breeds in Lanner Gorge, otherwise uncommon. Breeding occurs throughout the summer. A large swift which appears all-black in the sky, the tail moderately forked. Distinguished from the next species only with difficulty; seen from above the secondaries closest to the body are pale, contrasting with the rest of the wing and body. Breeds and roosts in rocky cliffs and *is often seen in the vicinity of these.* Otherwise may occur anywhere in the Park, usually flying at some height. Near colonies, flying flocks emit continual screams. **412**

EURASIAN SWIFT (Europese Windswael) *Apus apus.* Fairly common, non-breeding summer visitor. Distinguished from the previous species with difficulty; less white on the throat, from above more uniformly coloured. A fairly large, dark swift occurring in flocks anywhere. High-flying (except after storms) and wide-ranging. **411**

3 LITTLE SWIFT (Kleinwindswael) *Apus affinis.* Fairly common and widespread throughout the Park. A resident species breeding throughout the summer. A small, square-tailed swift with white throat and rump. Occurs in flocks, often with other swifts, especially in the vicinity of rest camps and high-level bridges where it roosts and nests. A high-pitched, excited twittering is made by the entire flock near the roost. **417**

4 WHITERUMPED SWIFT (Witkruiswindswael) *Apus caffer.* Fairly common August-April throughout the Park, absent in winter. Breeds in most rest camps. Has a distinctly forked tail, white throat and crescent-shaped white patch on the rump. The tail is more deeply forked than in (5), the rump-patch much smaller. Usually in flocks, often with other swifts, and is most noticeable in rest camps where it breeds and roosts under the eaves of huts, often taking over the mud nests of swallows. A thin, high-pitched scream is uttered on the wing. **415**

5 HORUS SWIFT (Horuswindswael) *Apus horus.* Locally common resident. Known to breed in the vicinity of Pafuri and the Olifants River region May-July. Otherwise occurs throughout the Park as a vagrant. Similar to the previous species but with a less markedly forked tail and a bold white rump which *wraps around the sides of the body.* Does not normally occur at rest camps and nests only in holes in earth banks. Makes a warbling trill. **416**

6 ALPINE SWIFT (Witpenswindswael) *Apus melba.* An uncommon vagrant occurring throughout the year in all regions. The largest swift, fast-flying and distinctly marked, being the only species in the region with a white belly. A mountain swift which wanders freely when not breeding. Makes a shrill screaming, but unlikely to be heard in the Park. **418**

PLATE 55

1 **BÖHM'S SPINETAIL (BATLIKE SPINETAIL)** (Witpensstekelstert) *Neafrapus boehmi.* An uncommon and localised resident species. Occurs mostly in the Pafuri and Shingwedzi regions. A nest with eggs has been recorded in April. A very short-tailed swift with fluttering, bat-like flight. The white rump and underparts are distinctive. Breeds in holes in baobab trees and may be seen near these, especially along Nyala Drive, Pafuri. Flight call a high-pitched 'ti-ti-ti-peep'. **423**

2 **MOTTLED SPINETAIL** (Gevlekte Stekelstert) *Telacanthura ussheri.* An uncommon, localised resident confined to the far north. Recorded breeding in May. Could be mistaken for the Little Swift (Plate 54) but is slightly larger and has a mottled not white throat. Tail spines not visible in flight. Often mixes with Little Swifts. Makes a chattering 'zi-zick', quite different from the Little Swift's screaming call. **422**

Mousebirds or colies. Family COLIIDAE. A family of long-tailed, frugivorous birds with crested heads. Apart from the tail feathers, which are stiff, the plumage is soft and hair-like. The zygodactylous feet, in which two toes face forward and two rearward, are an aid to clambering about trees when feeding. Mousebirds are found in parties of up to about a dozen individuals which keep in contact by call.

3 **SPECKLED MOUSEBIRD** (Gevlekte Muisvoël) *Colius striatus.* Common and widespread throughout the Park. A resident species, breeding in early summer. The fine vermiculations or speckling of the underparts are visible only at close range. The bill, with black upper mandible and bluish-white lower mandible, is diagnostic. Occurs in the denser, riparian vegetation and around well-wooded camps. Makes a rasping 'zwit, zwit'. **424**

4 **REDFACED MOUSEBIRD** (Rooiwangmuisvoël) *Colius indicus.* Common and widespread throughout the Park. A resident species breeding throughout summer. Rather paler in general colouring than (3) and with a bright red mask and feet. Unmistakable. Occurs in groups and calls both at rest and in flight. Frequents a wide range of habitats but is particularly common in riverside bush and on koppies where trees are fruiting. The call is a descending 'tree-ree-ree'. **426**

Trogons. Family TROGINIDAE. Colourful, forest-dwelling, dove-like insectivorous and frugivorous birds which nest in holes in trees. The feet are zygodactylous, two toes facing forward, two rearward.

5 **NARINA TROGON** (Bosloerie) *Apaloderma narina.* Rare, but is resident in the riverine forest at Pafuri where breeding occurs in summer. Has also been seen infrequently in the south. Beautiful and quite unmistakable, the combination of peacock-blue upperparts and crimson underparts (in the male) being unique. The blue regions of bare skin on the head of the male are most extensive during the breeding season. The female lacks the blue throat skin but retains the gape and eye colouring. Unlikely to occur away from dense riparian woodland. Floats among the larger trees in soft, buoyant flight and normally settles on a branch facing away from the observer, thereafter slowly turning its head to look back. Is often active at dusk. The call is a series of about eight hooting sounds, gradually descending in volume. **427**

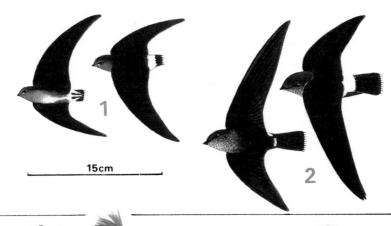

15cm

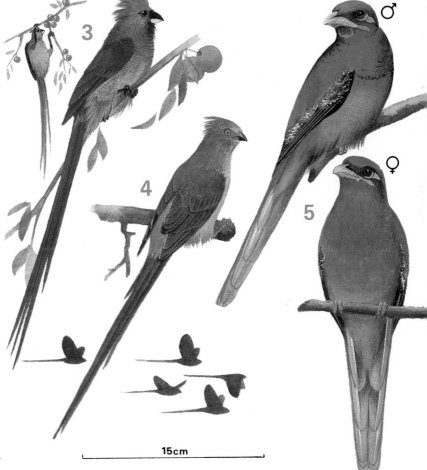

15cm

PLATE 56

Kingfishers. Family HALCYONIDAE. Of the nine kingfishers which occur regularly in the KNP only four are fish-eaters. The others feed on insects caught on the ground away from water, but some may dive to bathe occasionally. All kingfishers have large bills, small feet and legs unsuitable for walking. Many are brightly coloured. Hunting is usually undertaken from a vantage point from where they can watch the ground or water. When the prey is caught it is beaten vigorously on a stone or branch with sharp sideways flicks of the bill until stilled. Kingfishers breed in holes either excavated by themselves in earth banks or, in the woodland species, in a ready-made tree hole.

1 GIANT KINGFISHER (Reuse Visvanger) *Ceryle maxima.* A fairly common resident species which occurs at large rivers and wooded dams throughout the Park. Breeding occurs throughout the summer months. This large kingfisher is unmistakable, the only other predominantly black and white species (2) being very much smaller and lacking the rufous underparts; note that the male has the rufous breast, the female a rufous belly. Usually hunts from a branch overhanging the water but occasionally hovers and plunges to catch fish. May also fish from low-level bridges. Is also known to eat crabs. A very noisy species when disturbed, flying off with a loud 'kek-kek-kekkek'. **429**

2 PIED KINGFISHER (Bontvisvanger) *Ceryle rudis.* Common and resident. Occurs at pans, dams and rivers throughout the Park. Breeding occurs most months. An unmistakable black and white kingfisher, usually seen in small parties of 2-3 birds, repeatedly hovering over the water and plunging in. Sometimes hunts from bridges or telephone wires across rivers. When excited the call is a high-pitched 'kik kik kik kik'. **428**

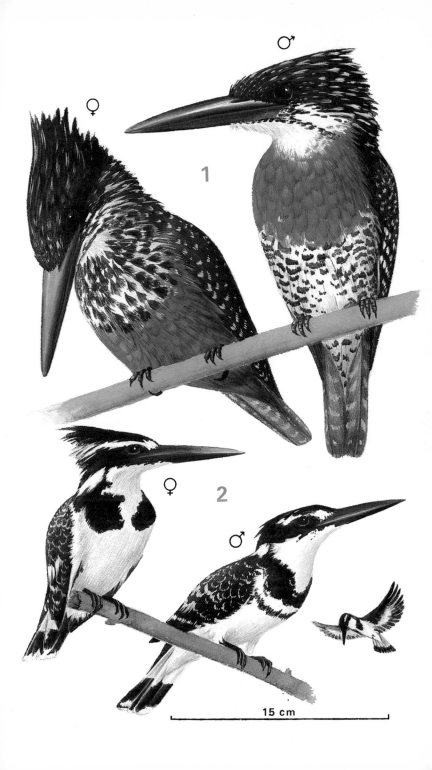

1

♀

♂

2

♀

♂

15 cm

PLATE 57

1 **WOODLAND KINGFISHER** (Bosveldvisvanger) *Halcyon senegalensis.* An intra-Africa migrant common throughout the Park during summer, arriving the first week of November and departing in April or later. Nests in holes in trees. A brilliant blue and white kingfisher closely resembling the rare Mangrove Kingfisher (3), being distinguished from that species by the red and black bill and black eye-stripe *extending to behind the eye*, as well as by call and behaviour. Immature birds frequently have *all red bills*, sometimes with a black tip, then identified by eye-stripe and blue (not grey) crown. This species is not a fish-eater but may sometimes dive into water to bathe. Prefers large trees such as are found along riverbanks where it catches insects and small lizards. Pairs greet each other with outstretched wings and upright posture. Can usually be located by its strident 'yimp-trrrrrrrrrr' call, the last part drawn out and descending. This call is repeated frequently throughout the day.　**433**

2 **GREYHOODED KINGFISHER** (Gryskopvisvanger) *Halcyon leucocephala.* An uncommon intra-Africa migrant arriving late October and departing in April. Is occasionally seen as late as June. Occurs all over the Park with breeding recorded in November. Its red bill, grey head and mantle, black back and chestnut belly should prevent confusion with other species. Prefers a woodland habitat, especially favouring the bush along dry watercourses. Feeds on various insects, lizards and small snakes. A quiet kingfisher, the call being described as a weak, descending 'chi-chi-chi-chi'.　**436**

3 **MANGROVE KINGFISHER** (Mangliedvisvanger) *Halcyon senegaloides.* Status unknown. A coastal species as its name implies, but moves inland along rivers in summer to breed. It has been reported in the Park a number of times although no breeding is recorded. Suspected sightings should be checked carefully against the description of the Woodland Kingfisher (1), especially the immature of that species which *may also have an all-red bill*. Note that in the Mangrove Kingfisher the *top of the head, nape, and mantle are grey* and there is a *black spot only in front of the eye,* not extending behind the eye as in (1).　**434**

15 cm

PLATE 58

1 **BROWNHOODED KINGFISHER** (Bruinkopvisvanger) *Halcyon albiventris.* A fairly common, widespread resident species. Normally breeds in early summer but this sometimes extends to as late as May. Occurs in woodland and riverine bush, even along dry watercourses. Perches on a low branch and flies down to seize insects on the ground. Inconspicuous while perched but, when flushed, flies in a fast direct path when the blue wings, tail and back become apparent. This species seldom catches fish, being predominantly insectivorous. The call is a loud, descending 'KIK, kik-kik-kik-kik' or, when agitated, a series on the same pitch 'kik-kik-kik-kik-kik . . '. **435**

2 **STRIPED KINGFISHER** (Gestreepte Visvanger) *Halcyon chelicuti.* A common and widespread resident kingfisher, occurring mainly in regions of large trees. Breeds in early summer. A small and inconspicuous species when not calling. The striped crown is diagnostic, the blue wings and tail being seen only in flight. Sits on the outer branch of a tree far from water and catches insects on the ground. Usually found in pairs which habitually call in duet: 'Tirrr-*deeeoo-deeeoo-deeeoo* '. **437**

3 .**PYGMY KINGFISHER** (Dwergvisvanger) *Ispidina picta.* Uncommon. Has been flushed from a nest hole at Pafuri in November, but has been seen over the length of the Park between November and March. Appears to be present in summer only. A very small, colourful bird, the red bill being conspicuous even in flight. Differs from the similar Malachite Kingfisher (5) in having a dark blue crown which *does not* touch the eyes, and purple cheeks. More likely to be seen away from water than the Malachite, but does frequent small pools and watercourses, perching on low branches from where it catches insects. Occasionally plunges into water, probably to bathe. Makes a sharp 'chit' when flushed. **432**

4 **HALFCOLLARED KINGFISHER** (Blouvisvanger) *Alcedo semitorquata.* A rare resident species. Has been recorded in both winter and early summer at scattered points throughout the Park, with sightings at several places on the Sabie River. Has bred near Skukuza in mid-summer. This is a very blue kingfisher and is especially conspicuous when flying. Note that the bill is black but so, too, is that of the immature Malachite Kingfisher (5). Perches low down over quiet waters and plunge-dives to catch fish. The flight is fast and direct. Calls 'peep' or 'seek-seek' when flushed. **430**

5 **MALACHITE KINGFISHER** (Kuifkopvisvanger) *Alcedo cristata.* Fairly common in suitable habitat; widespread and resident. Breeding takes place throughout the summer. A brightly coloured little bird which, however, is easily overlooked. Differs from the similar Pygmy Kingfisher in having a turquoise cap which *reaches the eyes.* The immature has a *black bill:* compare with (4). Found only in association with water, frequenting quiet pools, dams and rivers where it perches on a reed or low branch, plunging to catch small fish and water insects. Flies off low over the water in a fast, direct flight calling a sharp 'peep-peep'. **431**

15 cm

PLATE 59

Bee-eaters. Family MEROPIDAE. Colourful and graceful birds with long, curved bills and very short legs, they are aerial feeders subsisting on a variety of insects in addition to bees. They feed either by short flights from a perch or during prolonged sorties. In the former case the insect is usually brought back to the perch and beaten into immobility prior to being swallowed. The flight of the bee-eaters involves graceful aerobatics interspersed with short spells of gliding. They nest in burrows excavated in earth banks, often colonially. Most are gregarious and a number are migratory.

1 **LITTLE BEE-EATER** (Kleinbyvreter) *Merops pusillus*. A fairly common and widespread resident species. Breeds in summer. The smallest of our bee-eaters, predominantly green above and yellow to buff below, with dark brown on the upper breast. Usually found hawking insects from a low perch, frequently returning to the same perch to eat its prey. The voice is a soft 'kwip'. **444**

2 **CARMINE BEE-EATER** (Rooiborsbyvreter) *Merops nubicoides*. A very common non-breeding visitor during the period mid-December to late March. This species breeds in Zimbabwe during September-October and travels south as soon as the young are independent. The earliest reported arrival in the Park is 16 November, but mid-December is the norm, with birds appearing in the southern half of the Park before the northern. A very colourful and unmistakable bee-eater, carmine and pale blue with long tail-shafts. The immature is a drab version of the adult, more beige than carmine and lacks the tail-streamers or has them half-grown. This species frequently associates with other bee-eaters and is nearly always found in large flocks. Sometimes rests on roadways. The call is a throaty 'terk'. **441**

3 **EUROPEAN BEE-EATER** (Europese Byvreter) *Merops apiaster*. Common seasonally. A non-breeding summer visitor present in the Park from September (earliest record 22 September) to March, occasionally April. This distinctive bee-eater with chestnut-brown upperparts, pale blue underparts and yellow throat occurs in flocks all over the Park and mixes freely with other bee-eaters. May be abundant locally. The call is a liquid-sounding 'kwilp' often repeated in flight. **438**

4 **WHITEFRONTED BEE-EATER** (Rooikeelbyvreter) *Merops bullockoides*. A common resident species. Occurs throughout the Park but is usually restricted to the vicinity of rivers. Breeds colonially in September. Deep holes are burrowed in high riverbanks, the flock returning to roost in the holes even when not breeding. The white forehead and chin, red throat and cinnamon-coloured underparts are diagnostic. Does not have tail-streamers. It makes a variety of single-syllable notes sounding like 'kwoa-kwaai'. **443**

5 **BLUECHEEKED BEE-EATER** (Blouwangbyvreter) *Merops persicus*. Uncommon. Occurs at a few scattered water points in the Park during December-April but is fairly regular at Nwanedzi and on the floodpans of the Limpopo River, generally in small flocks. A large green bee-eater with tail-shafts. The blue eyebrow and cheeks are discernible only at close range or with binoculars. Usually seen hawking flying insects from a dead tree in water or near water. The call is a short 'prruik' or 'pree-oo'. **440**

132

15 cm

PLATE 60

Rollers. Family CORACIIDAE. Colourful, heavy-billed birds the size of a pigeon. They spend much of the day perched on a convenient post or branch, fly down to catch insects and other small prey on the ground and then return to kill the prey by beating it against the perch. They have harsh, croaking voices, very active flight displays and breed in holes in trees.

1 **RACKET-TAILED ROLLER** (Knopsterttroupant) *Coracias spatulata.* Uncommon and localised but probably resident. Found at all times of the year as far south as the Olifants River but regular only in the hilly country between Punda Maria and Pafuri. Similar to the Lilacbreasted Roller (3) but has plain blue underparts and spatulate tips to the tail-shafts. **448**

2 **BROADBILLED ROLLER** or Cinnamon Roller (Geelbektroupant) *Eurystomus glaucurus.* Fairly common, seasonal intra-Africa migrant occurring in the Park between October and late March. Found mainly in the far north, but also occurs in small numbers as far south as the Timbavati and Olifants Rivers. Breeding commences soon after arrival. A small roller, cinnamon in colour, with a conspicuous yellow bill. Is more inclined to catch insects in the air than other rollers and prefers the denser habitat of riverine forest. In courtship, pairs indulge in vigorous aerial pursuits with much harsh croaking, frequently continuing after nightfall. **450**

3 **LILACBREASTED ROLLER** (Gewone Troupant) *Coracias caudata.* A very common and widespread resident species. More plentiful in the open, lightly wooded habitat of the northern two-thirds of the Park, but numbers fluctuate in all regions. Breeding occurs September-December. A well-known and very colourful bird, often erroneously referred to as the 'Blue Jay'. Differs from the Racket-tailed Roller (1) in having a lilac breast and lack of prominent tips to the tail. In flight the wings appear electric blue. Vigorous aerial displays including rolls are performed in the breeding season to the accompaniment of harsh calls. In common with other rollers, it catches large insects, lizards, etc., on the ground, frequently eating them there. **447**

4 **EUROPEAN ROLLER** (Europese Troupant) *Coracias garrulus.* Common seasonally. A non-breeding Palaearctic migrant occurring in the Park early December-March. At times outnumbers the resident Lilacbreasted Roller (3) in some regions. May be identified by plain blue underparts and square tail. Perches prominently on a post, tree or wire and catches prey on the ground. **446**

5 **PURPLE ROLLER** or Mozambique Roller (Groottroupant) *Coracias naevia.* An uncommon resident species. Breeding has been recorded in all the months of summer. Widespread throughout the Park and seemingly more numerous in late summer. A large, dark-coloured roller with a square tail. Less active than other rollers and inclined to perch closer to the ground. Has a peculiar rocking display flight in which the wings seem to beat independently and during which a harsh 'kra-kra' call is emitted. In addition to large insects also eats lizards and small snakes. **449**

PLATE 61

Woodhoopoes and scimitarbills. Family PHOENICULIDAE. Medium-sized, glossy blue-green birds having long, graduated tails, long curved beaks and short legs. The feet are adapted for climbing about trees and clinging to the bark in search of insects. They also investigate the grass nests of weavers and sparrows in their search for insects and may throw out eggs or chicks in the process and therefore are mobbed by the adults of these species when their nests are approached. Woodhoopoes and scimitarbills breed in tree holes, either natural cavities or those made by woodpeckers, etc.

1 REDBILLED WOODHOOPOE (Gewone Kakelaar) *Phoeniculus purpureus.* A common and widespread resident species. Breeds October-July. A distinctive bird with its glossy plumage, long tail and curved red bill. White markings on wings and tail are conspicuous in flight. A sociable, nomadic species, always occurring in family parties of up to ten birds. Fly in straggling procession from tree to tree, landing low down on the trunk and working their way upwards before moving on again. The call is a high-pitched cackling started by one individual and taken up by the others to produce a cacophony of hysterical laughter. Very similar to the voice of the Arrowmarked Babbler (Plate 75) but less harsh, more musical. **452**

2 SCIMITARBILLED WOODHOOPOE (Swartbekkakelaar) *Phoeniculus cyanomelas.* Fairly common, widespread and resident. Breeding has been recorded in midsummer. Prefers areas of large trees along rivers and watercourses. Smaller and less colourful than the preceding species, it is less glossy with little white in its plumage and has a more sharply curved black bill. Usually occurs singly, probing about quietly on tree trunks and large branches. Feeds on insects and spiders and some vegetable matter. The call is not often heard outside the breeding season, a series of sounds repeated about ten times at intervals of half a second 'pwep-pwep-pwep-pwep . . .' **454**

Hoopoe. Family UPUPIDAE. The hoopoe is placed in a separate family to the woodhoopoes and differs from them in respect of its crested head, colouring, behaviour and call.

3 HOOPOE (Hoephoep) *Upupa epops.* Common, widespread and resident. Breeding occurs September-February. This well-known bird with its crested head and cinnamon-coloured plumage is also easily recognised in flight because of its black and white wings, which appear to flutter in the manner of a large butterfly, the flight being fairly slow with much undulation. When feeding it walks about unobtrusively, probing the ground for insects with its long curved bill. The crest is normally held lowered on the head, being raised only when the bird is attentive or alarmed. In addition to insects will also eat small frogs, lizards and burrowing snakes. Has a far-carrying, often repeated call 'hoop, hoop, -hoop, hoop, hoop'. **451**

1

2

3

15 cm

PLATE 62

Hornbills. Family BUCEROTIDAE. Medium to large insectivorous and frugivorous birds having heavy-looking, curved bills, sometimes with an ornamental casque on the upper mandible. Arboreal or terrestrial feeders, or both. Nest in holes in trees (among rocks in one species) and are well known for their practice of sealing the nest entrance with mud, faeces, etc. During egg incubation and development of the small young the female moults her feathers and is temporarily flightless. At this time the male is the sole provider. Later the female breaks out of the nest, reseals it, and helps to feed the growing young. The Ground Hornbill, largest member of the family, does not engage in nest-sealing. Hornbills fly in a heavy, clumsy manner; an undulating flight interspersed with gliding.

1 YELLOWBILLED HORNBILL (Geelbekneushoringvoël) *Tockus flavirostris*. Very common. A widespread resident species. Numbers fluctuate and it may be uncommon locally at times. Breeds October-April. A distinctive and well-known hornbill, the yellow bill making identification straightforward. Frequents camps and roadsides, becoming very tame and tolerant of moving vehicles. Favours dry savanna bush and mopane regions, and spends much time on the ground. The call is 'wurk, wurk, wurk, wurk, wurk, wukwukak, wukwukak, wukak, wukak, wurk, wurk, wurk . . .' This gradually works up into a crescendo and then fades away, often two birds calling simultaneously. **459**

2 REDBILLED HORNBILL (Rooibekneushoringvoël) *Tockus erythrorhynchus*. Resident and widespread but common only in dry, overgrazed regions. Otherwise uncommon or entirely absent in verdant regions during the summer. Breeding occurs November-April. Similar to (1) except for a red bill and smaller size. A ground-feeding hornbill most numerous where little rain has fallen and where the larger herbivores have grazed extensively. The voice is similar to that of (1) but rather lower in pitch 'wha, wha, wha, wha, wha, wha, kawacha, wacha, wacha, wacha, wach, wach . . .' **458**

3 CROWNED HORNBILL (Gekroonde Neushoringvoël) *Tockus alboterminatus*. Fairly common in a few restricted localities, favouring the more heavily wooded regions of the Park. Resident, breeding in early summer. May be confused with (2) but note predominantly brown plumage and larger size, plus casque on bill. Usually found in pairs. The call is a series of melancholy, piping whistles. **460**

4 GREY HORNBILL (Grysneushoringvoël) *Tockus nasutus*. A common and widely distributed species although populations tend to move away temporarily from regions where trees have lost their leaves. A plainly coloured hornbill with marked sexual differences about the head and bill, the male having the larger casque. Occurs in pairs or small parties, moving with characteristic dipping flight and much gliding between spells of wing-flapping. Makes a thin, piping mewing, a plaintive series of notes ascending and descending the scale 'phe, phephee, pheephee, pheeoo-pheeoo, phew, pheeoo-pheeoo . . .' This call, when made from a perch, is delivered with neck outstretched and wings flapping. **457**

15 cm

1

2

3

4 ♂ ♀

PLATE 63

1 **SILVERYCHEEKED HORNBILL** (Kuifkopboskraai) *Bycanistes brevis.* Rare vagrant to the extreme north of the Park, moving in from Zimbabwe only during periods of extensive rains. A very large, unmistakable hornbill associated with large trees in well forested regions. Feeds on fruits and insects. A noisy species at times, emitting a raucous, nasal braying 'haa, haa, haa, ha, ha, ha,ha, heh, heh, heh, heh . . .' the call fading away at the end and usually repeated by a number of individuals. **456**

2 **TRUMPETER HORNBILL** (Gewone Boskraai) *Bycanistes bucinator.* Fairly common along the permanent rivers and resident in these habitats, also ranging along the smaller watercourses in search of fruit-bearing trees. Breeds in early summer. Is usually first detected by the call and is mostly seen in small parties flying in straggling formation across rivers or from tree to tree in riverine forests. The male has the larger casque on its bill. An arboreal feeder on fruits and large insects. The call most commonly heard is a loud and melancholy nasal braying not unlike the cry of a baby 'heh - heh, heh - heh-h-h-h, heh, heh, heh, heh, hehhhhh . . .' **455**

3 **GROUND HORNBILL** (Bromvoël) *Bucorvus leadbeateri.* A common resident species, widespread throughout the Park. Breeds in summer. A huge terrestrial bird quite unlike other hornbills and unmistakable. Note that the female has the blue throat patch and the immature yellow skin on face and throat. Occurs in family parties of about eight birds which stride through the veld in search of food. Will fly into trees to roost or when alarmed. This bird is sometimes erroneously referred to as the Turkey Buzzard, an American species. It is neither turkey nor buzzard but a highly specialised African hornbill and one of the largest birds in the KNP. The Ground Hornbill feeds on almost anything it can seize and overpower; large insects, reptiles including tortoises, small mammals and birds, birds' eggs, etc. The call is usually heard in the early hours of the morning, a far-carrying grunting or hooting sound 'oomph, oomph-oomph'; when heard at a distance not unlike a lion roaring. **463**

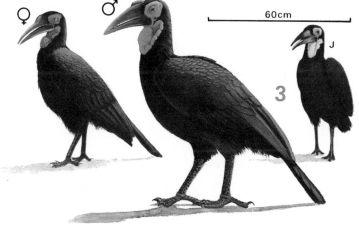

30 cm

60 cm

PLATE 64

Barbets. Family CAPITONIDAE. A family of small, stockily built and colourful birds related to the woodpeckers. They have stout, conical bills and feed on fruits and insects. The name 'barbet' refers to the tufts of hair-like feathers around their nostrils, gape and chin. Barbets excavate nest holes in trees just as do woodpeckers, although softer woods are probably preferred. Barbets have distinctive calls of a tooting or rattling nature which are often repeated for long periods. Tinker barbets are so named because their calls resemble the sound of a hammer on an anvil.

1 **GOLDENRUMPED TINKER BARBET** (Swartblestinker) *Pogoniulus bilineatus.* Rare and localised. Has been seen only along the Crocodile River in the extreme south, where it probably breeds. A very small barbet, almost completely black on its upperparts. Creeps about the trunks and branches of trees like a woodpecker. Would easily be overlooked were it not for its call 'kwerp kwerp kwerp kwerp kwerp', four to seven calls *followed by a pause.* **471**

2 **YELLOWFRONTED TINKER BARBET** (Geelblestinker) *Pogoniulus chrysoconus.* An uncommon resident species, widespread but most frequent in the north and south. Breeds throughout the summer. A very small barbet usually found in the leaf canopies of trees. The yellow to *orange* forehead is diagnostic. The bird can best be located by call, a monotonous and far-carrying 'purp purp purp purp . . .' repeated without pause for long periods on warm days. **470**

3 **PIED BARBET** (Bonthoutkapper) *Lybius leucomelas.* A fairly common and widely distributed resident species which breeds in summer. A smallish, black and white barbet with a conspicuous red forehead. Prefers the larger trees, especially riparian woodland and tree-surrounded dams. Frequents the upper branches where it feeds and calls. The most common utterances are a loud, nasal 'pehp, pehp, pehp', said to resemble the sound of a toy trumpet plus a ventriloquial 'poop poop poop poop', less loud than the previous call. **465**

4 **BLACKCOLLARED BARBET** (Rooikophoutkapper) *Lybius torquatus.* A common and widespread resident species which breeds throughout the summer. A striking and unmistakable bird, the red face and upper breast against a black surround being conspicuous. Normally occurs in pairs or small family groups. Individuals bob up and down or sway from side to side when greeting each other and frequently start their characteristic duet call. This commences with a subdued whirring sound 'skrrrr, skrrrr, skrrrr' and is followed by 'too-puddely, too puddely . . .' repeated about eight times, the first bird calling 'too' and the second 'puddely'. Also makes a harsh 'snaar' threat sound. **464**

5 **CRESTED BARBET** (Kuifkophoutkapper) *Trachyphonus vaillantii.* A common and widespread resident species which breeds throughout summer. An unmistakable yellow and black barbet, speckled with red and white and having a large yellow beak. Occurs in a variety of wooded habitats and may be seen in most camps. The call, heard frequently in the Park, is a continuing trill that may continue for long periods, sounding like a ringing alarm clock with the bell muffled. This call is slower, of higher pitch and more deliberate when the bird is agitated. **473**

PLATE 65

Woodpeckers. Family PICIDAE. Small, robust birds with straight, pointed bills, stiff tails and zygodactylous feet. They glean insects and their larvae from within burrows in trees and from beneath bark by tapping with their bills to loosen or chip the wood and by inserting their long sticky tongues. When feeding the tail is used as a prop. Woodpeckers nest in self-excavated holes in trees. Four woodpeckers occur in the KNP and all are very similar in appearance and are best identified by head and breast markings and by call. In addition to vocal communication woodpeckers use hollow branches to tap far-carrying territorial drumming signals.

1 CARDINAL WOODPECKER (Kardinaalspeg) *Dendropicos fuscescens.* A common and widespread resident species which breeds at almost any time of the year. A small, *streaky-breasted* woodpecker, the male with forehead brown, crown and nape red, the female with brown forehead, black crown and nape. Both sexes have a black moustachial streak. Found in a variety of habitats and even in small trees, working busily with almost continuous soft bill-tapping. Often joins mixed bird parties and will sometimes make short aerial sorties to hawk flying insects. The call is a high-pitched, chittering 'kekekekekekek'. **486**

2 GOLDENTAILED WOODPECKER (Goudstertspeg) *Campethera abingoni.* A common and widespread resident species which breeds in early summer. Larger than (1) but also with a *streaky breast*. The male has the entire crown and moustachial streak red, speckled with black; in the female the crown and moustachial streak are black speckled white but the nape is red. Often found along rivers and dry watercourses, and has a liking for dead wood. The call is diagnostic, a single, loud 'waaa'. **483**

3 BENNETT'S WOODPECKER (Bennettse Speg) *Campethera bennettii.* A fairly common resident species throughout the Park, breeding October-December. The only woodpecker in the Park with *spotted* underparts. The male has the entire crown and moustachial streak red. In the female the forehead and central crown are black, spotted with white, the rear crown and nape red while broad brown patches cover face and ear coverts, chin and throat. Frequently feeds on small tree stumps and logs close to or on the ground, even feeding on the ground where it probes into ant and termite holes. Calls 'wirr-it, wirr-it, wirr-it...' repeated five or six times. **481**

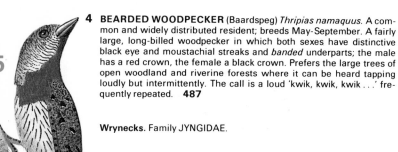

4 BEARDED WOODPECKER (Baardspeg) *Thripias namaquus.* A common and widely distributed resident; breeds May-September. A fairly large, long-billed woodpecker in which both sexes have distinctive black eye and moustachial streaks and *banded* underparts; the male has a red crown, the female a black crown. Prefers the large trees of open woodland and riverine forests where it can be heard tapping loudly but intermittently. The call is a loud 'kwik, kwik, kwik...' frequently repeated. **487**

Wrynecks. Family JYNGIDAE.

5 REDTHROATED WRYNECK (Draaihals) *Jynx ruficollis.* Rare. Seen on several occasions at Numbi Gate, a vagrant elsewhere. Identified by rust-brown throat patch plus brown-speckled upperparts with black broken line running from crown to mantle. Occurs in a variety of wooded habitats where it creeps about branches like a woodpecker, perches normally or hops on the ground. The call is a high-pitched 'kek-kek-kek-kek'. **489**

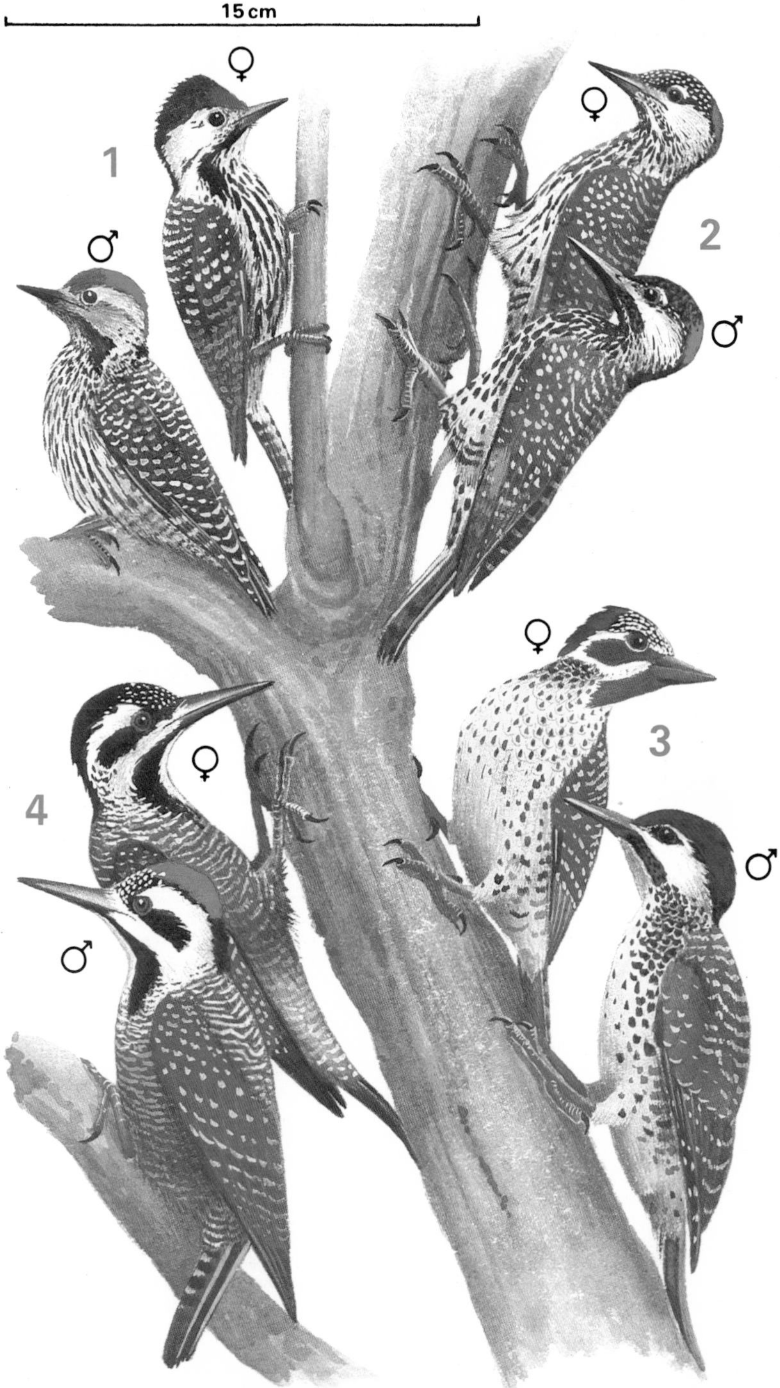
15 cm
1
♀
♂
2
♀
♂
3
♀
♂
4
♀
♂

PLATE 66

Honeyguides. Family INDICATORIDAE. A family of brood parasites which, in common with cuckoos, lay their eggs in the nests of other birds. Unlike young cuckoos the newly hatched chicks do not attempt to evict the eggs of their foster parents but, instead, are equipped with sharply hooked beaks with which they kill the young of the host. Related to barbets, they also have zygodactylous feet. Honeyguides, the breeding habits of which have not yet been fully studied, parasitise a variety of other species. Normally the sexes appear to lead separate lives, but males have regular call posts to which the females come in order to mate. The food of some species is beeswax and bee or wasp larvae, while others appear to be entirely insectivorous. In all species white outer tail feathers are diagnostic.

1 SHARPBILLED HONEYGUIDE (Skerpbekheuningvoël) *Prodotiscus regulus*. Rare, exact status uncertain. A single specimen has been collected at Numbi Gate but, in view of its cryptic coloration and unobtrusive habits, it may prove to be more widely distributed. A small, dull honeyguide. Perches quietly on trees from where it hawks flying insects, and is easily overlooked. When perched looks around with a bobbing head action, remaining on one perch briefly before moving on. Has an erratic, fluttering flight in which the white outer tail feathers and lateral rump are displayed. Two birds frequently chase each other in long, erratic flights. Parasitises various warblers. The call is a gutteral 'zeet' uttered while perched and during chases, plus a high-pitched trill lasting about seven seconds 'trrrrrrrrr'. **478**

2 LESSER HONEYGUIDE (Kleinheuningvoël) *Indicator minor*. Uncommon resident, widespread throughout the Park and breeding in summer. A small, unobtrusive bird. Frequently occurs in riverine forest. Feeds mainly on beeswax and insects, including bee larvae, and is known to parasitise Pied, Blackcollared and Crested Barbets as well as the Yellowthroated Sparrow. The call is 'klew, klew, klew . . .' uttered ten to forty times. **476**

3 SCALYTHROATED HONEYGUIDE (Gevlekte Heuningwyser) *Indicator variegatus*. Rare but exact status unknown. Has been recorded over the length of the Park, mostly in summer. Another dull, nondescript honeyguide of unspectacular appearance. Frequents thick riverine forest and calls from the topmost branches of large trees; a high-pitched 'foyt-foyt-foyt' plus, from regularly used call-sites, a bubbling, *ascending* frog-like 'ghrrrrrr . . .' which may last several seconds. Known to parasitise woodpeckers but KNP records are lacking. **475**

4 GREATER HONEYGUIDE (Grootheuningwyser) *Indicator indicator*. Uncommon but widespread throughout the Park, parasitising hole-nesting species during summer. The sexes and immatures all differ as illustrated. Normally unobtrusive except for the male's far-carrying call uttered for long periods from a regularly used perch. Has the habit, common to certain honeyguide species, of guiding or leading human beings to a bees' nest by uttering a continual chattering call while fluttering ahead in the hope of gleaning the wax and grubs from the opened nest. Feeds also on other insects. The normal call from regularly used call-sites is a much repeated 'whit-purr, whit-purr, whit-purr . . .' interpreted as 'vic-terr'. When guiding, makes an excitable rattling call like the sound of a matchbox being shaken. Known to parasitise bee-eaters, woodpeckers, barbets, kingfishers, hoopoes, swallows, starlings and hole-nesting sparrows. **474**

1

2

3

4 J

♀ 4 ♂

PLATE 67

Larks. Family ALAUDIDAE. Small, terrestrial birds of sober plumage, similar in many respects to pipits, Plates 69-70, but usually having stouter bills. Most larks have distinctive songs or calls in the breeding season, many delivered during a display flight. Larks feed on seeds and insects. The sexes are alike (except in finch-larks) and they build their nests in or under a grass tuft.

1 MONOTONOUS LARK (Bosveldlewerik) *Mirafra passerina*. Very common seasonally, being a breeding visitor following good summer rains. May occur anywhere in the Park but prefers regions of grassland or open bushveld. A small inconspicuous lark unless calling, spending much time on the ground where it runs with facility. Numbers may suddenly appear in a locality following rains and apparently commence breeding immediately; the males are then conspicuous as they deliver their monotonous call from the top of a small bush throughout the day and frequently at night. When calling the white throat is conspicuous, see illustration. The call is a frequently repeated 'chlorit-wee' or 'corr-weeoo-weeoo'. **493**

2 SABOTA LARK (Sabotalewerik) *Mirafra sabota*. A very common resident lark, especially in the central regions, but occurs everywhere. Breeds in summer. A fairly boldly marked lark, with a distinct white eyebrow, bold breast markings and a stout conical bill. Frequently feeds at the roadside and is not easily alarmed by vehicles. Also perches on bushes readily and, when breeding, sings from such a perch. Has a rather harsh chirruping call. In the breeding season has a pleasant song in which it imitates the calls of other birds. **498**

3 CLAPPER LARK (Hoëveldklappertjie) *Mirafra apiata*. Status uncertain. Has been recorded rarely at scattered locations and has been seen in territorial display. A very rufous, thick-billed species with erect stance found in grassland or open bushveld. Unobtrusive unless displaying when it flies upwards, hovers briefly while wing-clapping and then drops steeply while uttering a drawn-out 'fooeeeee'. **495**

4 FLAPPET LARK (Laeveldklappertjie) *Mirafra rufocinnamomea*. Fairly common, resident and widespread throughout the Park. A fairly rufous species with boldly defined markings on its upperparts, but of shy disposition and not easily seen unless displaying during summer. At this time males cruise about at a height of about 100 metres making frequent audible wing-snaps. These displays may commence soon after dawn and continue throughout the day, the sound resembling a muffled 'trrrrrrrr' delivered every few seconds. Usually found in hilly, lightly bushed regions. Makes a softly whistled 'tuee-tui' from the ground or a low perch. **496**

5 FAWNCOLOURED LARK (Vaalbruinlewerik) *Mirafra africanoides*. Common within a very restricted habitat, found only in the Nwambiya sandveld in the northeast of the Park where it is resident. As its name suggests, a distinctly fawn coloured bird, with a white eyebrow and underparts. Occurs in sandy regions, especially tracks and firebreaks in otherwise quite dense bush. The song is comprised of a jumble of sweet, twittering phrases ending in a drawn-out 'cheeeez'. **497**

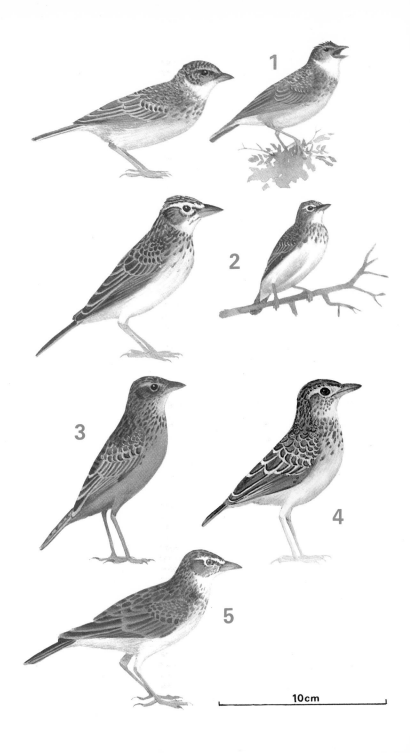

10cm

PLATE 68

1 **REDCAPPED LARK** (Rooikoplewerik) *Calandrella cinerea*. Uncommon. This lark has been seen at a few widely scattered points in the Park. A distinctive lark, with rufous crest and shoulder patches, white eyebrow and underparts. Occurs in areas of sparse ground cover where overgrazing, burning, etc., has occurred and moves about busily feeding and calling with occasional wing-flutters. During the breeding season the male has a musical song uttered while hovering in the air. Otherwise a continuous twittering is made while feeding, especially noticeable when in flocks. **507**

2 **RUFOUSNAPED LARK** (Rooineklewerik) *Mirafra africana*. Fairly common and resident in grassland and open bushveld throughout the Park and identifiable by call during the period August-March. A fairly large lark with a rufous crest and flight feathers, a prominent eyebrow and breast markings. Readily located in the summer by its habit of calling from a bush-top or other prominent perch; a frequently repeated, plaintive 'tseep-tseeooo'. Also has a display flight in the breeding season when it ascends into the air mimicking the calls of other birds interspersed with notes of its own. **494**

3 **DUSKY LARK** (Donkerlewerik) *Pinarocorys nigricans*. Uncommon. A non-breeding summer visitor recorded November-April, its movements apparently dictated by rainfall. Recorded throughout the Park but unpredictable. A large, distinctive lark resembling a Groundscraper Thrush (Plate 75) in having dark upperparts, distinctive facial markings and a boldly speckled breast. Occurs in fairly open country and is sometimes common in the central region. The call is unrecorded in the Park. **505**

4 **CHESTNUTBACKED FINCHLARK** (Rooiruglewerik) *Eremopterix leucotis*. Uncommon to locally common. A resident species subject to fluctuations in numbers. Occurs throughout the Park but is rare in the extreme south. Has been seen with small chicks in June, but breeding is probably geared to rainfall. Very small, finch-like larks, normally occurring in flocks. Both sexes have the whitish bill and chestnut-coloured wing coverts. Frequents open terrain with sparse grass cover and flocks are often flushed from gravel roads. The call is a sharp, rattling 'chip-chee-w' plus a sweet song in fluttering flight. **515**

10 cm

1

2

3

♂

♀

4

PLATE 69

Pipits, longclaws and wagtails. Family MOTACILLIDAE. Small, insectivorous birds of mainly terrestrial habits (water-associated in wagtails) in which the sexes are alike. All have white or pale buff outer tail feathers, are lark-like in both appearance and behaviour, and several are so similar as often to make positive field identification impossible. Most pipits utter a 'chissik' call on take-off, while their flight is low and undulating. At least six species occur in the KNP and all, except Richard's Pipit, are rare and apparently localised. Longclaws are pipit-like in behaviour but have distinctive, colourful plumage. One species occurs in the Park. Wagtails are the best known of this family because of their trusting nature but only the Pied Wagtail is fairly common within the Park.

1 **RICHARD'S PIPIT** (Gewone Koester) *Anthus novaeseelandiae.* An uncommon resident species recorded throughout the Park at all times of the year. This pipit has fairly bold facial markings, boldly streaked breast and *white outer tail feathers.* The legs appear long for the size of bird. Occurs in regions of lush grassland where it frequently feeds at the roadsides. Takes off with the 'chissik' call and proceeds with characteristic dipping flight, usually resettling nearby. Also sings in flight, 'tri-tri-tri-tri' during each dip. **716**

2 **YELLOWTHROATED LONGCLAW** (Geelkeelkalkoentjie) *Macronyx croceus.* Fairly common in the south-western region, otherwise uncommon and occurring sparsely throughout the Park. A resident species which breeds in summer. Could be confused with the Bokmakierie (Plate 90), but has brown upperparts (not green) and pinkish legs (not grey). Occurs in pairs in park-like terrain, especially in areas of lush grass near vleis and dams. Has a short, laboured, fluttering flight during which it mounts upwards, calls 'wheeh', and then resettles. Perches in trees readily, particularly when singing. The song is 'tree, tree, tree, tree-trit-trit, tree-trit-trit'. **728**

3 **LONGBILLED PIPIT (NICHOLSON'S PIPIT)** (Nicholsonse Koester) *Anthus similis.* Rare and probably seasonal, but exact status uncertain. Larger than (1) and tending to more grey-brown on upperparts. The moustachial streaks are obvious, the breast streaked though not boldly so, the margins of the outer tail feathers buff-coloured. Prefers stony ground, especially on hillsides, and calls from some low perch such as a rock or bush; a metallic 'kilink' or 'chreep-chroop'. **717**

4 **PLAINBACKED PIPIT** (Donkerkoester) *Anthus leucophrys.* Rare and probably seasonal, but exact status uncertain. Usually occurs in the far north in autumn. Best identified by the absence of markings on the mantle, the almost complete absence of a moustachial streak and indistinct or entirely absent breast streaking. Prefers open, sparsely grassed terrain in hilly regions. It makes a sparrow-like 'jreet-jroot' from a low perch. **718**

5 **BUFFY PIPIT** (Vaalkoester) *Anthus vaalensis.* Exact status uncertain but probably a seasonal visitor. Occurs mostly during late summer in grasslands of the northern and central regions. Slightly larger than the preceding species and generally more buffy, but this is variable; see illustrations. The moustachial streak is present but not pronounced, breast streaking variable and often indistinct. Has the habit of running a short distance and then standing in a very vertical stance, with the chest thrown out. Bobs its tail frequently. Inhabits grassy plains and perches readily on ant-hills. **719**

PLATE 70

1 **BUSHVELD PIPIT** (Bosveldkoester) *Anthus caffer.* Uncommon resident species recorded over the length of the Park. A small, inconspicuous pipit. Occurs in regions of sparsely grassed bushveld and when flushed flies off in an erratic fashion. The song, made from a tree, is a sibilant 'skeer-trurp, skeer-trurp, skeer-trurp-skee, skeer-trurp-skee-skee . . .' with alternating higher and lower notes. **723**

2 **STRIPED PIPIT** (Gestreepte Koester) *Anthus lineiventris.* Uncommon and localised. Probably a summer visitor, but status uncertain. Normally frequents hilly regions with rocks and trees, having been recorded mostly in the south-west of the Park during August. A distinctive, large pipit with yellow edges to the flight feathers and boldly streaked underparts. Searches actively for insects among rocks, under bushes and at the roadside, occasionally running or flying a short distance. Perches on trees with its body parallel to the branch from where it utters a loud, thrush-like whistling song. **720**

3 **CAPE WAGTAIL** (Gewone Kwikkie) *Motacilla capensis.* Uncommon. Appears to be a casual visitor. Solitary individuals have been recorded at various rivers and dams throughout the Park. The normal form (a) is most frequently seen but (b), lacking the chest band, has been recorded on the Olifants River. Frequents shorelines where it feeds on insects and small crustaceans and has the very characteristic habit of bobbing its tail up and down. The call is a cheerful double note 'tseep-ep' or 'tsee-u'. **713**

4 **AFRICAN PIED WAGTAIL** (Bontkwikkie) *Motacilla aguimp.* Fairly common and resident at rivers and large dams throughout the Park. Breeds in early summer. A distinctive black and white wagtail, larger than (3) and longer tailed. This is the common wagtail of the Park's waterways, and it occurs also in riverside camps where it forages on the lawns and breeds in eaves and roofs of camp buildings. Has a variety of cheerful whistles, 'tu-weee, tu-tu-tu' or 'twip-twip-twip, weep-weep' etc. **711**

5 **LONGTAILED WAGTAIL** (Bergkwikkie) *Motacilla clara.* Rare. Has been seen only on the Sabie River near Skukuza and in Lanner Gorge on the Luvuvhu River where it may be resident. Differs from (3) and (4) in having a much longer tail and being more blue-grey and white in appearance. Prefers fast-flowing rivers and streams with rocks. Bobs its tail frequently. Calls 'chirrup' or 'chissik' on take-off and sings a cheerful, piping 'ti-tuu-ui-tui-tui'. **712**

10cm

PLATE 71

Black birds. Three small, entirely black birds occur in the Kruger National Park, and are similar to each other though unrelated. They are the Forktailed Drongo (Family DICRURIDAE), Black Flycatcher (Family MUSCICAPIDAE) and Black Cuckooshrike (Family CAMPEPHAGIDAE). Because of confusion surrounding their identities they are presented together on this plate for ease of comparison.

1 FORKTAILED DRONGO (Mikstertbyvanger) *Dicrurus adsimilis.* A very common and widespread resident, breeding September-January. Frequents all habitats and is usually conspicuous in rest camps. Distinct from other black birds in having a fish-like tail. An active and pugnacious species, attacking and pestering even eagles that enter its territory. Feeds in the manner of a flycatcher, by darting out from a perch to seize flying insects and performing aerial acrobatics during the chase. In flight the wings appear pale, as do those of the next species. Makes a variety of unmusical twanging and rasping sounds interspersed with attempts at copying the calls of other birds, especially those of owls and other birds of prey. **541**

2 BLACK FLYCATCHER (Swartvlieëvanger) *Melaenornis pammelaina.* Fairly common and widespread. A resident species preferring woodland regions and occurring in many rest camps. Breeds in early summer. Smaller than (1) and with only a small notch in the tail, not a distinct fork. The immature, as illustrated, is distinctly spotted with buff on a dull, blackish-brown plumage. Hawks flying insects from a tree-perch or seizes them on the ground in the same fashion as (1). The call is a weak, sibilant 'swee-sweer'. **694**

3 BLACK CUCKOOSHRIKE (Swartkatakoeroe) *Campephaga flava.* Uncommon but widely distributed. A summer, breeding visitor, present in the Park August-May; a few individuals, usually females, remain all year. Only the male is black, with a *rounded* tail and a distinct orange-yellow gape. The yellow shoulder patch is diagnostic when present (a), but many individuals lack this (b). The female is distinctively marked, as illustrated, but could be mistaken for the Yellowspotted Nicator (Plate 74). Differs from that species in having barred underparts. The behaviour is quite different to that of (1) and (2). This species is quiet and unobtrusive, creeping about in dense tree canopies where it gleans insects from the leaves. The call is not often heard, a very high-pitched tinkling sound somewhat resembling the bell of an alarm clock. See Plate 72 for other cuckooshrikes. **538**

PLATE 72

Cuckooshrikes. Family CAMPEPHAGIDAE. Insectivorous, heavy-billed birds of cuckoo-like appearance. Three species occur in the KNP. Cuckooshrikes mostly inhabit the larger trees of woodland or riverine forest, and build bowl-shaped nests of lichen.

1 WHITEBREASTED CUCKOOSHRIKE (Witborskatakoeroe) *Coracina pectoralis.* Uncommon resident. Recorded throughout the Park, most commonly in the north. Breeds in summer. Both sexes are similar as illustrated but the grey of the throat is hardly discernible in the female. A lethargic bird which moves from branch to branch with long hops, peering closely at leaves in search of insects, or makes short aerial sallies. Usually in pairs. The call is a softly whistled 'duid-duid' by the male, and a trilling 'che-e-e-e-e' by the female. **539**

2 GREY CUCKOOSHRIKE (Bloukatakoeroe) *Coracina caesia.* Rare. Has been recorded in the far north where it is probably resident in small numbers, and also in the south where it is thought to be a migrant from the escarpment forests. Within the Park is usually seen in riverine forests and the dense woodland of the Punda Maria and Pafuri regions. The female is slightly paler and lacks the black mark between eye and bill, otherwise sexes are alike. Pairs, both in flight and while feeding, emit a high-pitched and prolonged 'peeeeoooo'. In addition they make a variety of chittering and trilling sounds plus a weaver-like chattering. **540**

BLACK CUCKOOSHRIKE See Plate 71.

Crows. Family CORVIDAE. Large, predominantly black, omnivorous scavenging birds. Three species occur in the KNP, mainly along the western boundary, mostly entering on daily foraging trips from nearby settlements and agricultural lands.

3 PIED CROW (Witborskraai) *Corvus albus.* Locally common, especially in the north. Has bred in early summer at Skukuza. The only crow with white breast and collar; distinctive both at rest and in flight. In the Park frequents rest camps, camp sites, staff camps, etc., especially adjacent rubbish dumps. Will also attend animal carcases with vultures when the opportunity arises. The call is a loud 'kwaak', repeated frequently in flight. **548**

4 BLACK CROW or Cape Rook (Swartkraai) *Corvus capensis.* Rare. Likely to be seen only in the far north. Fractionally larger than (3) and entirely glossy black with a large, pointed bill. Otherwise its behaviour in the Park can be expected to be the same as the other crows. It makes a high-pitched 'kaaa'. **547**

5 WHITENECKED RAVEN (Withalskraai) *Corvus albicollis.* Rare generally but common in the Punda Maria region. Largest of the three crows, having a very heavy bill and a white collar which, however, is not easily seen in flight, when the broad wings and broad, rounded tail distinguish it from the other crows. Habits much as for (3) and (4). Will visit kills, especially road casualties. The voice is a loud 'kraak'. **550**

1 ♂

2

3

4

5

PLATE 73

Orioles. Family ORIOLIDAE. Striking golden-yellow birds with pink bills and clear, liquid calls. All are insectivorous and frugivorous, and find their food in the upper canopy of large trees. Of the three species that occur in the Kruger National Park, only one is resident.

1 **EUROPEAN GOLDEN ORIOLE** (Europese Wielewaal) *Oriolus oriolus.* An uncommon Palaearctic migrant, occurring throughout the Park between October and March. The male is the only oriole with black wings. The female is similar to the immature illustrated but whiter on the underparts; less yellow than the female or the immature of the African Golden Oriole (2). A bird of wooded regions but nowhere plentiful. The call is a ringing and mellow 'weela-weeoo' plus a churring alarm note common to all orioles.   **543**

2 **AFRICAN GOLDEN ORIOLE** (Afrikaanse Wielewaal) *Oriolus auratus.* Uncommon intra-Africa migrant. Most plentiful in seasons of good rain and then largely confined to the north. Occurs November-May. The most yellow of the orioles, with very little black on the wings. Note that the black mask extends from the bill to well beyond the eye, even in the immature. The female is olivaceous yellow above and paler below than the male. A bird of the denser, forested regions, it prefers to remain in the thick leafy canopies of trees. The calls are a cheerful, liquid whistle, 'wee-er-wul', a prolonged 'aa-aa-aa-er' and a variety of mewing and squalling cries. The alarm call is a harsh 'mwah-mwah'.   **544**

3 **BLACKHEADED ORIOLE** (Swartkopwielewaal) *Oriolus larvatus.* A common resident, widespread throughout the Park. Breeds in early summer. The only oriole with a completely black head. A larger bird than any of the black-headed weavers (Plate 99) and having a pink bill. The sexes are alike. The immature shows traces of the adult black head at all stages. Prefers well-wooded localities where it spends its time in the leafy canopies of trees in search of fruits, caterpillars and other insects. Calls frequently, a loud, liquid-sounding 'pheeoo' or 'phea-pheeoo'. Has a harsh alarm call 'cherrr'.   **545**

160

15cm

PLATE 74

Bulbuls. Family PYCNONOTIDAE. This family of small birds is widespread in Africa and contains many diverse species. Largely frugivorous and insectivorous and inhabit woodland and forest. Some species are secretive and seldom seen, others like the ubiquitous Blackeyed Bulbul or Toppie are common and very well known. Their nests are fragile basins of fine tendrils.

1 **BLACKEYED BULBUL** or Toppie (Swartoogtiptol) *Pycnonotus barbatus.* A common and widespread resident species. Breeds October-December. This cheerful and confiding species is a well-known garden bird in many parts of the country, its black tufted head and yellow vent being diagnostic. Is common in most rest camps and picnic spots. The calls are many and varied, the most common resembling the words 'Wake up, Geoffry'. At sunset it maintains a continuous 'chit, chit, chit . . .' This call is also repeated in an agitated manner when a snake, mongoose or similar predator is sighted, which causes other small birds to gather and add their own calls to the general commotion.   **568**

2 **SOMBRE BULBUL** (Gewone Willie) *Andropadus importunus.* A common resident species in certain restricted habitats, breeding in summer. Occurs throughout the Park and is particularly plentiful in the moister regions, inhabiting dense bush along rivers and even small watercourses provided that the cover is sufficiently thick. This bird is heard more than it is seen. Its cryptic colouring blends so well with the vegetation of its habitat that, even when perched in the open, it is difficult to see. Usually calls from within foliage, a strident 'Willie!' repeated frequently. In the breeding season the first call is followed by a babbling trill, the full phrase sounding like 'Willie! Come out and fight! Sca-a-a-red'; the last sound being faint and barely audible.   **572**

3 **YELLOWSPOTTED NICATOR** (Geelvleknikator) *Nicator gularis.* An uncommon resident species confined to the heavily wooded regions of Pafuri, the adjacent Limpopo riverine forests, Nwanedzi, Orpen Dam and a few other points in the east of the Park. A secretive bird which spends much time in matted bush. Could be confused with the female Black Cuckooshrike (Plate 71) but lacks the barred underparts and has a heavier bill. The call is a pleasant, jumbled warble difficult to describe but with notes of both high and low pitch.   **575**

4 **YELLOWBELLIED BULBUL** (Geelborswillie) *Chlorocichla flaviventris.* An uncommon but widespread resident recorded at various points throughout the Park. Prefers dense bush but will emerge if undisturbed. May be seen at Punda Maria and Nwanedzi camps where it often hops about the ground in the early mornings. An unmistakable species with its yellow underparts and greenish upperparts. The call is a loud, high-pitched nasal 'pur, pur, pur, pur, peh, peh, peh, peh, peh . . .'   **574**

5 **TERRESTRIAL BULBUL** (Boskrapper) *Phyllastrephus terrestris.* Uncommon but a widely distributed resident species. Prefers heavily wooded regions, especially the densely bushed slopes along watercourses and koppies. A drab bird, always occurring in parties of six or more, scratching about among dead leaves and other ground debris. Secretive and easily overlooked if not heard. Feeding parties maintain a continual chuckling 'wik, wak, wak, wok, wackle, wak, wog . . .'   **569**

15 cm

PLATE 75

Babblers (family TIMALIIDAE); **thrushes, chats and robins** (family TURDIDAE). Divided into two families on morphological grounds but closely related and similar in general behaviour. All are ground feeders and insectivorous while the robins are among our finest songsters. Babblers, thrushes and chats are fairly bold, confiding birds whereas robins are mostly shy and secretive.

1 ARROWMARKED BABBLER (Pylvlekkatlagter) *Turdoides jardineii.* A common resident species. Occurs in all regions, preferring riverine bush. Breeds any month of the year. Always in parties of several birds, appearing plain, dusky brown in the field except at close range. Spends much time on the ground, scratching about in search of insects. At times very noisy, the call being an excitable whirring chatter started by one individual and taken up by all the others until it resembles hysterical giggling, similar to the call of the Redbilled Woodhoopoe (Plate 61) but harsher. **560**

2 GROUNDSCRAPER THRUSH (Gevlekte Lyster) *Turdus litsitsirupa.* Fairly common and resident, occurring all over the Park in open, park-like regions. Breeding recorded in early summer. Boldly spotted underparts are diagnostic; cf. Dusky Lark (Plate 68). Feeds on the ground, running a short distance then standing still with an erect stance. Displays brown wing feathers in flight. Sings from a tree; a continuing melody of mellow phrases such as 'trroo-trroo, tweet, tweet . . . chichiruchee . . . tru-chitru, trit, trit . . .' with continual variations. **580**

3 KURRICHANE THRUSH (Rooibeklyster) *Turdus libonyana.* A fairly common and widespread resident; breeds September-December. The orange legs and beak, and orange flanks, together with black moustachial streaks, are diagnostic. Favours large tree woodland in moister regions, being absent in arid areas. Often noisy at dawn and dusk, when it flies about emitting a loud 'peet-peeoo, peet-peeoo'; also has a loud, deliberate song delivered in short bursts 'wheet-weedle, wheet-weet-weet . . .' normally only heard in the breeding season. **576**

4 FAMILIAR CHAT (Gewone Spekvreter) *Cercomela familiaris.* Uncommon and localised but resident where it occurs. Recorded at scattered points throughout the Park. A drab little bird which reveals an orange-coloured rump and outer tail feathers when it flies. Has the habit of flicking its wings when perched. Tame and tolerant of a close approach. Frequents rocks and posts from where it flies to the ground to seize insects. Not very vocal. Call note a soft 'chak-chak'. **589**

5 MOCKING CHAT (Dassievoël) *Thamnolaea cinnamomeiventris.* Fairly common and resident in suitable rocky habitats. Breeds September-December. A distinctive species mostly restricted to rocky outcrops, but has adopted certain camps such as Punda Maria, Letaba, Olifants and Nwanedzi. Occurs in family parties and becomes tame in association with humans. Has a variety of melodious call notes and an attractive song, including imitation of other species. **593**

PLATE 76

Tits. Family PARIDAE. A widespread group of small, insectivorous birds having short, stout bills, the nostrils obscured by bristles. Arboreal by nature, they breed in holes in trees. Included on this plate for easier comparison with the black chats.

1 SOUTHERN BLACK TIT (Gewone Swartmees) *Parus niger.* A common and widespread resident. Breeds November-December. A small black bird with white wingbars. Occurs in a variety of broadleafed bush habitats (less so in *Acacia* veld) where it may be seen actively searching foliage and bark for insects. At times *runs about tree trunks in the manner of a woodpecker.* The harsh call, uttered frequently, has an impatient quality about it, a rapid 'twiddy-zeet-zeet-zeet', the first phrase shrill, the others rasping. **554**

2 MOUNTAIN CHAT (Bergwagter) *Oenanthe monticola.* A rare and localised species recorded only in the vicinity of Maschicindzudzi Hill west of Pafuri, and a hill near Phalaborwa Gate. The male is variable as illustrated (a and b) but always has the white rump, undertail coverts and shoulder patches. Old females may also have white on the shoulders. A terrestrial bird which inhabits rocky locations in hills. Normally a quiet species but has a pretty song in the breeding season. **586**

3 ARNOT'S CHAT (Bontpiek) *Thamnolaea arnoti.* Fairly common locally, restricted to the mopane woodlands in the north. A resident species with breeding recorded in November. The white cap of the male, white throat of the female and lack of any white in the tail region separate this chat from (2) which, in any case, occupies a different habitat. Occurs only in tall mopane trees *(Colophospermum mopane),* not in the mopane scrub which is characteristic of much of the northern regions. Feeds on the lower branches of the trees and on the ground beneath them, and frequently occurs in small parties. Has a pretty song involving a musical 'feeeee', first ascending and then descending the scale. **594**

4 CAPPED WHEATEAR (Hoëveldskaapwagter) *Oenanthe pileata.* Uncommon. Has been recorded on grass flats throughout the Park and appears to be regular at Nshawu Dam. Unmistakable if seen, but a small terrestrial species, and easily overlooked. Frequents bare ground around pans, freshly burnt and heavily grazed open regions where grass is sparse, airstrips, etc. Struts about busily with much wing- and tail-flicking, sometimes perching momentarily on anthills, stones and low bushes. Has a pretty song, including mimicry, uttered in outbursts while fluttering some metres above ground, after which it descends again. **587**

PLATE 77

1 STONECHAT (Gewone Bontrokkie) *Saxicola torquata*. An uncommon visitor recorded April-September in most regions where it occurs, with one sighting for December. Exact status uncertain but may breed within the Park. Is most plentiful in the south but records indicate a wide though scattered distribution. A small, robin-like species, the female being a drab version of the male. Both show white wing-bars and white rump in flight. Prefers open areas close to water, where it perches on a low bush or tall weed and flies down to pick up insects. The chief call is a grating 'tsak, tsak' which resembles the sound of two stones being banged together. **596**

2 CAPE ROBIN (Gewone Janfrederik) *Cossypha caffra*. Rare, and exact status uncertain. Has been seen in the south-west of the Park and at Shingwedzi, all sightings in August. Is believed to be a non-breeding altitudinal migrant, coming to the lowveld during winter. Note that the orange colouring is confined to the upper breast, rump and tail. Frequents dense bush near rivers but feeds in the open frequently. Has a pleasant and continuing song in which the phrase 'Jan-fred-erik' is often repeated. Emits a scolding 'waa-deda' when alarmed. **601**

3 WHITETHROATED ROBIN (Witkeeljanfrederik) *Cossypha humeralis*. A fairly common and widespread resident, but secretive, keeping to the dense bush of riverbanks and koppies. Breeds in early summer. A distinctive and attractive little robin, sometimes confused with the Boubou Shrike (Plate 88) but differing from that species in having a white eyebrow and grey, not black, mantle and back. A common call, heard in the early hours, is a much repeated 'tree-trrirr, tree-trrirr; cf. Natal Robin (Plate 78), but also a beautiful though subdued song. **602**

4 HEUGLIN'S ROBIN (Heuglinse Janfrederik) *Cossypha heuglini*. An uncommon and localised resident. Is recorded regularly only in dense riverine bush. Breeds in early summer. The only robin in the Park with completely orange underparts and a white eyebrow. A secretive species which reveals its presence by frequent song. A variety of pleasant phrases starting quietly and increasing in volume to reach a crescendo; 'bewik-troo, bewik-troo, bewik-troo, bewik-troo . . .' and 'don't-you-do-it, don't-you-do-it . . .' etc.; the actual sounds within the crescendo are variable with individuals and locality. **599**

♀

♂

1

2

3

4

PLATE 78

1 **NATAL ROBIN** (Nataljanfrederik) *Cossypha natalensis.* Uncommon, secretive and localised, but a resident species. Breeds in early summer. Is most common in the far north but occurs throughout in suitable habitat. A bird of the dense thickets near rivers and large dams, it ventures into the open during the early mornings and at dusk. Unmistakable when seen since it is the most orange in colour of the Park's robins, and lacks a white eyebrow. Has the habit of lifting its tail high after landing on a perch. Has a monotonous call note 'tree-trrirr' rising and falling, which may be repeated for long periods; cf. the similar call of the Whitethroated Robin (Plate 77). Also has a beautiful singing repertoire and is a capable mimic. **600**

2 **WHITEBROWED (SCRUB) ROBIN** (Gestreepte Wipstert) *Erythropygia leucophrys.* A common and widespread resident species which breeds in early summer. Occurs all over the Park and is easily located by song, which can be heard in all seasons. A rather shy and secretive species which keeps to thorn thickets surrounded by long grass but which, on the other hand, sings for long periods from an exposed perch. A small, brown robin with heavily speckled breast. When flushed flies off about a metre above the ground and displays a white-rimmed tail and white wing-bars as illustrated. The song is a loud series of repeated phrases delivered for long periods on sunny mornings: 'pirit-pirit, tertwee . . .pirit-pirit, tertwee . . .chee, chee, choo, chu-itchu-it . . . chiroo-chu, chu-chiroo . . . perpwee, perpwee, tirrit-tirrit . . .' **613**

3 **BEARDED ROBIN** (Baardwipstert) *Erythropygia quadrivirgata.* Uncommon but widespread and resident. Is found regularly only in well wooded regions, especially riverine forests. Breeds October-January. In this robin the black beard streaks on either side of the white throat are diagnostic, as are the orange and white underparts. Habitually sings from a prominent perch in the mornings but otherwise feeds on the ground, seeking insects in leaf debris beneath trees. The song is loud and clear, being a series of pleasant phrases each repeated three or four times with much variation. Examples are 'pee pee pee terr treee . . . chiroo chiroo chiroo . . . witchoo witchoo witchoo . . . tirroo tirroo tirroo . . . pee pee pee pee . . . chu-it chu-it chu-it . . .', some phrases rising in crescendo. **617**

4 **BROWN ROBIN** (Bruinwipstert) *Erythropygia signata.* Rare. A very localised species seen only at Pafuri and Nwanedzi, but probably resident in these and other densely wooded habitats. The generally brown colouring and liking for the most dense and gloomy thickets should serve to identify this robin. It will emerge from cover to feed in open ground adjacent to thick bush if undisturbed, and may be seen in these circumstances at the Pafuri picnic site. A fine songster with a series of sweet, high-pitched phrases 'teeree-tee-oo, teeree-teee, sweetee-teee, ti-teeree-teeoo . . .' each set of phrases starting on the same note. **616**

1

2

3

4

10cm

PLATE 79

Warblers. Family SYLVIIDAE. A large group of insectivorous small birds of mostly sombre colouring. Many have well-developed and attractive warbling songs and can often be better identified by these than by plumage. Some visit us as non-breeding Palaearctic migrants.

1 WILLOW WARBLER (Hofsanger) *Phylloscopus trochilus.* Common throughout the Park September-April. A non-breeding Palaearctic migrant. A small, active warbler with greenish-brown upperparts, pale yellow to white underparts, a distinctive eyebrow and scalloped tail. A leaf-gleaner, it works its way busily through the mid-and upper strata of trees and bushes. Calls frequently while feeding, a querulous 'foo-wee'. Also has a pleasant, warbling song, a descending jumble of notes.   **643**

2 ICTERINE WARBLER (Spotvoël) *Hippolais icterina.* An uncommon but widespread non-breeding Palaearctic migrant recorded November-March. Similar in general colouring to the previous species but larger, more yellow below, the wing feathers being clearly emarginated to with pale yellow. Works its way busily through the upper branches of small trees, usually singing as it moves about; a repetitive, vehement jumble of warbling notes, some pleasant, some harsh.   **625**

3 GARDEN WARBLER (Tuinsanger) *Sylvia borin.* An uncommon, non-breeding Palaearctic visitor. Has been recorded at points throughout the Park. An entirely plain-coloured warbler, lacking in distinctive markings. Shy and secretive, it is best identified by its quiet, babbling song uttered from within a thick bush; a sustained, low-pitched warbling of even notes continued for long periods.   **619**

4 THRUSH NIGHTINGALE (Lysternagtegaal) *Luscinia luscinia.* Rare. A non-breeding Palaearctic migrant, occurring sparsely throughout the Park in summer. A robin-sized warbler (to which family it properly belongs) with plain upperparts, the tail slightly rufous in colour, and whitish underparts with faintly mottled breast. Usually remains concealed in dense thickets close to rivers or other damp situations. The song is a rich melody of beautiful but variable notes including a few harsh ones.   **609**

5 OLIVETREE WARBLER (Olyfboomsanger) *Hippolais olivetorum.* A rare, non-breeding Palaearctic migrant, recorded only at Pafuri and on the Olifants River. A large, greyish warbler with white eyebrows and wing feather emarginations plus fairly large bill with yellowish lower mandible. A secretive species inhabiting dense riverside thickets. The song is louder and deeper than that of most warblers; a continuing jumble of notes with sharp, 'tck-tch' sounds interspersed.   **626**

6 BROADTAILED WARBLER (Breëstertsanger) *Schoenicola brevirostris.* Rare. Status unclear. Recorded in the north and south during summer but could prove to be more widespread. Distinguished by its voluminous black tail with buff-tipped feathers. Frequents tall grass, reeds and tangled vegetation. Secretive but sometimes perches conspicuously in a *vertical position.* If flushed makes off with bobbing flight, then drops down. The voice is a weak 'trreet trreep trreep' or 'zink zink zink' repeated rapidly.   **642**

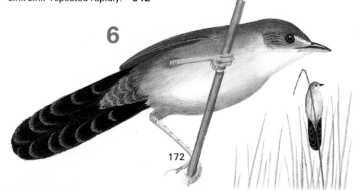

10cm

PLATE 80

1 GREY PENDULINE TIT (Gryskapokvoël) *Anthoscopus caroli*. (The only representative in the KNP of the family REMIZIDAE, placed with the warblers for purposes of comparison.) An uncommon but widespread resident species. Breeds in early summer. The smallest bird in the Park. Occurs in small parties which work their way through trees, usually near the upper canopy, and then stream after one another to the next tree. Roosts commonly in weaver nests. Makes a squeaky 'tsweewhee', the first note higher than the second.   **558**

2 BURNTNECKED EREMOMELA (Bruinkeelbossanger) *Eremomela usticollis*. An uncommon but widespread resident species which breeds in summer. In some individuals the brown throat-bar may be absent or very faint, probably a seasonal variation. Whitish eye with red surround and creamy underparts diagnostic. Usually occurs in pairs in thornveld, often in mixed bird parties working their way actively through the canopies. Makes a musical 'zip-zip-zip' or 'dyup-dyup-dyup-dyup'.   **656**

3 YELLOWBELLIED EREMOMELA (Geelpensbossanger) *Eremomela icteropygialis*. A fairly common resident species occurring throughout the Park. Breeds in early summer. A very small, short-tailed species with distinctive yellow belly and vent. Has a thin white ring around the eye; cf. Cape White-eye (Plate 96). An active little bird, often occurring in small groups and frequently with bird parties. Usually found in small, low thorn bushes where it works its way through the lower branches. Has a chittering jingle of four syllables 'chirri-cheechee-choo' or 'How are you two?' plus a plaintive 'see-see' and a scolding 'chee-chiri-chee-chiri-chit'.   **653**

4 GREENCAPPED EREMOMELA (Donkerwangbossanger) *Eremomela scotops*. Uncommon resident. Occurs sparsely throughout the Park, especially in riparian habitats. Can be mistaken for a Cape White-eye (Plate 96) to which it has similar habits and often associates, but note red not white eye-ring. Usually occurs in large fig trees where it searches for insects amongst the fruit and leaves. Also flies out to hawk insects in the air. Restless, noisy little birds frequently chasing and fighting while feeding. A variety of calls are recorded, a twittering 'nyum-nyum nyum' or a repeated, monotonous 'tip tip tip . . .' plus a liquid song of five or six notes.   **655**

5 YELLOW WARBLER (Geelsanger) *Chloropeta natalensis*. Rare but probably resident. Sightings have been made at points throughout the Park, mostly in summer. Could be mistaken for one of the yellow weavers (Plates 98-99) occurring as it does in the same riverine habitat. Prefers reeds and riverside herbage and often flies to an uppermost point to view the surroundings if disturbed. Makes a clear but brief warble 'chudlee-chudlee-wupdudulee-dudlee', also 'twee-twee-twee' followed by a warble.   **637**

10 cm

PLATE 81

1 **EUROPEAN SEDGE WARBLER** (Europese Vleisanger) *Acrocephalus schoeno-baenus.* Uncommon. A non-breeding Palaearctic migrant present November-March. Recorded in the northern regions of the Park but thinly distributed. The only reed warbler with distinctly marked upperparts, including well-striped crown and faintly blotched chest. Fairly shy and secretive, inhabiting emergent waterside grasses, sedges and reeds, but will often reveal itself briefly in order to view the observer. The normal call is a soft 'tuc' repeated about every three seconds. The song is a loud, rambling warble, a mixture of sweet and harsh notes and mimicry. **634**

2 **AFRICAN MARSH WARBLER** (Kleinrietsanger) *Acrocephalus baeticatus.* An uncommon, breeding, intra-Africa migrant recorded August-March. Some individuals may overwinter in the Park. A small warbler, pale on the underparts with no distinct eyebrow. Inhabits sedges and other vegetation both in and away from water. The song is a slow, monotonous warbling 'chuck chuck weee chirruc churr werr weee weee chirruc . . .' for long periods. **631**

3 **CAPE REED WARBLER** (Kaapse Rietsanger) *Acrocephalus gracilirostris.* A fairly common and widespread resident species. Breeds in summer. Very similar to (2) but slightly larger and with a pale eyebrow. Inhabits reedbeds on the edges of dams, pans and rivers. Being curious of any disturbance will usually reveal itself briefly. Has a very pretty short song uttered frequently, a mellow 'chirroo chirroo tiriririri', slowly at first, then fast. **635**

4 **AFRICAN SEDGE WARBLER** (Kaapse Vleisanger) *Bradypterus baboecala.* An uncommon but widespread resident species which breeds in summer. The upperparts rather darker than others in this group, the eyebrow well defined, faint chest markings present and the tail broad and rounded, the individual feathers much wider than in other warblers. Creeps about in matted rushes and other waterside herbage; shy but inquisitive. Usually heard more frequently than seen, a characteristic waterside sound resembling that made by a stick held against the spokes of a revolving wheel 'tuc tuc tuc tuc tuc . . .' first slowly, then fast. **638**

5 **GREAT REED WARBLER** (Grootrietsanger) *Acrocephalus arundinaceus.* Rare, but recorded all over the Park. A non-breeding Palaearctic migrant present September-March. A large reed warbler with distinct eyebrow, resembles a larger version of (3), the bill proportionately stouter. Occurs in tall reedbeds at the water's edge. Has a loud and far-carrying warble, frog-like with many notes of a croaking nature 'karra karra krik krik krik gurk gurk gurk tuckle tuckle . . .' **628**

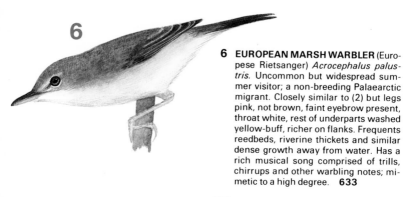

6 **EUROPEAN MARSH WARBLER** (Europese Rietsanger) *Acrocephalus palustris.* Uncommon but widespread summer visitor; a non-breeding Palaearctic migrant. Closely similar to (2) but legs pink, not brown, faint eyebrow present, throat white, rest of underparts washed yellow-buff, richer on flanks. Frequents reedbeds, riverine thickets and similar dense growth away from water. Has a rich musical song comprised of trills, chirrups and other warbling notes; mimetic to a high degree. **633**

2

1

3

4

5

10cm

PLATE 82

1 BARTHROATED APALIS (Bandkeelkleinjantjie) *Apalis thoracica.* Uncommon resident species recorded only in the eastern regions. Breeds in summer. A distinctive warbler, the pale eye and chest band being diagnostic, the latter slightly less wide in the female. Usually occurs in pairs feeding in the middle strata of bushes in wooded kloofs and on hillsides. Not a shy species and is often seen in bird parties. The call is a fairly loud 'pill-pilli-pilli-pilli . . .' **645**

2 YELLOWBREASTED APALIS (Geelborskleinjantjie) *Apalis flavida.* A resident species, fairly common throughout the Park and breeding all summer. Unmistakable, the yellow breast-band with black bar (male only) being characteristic. Occurs in pairs, often with bird parties, in both lush riverine bush and quite dry regions. Frequents many camps. The normal song is 'skee-skee-skee-chizzik-chizzick' replied to by the mate in higher pitch 'krik-krik-krik . . .' **648**

3 RUDD'S APALIS (Ruddse Kleinjantjie) *Apalis ruddi.* Uncommon, localised resident. Occurs in the Nwambiya sandveld; could occur near Pafuri. Differs from (1) in having dark eyes, yellow-green upperparts. The call is a rapid and simultaneous 'tritritritritrit . . .' and 'punk-punk-punk . . .' by two birds. Frequents dense bush and thickets, but is not secretive. **649**

4 LONGBILLED CROMBEC (Stompstert) *Sylvietta rufescens.* A common resident warbler found throughout the Park. Breeds in summer. An unmistakable, almost tailless species, frequently found in mixed bird parties. Occurs in dry thornveld and woodland regions, and is common about most camps. The call is a loud, imperative 'tree-cheer, tree-cheer, tree-cheer . . .' **651**

5 BLEATING WARBLER (Kwê-kwêvoël) *Camaroptera brachyura.* Fairly common and widespread resident. Found throughout the Park in suitable habitat. Breeds in summer. Upperparts entirely dark olive-green. A very small warbler which carries its tail high over its back much of the time. Occurs in dense riverine bush and well-wooded kloofs, usually in the lower strata. Often reveals its presence by call: when alarmed makes a kid-like bleating 'kwe'; the territorial call, heard in the summer months, is a loud 'chirrup chirrup chirrup . . .' sounding like two stones being clapped together and continued for long periods from high in a bush. **657**

6 STIERLING'S BARRED WARBLER (Stierlingse Sanger) *Camaroptera stierlingi.* Uncommon but resident and recorded throughout the Park. Breeds in summer. A very small warbler with heavily barred underparts. Flirts its tail over its back like (5). Occurs in scrub and open woodland, creeping about in thorny thickets. The voice is an insect-like 'biritbiritbiritbirit', not loud but far-carrying. **659**

7 TITBABBLER (Bosveldtjeriktik) *Parisoma subcaeruleum.* Rare. Recorded only a few times at scattered points throughout the Park. Identified by pale eye, spotted breast and chestnut coloured vent. Occurs in almost any woodland, thornveld, wooded hillsides and riverine bush. Forages restlessly, mostly in tree canopies, gleaning insects from leaves and branches. Has several clear song phrases, typically 'cheriktiktik' or 'chuu-ti chuu-ti chuu-chuu'. **621**

10 cm

PLATE 83

The **cisticolas** (pronounced cisTIKola) are a group of small grass warblers with confusingly similar plumage patterns. Breeding and non-breeding plumages frequently differ, the tails are shorter when breeding, and females often differ from males. Best identified by call and behaviour. The four species on this plate represent a group known as the cloudscraper cisticolas from their habit of making high aerial cruises in the breeding season, which is summer. Those on Plates 84 and 85 call mostly from a perch.

1 **FANTAILED CISTICOLA** (Landeryklopkloppie) *Cisticola juncidis.* Uncommon but occurs throughout the Park in suitable habitat. Females resemble non-breeding males. A species of open grasslands, often near damp regions. During the summer the male cruises above its territory at a height of about 50 metres with dipping flight and calling 'tink . . . tink . . . tink . . . tink . . .' each call synchronising with a dip in flight. **664**

2 **DESERT CISTICOLA** (Woestynklopkloppie) *Cisticola aridula.* Uncommon. Recorded only in the northern grasslands where it is probably resident. Non-breeding males and females are similar. Breeding females less heavily mottled on upperparts than males at the time. Inhabits open grassland. In summer the male makes a repetitive, high-pitched 'ting . . . ting . . . ting . . .' from a low perch or while cruising over the grass. If alarmed darts about erratically at low height uttering sharp 'tuc . . . tuc . . .' sounds and snapping its wings. **665**

3 **CLOUD CISTICOLA** (Gevlekte Klopkloppie) *Cisticola textrix.* Recorded only in the northern grasslands where it is probably resident. A very short-tailed, long-legged species. Non-breeding plumage similar in both sexes. In breeding plumage the female has a more mottled crown than the male, no dark spot before the eye and lacks pectoral spots. In the summer the male rises high into the air, usually out of normal sight, and cruises above its territory uttering a whispy 'see see seesee chick chick chick' repeated at two- or three-second intervals. Descends in an almost vertical plunge uttering a rapid 'chick-chick-chick-chick . . .' **666**

4 **AYRES' CISTICOLA** (Kleinste Klopkloppie) *Cisticola ayresii.* Rare. Recorded only in the north and the south-west. True status uncertain. Sexes similar in non-breeding plumage. In breeding plumage female has the crown heavily mottled, spot before eye absent. A species of the higher plateaus; in the Park may prove more common in hilly regions. In the summer the male mounts in the air and cruises about repeatedly calling in strophes of four to six wispy, high-pitched notes at three second intervals 'tsee-tsee-tsee-tsee'. This is interspersed with violent swerves and dives accompanied by wing-snapping. Descends in a rapid dive while uttering a hissing 'tsic-tsic-tsic-tsic . . .' plus volleys of wing-snaps. **667**

N-Br ♂   Br ♂   **1**

N-Br ♂   Br ♂   **2**

N-Br ♂   Br ♂   **3**

N-Br ♂   Br ♂   **4**

10cm

PLATE 84

1 BLACKBACKED CISTICOLA (Swartrugtinktinkie) *Cisticola galactotes.* Fairly common within a restricted range. Occurs in small numbers on rivers, dams and vleis throughout the Park. Has been seen feeding newly fledged young in June. Easily confused with (2) because of similar dark upperparts, the crown with almost total lack of markings. In summer plumage differs from (2) in more grey about the back, a dark spot between eye and bill and a shorter tail. In winter is less black on the upperparts than (2), crown less brightly rufous. The inside of the mouth is black at all times. The juvenile is sulphur-yellow below as illustrated. Inhabits reeds and other vegetation over or near water, plus bushes on flood grounds. Normal call a feeble, rasping 'zreeee . . .' or 'chit, chitchit' and 'trrrp trrrp trrrp' plus a loud and far-carrying 'prrrit prrrit prrrit'.   **675**

2 LEVAILLANT'S CISTICOLA (Vleitinktinkie) *Cisticola tinniens.* Status uncertain. Recorded only at Nwanedzi and Lower Sabie camps, the last record in early June. Very similar to the winter plumage of (1), with little seasonal or sexual variation. A waterside species, frequenting the fringes of pans, dams and the smaller streams, less common on large rivers. Occurs in sedge and similar low herbage in addition to reeds. Has a chirpy, warbling call 'chi chi cherrrueee'.   **677**

3 RATTLING CISTICOLA (Bosveldtinktinkie) *Cisticola chiniana.* Very common. A resident species, occurring throughout the Park and breeding in summer. A very 'typical' cisticola in general colouring, with few characteristic features except that the inside of the mouth, conspicuous when the bird is calling, is black. Best identified by behaviour and voice. The male is very conspicuous for much of the year, perching on the top branch of a bush and calling continuously. During the short non-breeding period form family groups, creeping about in matted thornbush and giving their typical alarm call when disturbed. The territorial call is a loud 'chi chi chi CHRRRRRRRR' repeated ad lib at short intervals; the last part of the call is the rattling sound which gives rise to the name. The alarm call is 'cheee cheee . . .'   **672**

4 TINKLING CISTICOLA (Rooitinktinkie) *Cisticola rufilata.* Has been identified only in the vicinity of Olifants camp, and is apparently resident in the surrounding hills. A slenderly built, very rufous cisticola, particularly in its winter plumage. The crown and tail markedly reddish at all times; inside of mouth black. A very secretive species, extremely difficult to locate and watch, diving into thick cover at the first alarm. Its shy habits may conceal a wider distribution. The male has a song consisting of a series of high, tinkling, bell-like notes. The alarm call, by either sex, is a series of high, twittering notes 'dee dee du du e e e'.   **671**

5 WAILING CISTICOLA (Huiltinktinkie) *Cisticola lais.* Status uncertain. Recorded only at Olifants Gorge and the Punda Maria region. A boldly patterned cisticola, especially in summer when the rufous crown contrasts with the greyish back. In winter lacks the greyish upperparts, being more reddish streaked black, the tail considerably longer. A bird of open or lightly wooded hillsides, often where scattered rocks occur. Reveals its presence by its agitated behaviour and alarm call; a plaintive 'wheeeet' or 'to-wee-yeh', repeated continually and rising in volume, loud and far-carrying. The song is a variety of notes in which the wailing alarm call predominates.   **670**

PLATE 85

1 LAZY CISTICOLA (Luitinktinkie) *Cisticola aberrans*. Fairly common but localised. Recorded only in the hilly regions of the south-west. No breeding records. A moderately large, long-tailed cisticola, the back and mantle only faintly mottled, the crown a rich rufous. Inhabits rocky regions with bush on hillsides or streams in these localities. A noisy species when alarmed, hopping about in agitated manner on rocks and below bushes and flirting its tail above its back and calling loudly. The palate is black. The call is a loud 'breeerp' or 'tu-hweee' or 'kweee-et' etc. **679**

2 NEDDICKY (Neddikkie) *Cisticola fulvicapilla*. Common throughout the Park. A resident species but breeding unrecorded. A small, plain-backed species with prominent rufous cap. Occurs in a variety of bushveld habitats and is located fairly easily by call. In the summer the male calls for long periods from a bush top, a monotonous 'chirrup-chirrup-chirrup . . .' Alarm call uttered by both sexes while flitting about in long grass or matted bushes is 'tik-tik-tik-tikkity-tikkity . . .' similar to the sound made by running a fingernail across the teeth of a comb. **681**

3 REDFACED CISTICOLA (Rooiwangtinktinkie) *Cisticola erythrops*. Common throughout the Park in suitable habitat. Resident but breeding unrecorded. A plain-backed cisticola, the crown almost concolourous with rest of upperparts. The rufous face and underparts are conspicuous in non-breeding plumage, less obvious at other times. Inhabits reeds and low growth at riversides, the larger dams, pans and floodplains. Is found at all permanent rivers in the Park, and is easily identified by call but usually remains concealed. The voice is a loud crescendo 'wink *wink* WINK' with variations. **674**

4 CROAKING CISTICOLA (Groottinktinkie) *Cisticola natalensis*. Fairly common but localised. Most records are for the southern half of the Park with the greatest concentration in the hilly south-west. Breeds in summer. Largest of the cisticolas, being short-tailed and drab during summer, when the male is noisy and conspicuous. The alarm call is a frog-like 'tee-YRRR'. When breeding the male's display flight is performed a few metres above ground, the bird cruising about at random with a loose wing-action and uttering a harsh 'cru-cru-cru-cru . . .' Also calls from a bush, a harsh 'CHEE-FRO' or 'chip-MUNK'. **678**

Prinias. Small, insectivorous, long-tailed warblers with the habit of flirting their tails over their backs.

5 TAWNYFLANKED PRINIA (Bruinsylangstertjie) *Prinia subflava*. Common and widespread, breeding throughout summer. A very small, long-tailed bird with a distinct eyebrow. Found in a variety of habitats, especially near water in small parties. Song 'fillip-fillip-fillip . . .' repeated; the alarm call, taken up by all members of the group, is a mewing, kitten-like 'skeeer, skeeer . . .' **683**

1

2

3

J

N-Br

N-Br

4

Br

5

10cm

PLATE 86

1 **MASHONA HYLIOTA** (Mashonahyliota) *Hyliota australis.* Uncommon and local-ised but resident, breeding in summer. Recorded only in the Punda Maria and Pafuri regions. Blackish upperparts with bold white wing-bars and yellowish underparts distinctive. Usually in pairs in the upper canopy of trees in broadleafed woodland. Active leaf-gleaners often found in mixed bird parties. Has a two-syllabled chittering whistle and a trilling warble. **624**

Flycatchers. Family MUSCICAPIDAE. Small, insectivorous birds having broad and flattened bills with prominent bristles protruding from the base. Many catch insects by repeated sallies from a perch, some are soberly coloured while others are attractively patterned or ornamented.

2 **MARICO FLYCATCHER** (Maricovlieëvanger) *Melaenornis mariquensis.* Uncom-mon. Has been seen at various points in the northern regions. No breeding recorded. Underparts conspicuously *clear white* (cf. 3), upperparts brown; immature (not recorded in KNP) heavily spotted and streaked as illustrated. Frequents *Acacia* thornveld, hawking insects from some low branch. Calls a soft 'chew-week'. **695**

3 **MOUSECOLOURED (PALLID) FLYCATCHER** (Muiskleurvlieëvanger) *Melae-nornis pallidus.* An uncommon resident. Recorded throughout the Park, breeding in early summer. Very plainly coloured with little contrast between upper and underparts; cf. (2). Occurs mostly in broadleafed woodland where it hawks insects from a low branch. The rambling, raspy song is not often heard. **696**

4 **SPOTTED FLYCATCHER** (Europese Vlieëvanger) *Muscicapa striata.* Common to very common non-breeding Palaearctic migrant present October-March. A small drab bird with streaks or smudges on its breast; differs from (5) in having a streaky crown. Perches on a low branch under a tree from where it hawks insects. Flicks its wings frequently. The call is a sibilant 'tzee'. **689**

5 **DUSKY FLYCATCHER** (Donkervlieëvanger) *Muscicapa adusta.* Uncommon resi-dent, widespread in suitable habitat. Breeds in early summer. Small and drab, the smudges on the breast less obvious than in (4), the crown lacking stripes. Found in moist, forested areas, usually in a riparian habitat. Habits same as (4) but flicks wings less often. Makes a sibilant 'zeeet'. **690**

6 **FANTAILED FLYCATCHER** (Waaierstertvlieëvanger) *Myioparus plumbeus.* Fairly common and widespread resident. Breeds during summer. Very similar to (7) but has *white outer tail feathers,* different behaviour. Moves actively through the mid-stratum of the bush foraging and calling. Frequently fans its tail while raising and lowering it. Also flicks its wings. May be located by the repeated call, a loud, cheerful 'teee-reee', the second syllable lower than the first. **693**

7 **BLUEGREY FLYCATCHER** (Blougrysvlieëvanger) *Muscicapa caerulescens.* Un-common resident sparsely distributed throughout the Park. Breeds in early summer. Very similar to (6) but less active, having the same quiet ways as (3), (4) and (5). Occurs in riverine forests as well as drier woodland. The call is a sibilant, husky 'tsip-tsip-tsip-tsip-tse-tslipsip'. **691**

BLACK FLYCATCHER *Melaenornis pammelaina.* See Plate 71.

10 cm

PLATE 87

1 BLUEMANTLED FLYCATCHER (Bloukuifvlieëvanger) *Trochocercus cyanomelas.* Rare. Recorded June-December in the far north and at scattered localities elsewhere. Exact status uncertain. The male with its black throat, black crested head and white underparts is distinctive. The female could be confused with other small grey flycatchers but the crested head is diagnostic. Frequents riverine and other evergreen forests. Always extremely active, swivelling from side to side with fanned tail and flitting about restlessly. The call is a sharp 'zwee-zwer' identical to the call of (2) and often the only clue to its presence.   **708**

2 PARADISE FLYCATCHER (Paradysvlieëvanger) *Terpsiphone viridis.* Fairly common throughout the Park October-March; individuals present in small numbers April-September. Bulk of population summer-breeding visitors only. A striking, colourful little bird, the male with its long tail-streamers being especially noticeable. Highly active and vociferous, usually found among large trees in a riparian habitat. The normal call is a sharp 'zwee-zwer' exactly similar to the call of (1). The song of the male is a lively trill 'wee-te-tiddly-wit-wit'.   **710**

3 CHINSPOT BATIS (Witliesbosbontrokkie) *Batis molitor.* Common throughout the Park and resident, breeding in early summer. In this species the female has the russet gorget and chin-spot; the male has a broad black gorget. Occurs in a variety of habitats and is frequently seen in camps, its call being one of the first sounds after sunrise. Invariably in pairs, frequently in bird parties. Variable song notes are uttered, the most common being a much repeated 'phe-phy-phu' sounding like 'three blind mice'.   **701**

4 WATTLE-EYED FLYCATCHER (Beloogbosbontrokkie) *Platysteira peltata.* An uncommon resident species, frequent only in the Pafuri region with scattered sightings further south. Breeds all summer. The male has a *narrow* breast-band and a completely black hood; both sexes have a red wattle or flange above and in front of the eye. A species of dense riverine thickets, it seldom ventures to higher levels. The song is a tinkling 'er-er-fea-er-er-fee-fea'; the call 'chit-chit-chit'.   **705**

5 FISCAL FLYCATCHER (Fiskaalvlieëvanger) *Sigelus silens.* Uncommon, exact status uncertain. Records cover the length of the Park, mostly in winter. No evidence of breeding. A large black and white flycatcher which resembles the Fiscal Shrike (Plate 88) but differs in having a more slender bill and a white wing-bar *not extending to the shoulder* as in the shrike. Habitually perches at the extremity of a lateral branch from where it flies down to seize insects on the ground. The song is a series of rather feeble, sibilant notes.   **698**

6 FAIRY FLYCATCHER (Feevlieëvanger) *Stenostira scita.* Rare vagrant April-August; few sightings, two in the Nshawu area. A very small grey, black and white bird, the white wing-bar and outer tail feathers conspicuous, pink belly inconspicuous. Highly active leaf-gleaner in a variety of bushy habitats, bobbing and fanning its tail frequently. Call a sibilant 'kisskisskiss' and similar squeaky sounds.   **706**

10 cm

PLATE 88

Shrikes, bush shrikes and allies. Family LANIIDAE. Insectivorous or partially carnivorous birds with stout, hooked or slightly hooked bills. Members of the various genera are illustrated according to plumage similarity.

1 FISCAL SHRIKE (Fiskaallaksman) *Lanius collaris.* Rare, exact status uncertain. Has been seen at a number of localities within the Park both in summer and winter. A heavy-headed, heavy-billed bird with white wing-bars *extending to the shoulders;* cf. Fiscal Flycatcher (Plate 87). The female only has rufous flanks. Perches with erect stance on bush or post and captures its prey on the ground. Likely to occur in lightly bushed terrain. The call is a harsh 'gercha, gercha'. Also has a rambling, rather discordant song. **732**

2 BRUBRU (Bontroklaksman) *Nilaus afer.* A common and widespread resident species, breeding in early summer. A small black and white bird with rufous flanks. An active species of *Acacia* veld and mixed woodland. Occurs in pairs, calling continuously while foraging in the tree canopies. The male makes a drawn-out whistling 'trioooo'; the female replies with a softer, wheezy 'wheee'. **741**

3 PUFFBACK (Sneeubal) *Dryoscopus cubla.* Common and widespread resident in a variety of wooded habitats. Breeds in early summer. Both sexes have wine-red eyes. When excited the male puffs out its back feathers as illustrated. An active and noisy species. Gleans insects from the leaf canopy of trees. Males frequently call a loud 'chic-weeu, chick-weeu . . .' **740**

4 SOUTHERN BOUBOU (Suidelike Waterfiskaal) *Laniarius ferrugineus.* Fairly common and widely distributed resident, breeding in early summer. Very similar to (5); separated by call. Inhabits dense riverine and hillside bush, seeking insects in the lower stratum and on the ground. Has a variety of pleasant, ringing calls delivered in duet by both sexes, such as 'boo-boo' replied to by 'whee'; 'ko-ko-ko' replied to by 'wheeoo'. **736**

5 TROPICAL BOUBOU (Tropiese Waterfiskaal) *Laniarius aethiopicus.* Fairly common resident within a restricted range. There are no breeding records. Occurs only in the north, being most common in the Pafuri region and the Nwambiya sandveld; also recorded near Shingwedzi. Differs from (4) in having underparts more uniformly pinkish, less rufous on flanks, otherwise very similar. Habits as (4) but tends to occur near water more frequently. Pairs call in duet with rapid delivery; usually three liquid, bell-like notes answered by 'hueee' but many variations occur. **737**

15 cm

PLATE 89

1 LONGTAILED SHRIKE (Langstertlaksman) *Corvinella melanoleuca*. Fairly common and widespread resident which breeds September-January. Unmistakable, the long tail being diagnostic. Prefers semi-grassland or open, wooded habitats. Usually occurs in small parties of three to five birds which perch on low bushes. Feeds on insects and small reptiles. The call is 'prooit-preeoo, prooit-preeoo-preeoo'. **735**

2 REDBACKED SHRIKE (Rooiruglaksman) *Lanius collurio*. A fairly common non-breeding Palaearctic migrant present in the Park October-April. Widespread but most numerous in the north. The male is distinctive, the female less so; the concentric marks of the underparts are sometimes quite faint. (Occasionally individuals are seen with an incomplete or full white wing-bar. This is a form of partial albinism.) Perches openly on a low branch in any bushveld habitat and flies to the ground to seize insects. Changes its perch frequently. The call is a harsh 'chak, chak'. **733**

3 WHITECROWNED SHRIKE (Kremetartlaksman) *Eurocephalus anguitimens*. Fairly common in the Park but distribution patchy. A resident species, breeding in summer. A large unmistakable shrike, its white crown and dark mask distinguishing it from all others. Occurs in open woodland, especially where baobab trees occur. Groups of three to five birds perch on prominent branches or telephone wires from where they watch the ground for insects. Makes a curious 'kwep, kwep' sound. **756**

4 LESSER GREY SHRIKE (Gryslaksman) *Lanius minor*. An uncommon, non-breeding Palaearctic migrant occurring October-April. May be seen with full black mask as in illustration (a) or with grey forehead as in illustration (b). Occurs in a variety of woodland habitats or in grassland. Perches on a low bush or post from where it catches insects on the ground. Normally silent in Africa. **731**

5 CRIMSON BOUBOU (Rooiborslaksman) *Laniarius atrococcineus*. Rare. Exact status uncertain. Several sightings have been made in the far north where it may prove to be resident in small numbers. Unmistakable. Upperparts identical to Southern Boubou (Plate 88), underparts bright crimson. Occurs in the lower stratum of thornveld, spending much time on the ground. Pairs call in duet, a sharp 'qui-quip-chiri'. **739**

192

15 cm

PLATE 90

1 ORANGEBREASTED BUSH SHRIKE (Oranjeborsboslaksman) *Telophorus sulfureopectus*. A common and widespread resident species. Breeds in early summer. Frequents regions of thick bush, especially along rivers, and usually in pairs foraging in the mid-stratum. Reveals its presence by call, a much repeated 'pooo pooo pooo poooooo' or 'pipit-eeez, pipit-eeez . . .' **748**

2 BLACKFRONTED BUSH SHRIKE (Swartoogboslaksman) *Telophorus nigrifrons*. Rare. Exact status uncertain. Recorded only at Punda Maria and Pafuri. Similar to (1) but of entirely different habits. A species of evergreen forests, frequenting the tree canopies and difficult to locate except for its call 'doh-me' as in the tonic sol-fa scale. **749**

3 BOKMAKIERIE *Telophorus zeylonus*. Rare. Has been recorded only at Numbi Gate, near Skukuza and Muzandzeni picnic place west of Satara. A non-breeding nomad not normally associated with the KNP. Well known in many parts of the country for its joyful call, the onomatopoeic 'bok-makiri' plus 'bok bok-chit' or 'whit, wit-wit'. **746**

4 GORGEOUS BUSH SHRIKE (Konkoit) *Telophorus quadricolor*. Fairly common. Recorded at scattered locations throughout the Park. A resident species; no breeding recorded but a sub-adult seen in July. Beautiful and quite unmistakable if seen, but very shy, remaining in dense bush. Best located by call, heard frequently in favoured haunts, a melodious, liquid 'kong-kong-koit' or 'kong-kong-koit-a-koit'. **747**

5 GREYHEADED BUSH SHRIKE (Spookvoël) *Malaconotus blanchoti*. A common resident species, occurring throughout the Park. Similar colouring to (1) and (2) but much larger and heavier-billed, less spritely in its movements. Frequents fairly dense bush and reveals its presence by its call, a far-carrying, mournful 'phooooo, phooooo, phooooo-it'. Also makes a continuous clicking sound interspersed with a high-pitched 'kwerk'. **751**

6 OLIVE BUSH SHRIKE (Olyfboslaksman) *Telophorus olivaceus*. Rare. Seen only in the Punda Maria and Pafuri regions; no breeding recorded. Secretive, frequenting the lower stratum of dense hillside or riverine bush; more often heard than seen. The call is about six notes of varying pitch 'phwee-phwe-phwe-phwe-phwe-phwe' or 'tee-tew-tew-tew-tew-tew' or 'tee-toy-toy-toy-toy-toy' and a descending 'CHE-*che*che-che-che-che'. **750**

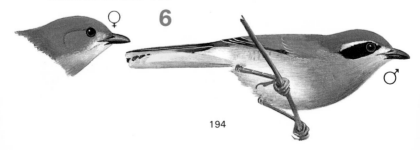

15 cm

2 ♂

1

3

♂

4

5

PLATE 91

1 **THREESTREAKED TCHAGRA** (Rooivlerktjagra) *Tchagra australis.* A common and widespread species, occurring in a variety of habitats and breeding in summer. Very similar to (2) and frequently confused with it. The top of the head is *brown* and the white eyebrow is edged by a thin black line above and a broad one below. A bird of the lower bush stratum, it spends much time on the ground. If disturbed flies into the next bush displaying reddish-brown wings and white terminal spots on the tail exactly similar to (2). The territorial call is made during a display flight. The bird flies up above the trees and then glides down with quivering wings calling 'tui-tui-tui-tui-tui- . . .', descending the scale.   **743**

2 **BLACKCROWNED TCHAGRA** (Swartkroontjagra) *Tchagra senegala.* Common resident, widespread throughout the Park. Prefers rather denser woodland than (1) but the two overlap in many regions. Breeds October-January. Very similar to (1) but larger, with a heavier bill and a *black* crown above the white eyebrow. Creeps about in the lower stratum and on the ground. When flushed shows the same colour pattern as (1) but has a heavier flight. The call is one of the characteristic sounds of the bushveld, a loud, ponderous and flat-sounding 'trichi CHEER-tcharoo, trichi CHEER-tcharoo, cheeroo, cheeroo'. Also has a variety of grating, churring and whistling calls delivered by pairs in duet.   **744**

Helmetshrikes. Family PRIONOPIDAE. Small, social shrikes, occurring in woodland and forest, all being insectivorous leaf and ground foragers and occurring in groups of six to twenty birds. Helmetshrikes have brightly coloured legs and bills, and eyes surrounded by fleshy wattles. The head feathers are long and loose and project forward over the bill. Their calls are a communal chattering accompanied by bill-snapping.

3 **REDBILLED HELMETSHRIKE** (Swarthelmlaksman) *Prionops retzii.* Uncommon but widespread throughout the Park and resident. There are no breeding records but a party has been seen feeding a thickbilled Cuckoo (Plate 46) foster-chick in April. Occurs in heavily wooded regions and is nomadic to some degree. An unmistakable black bird with white on the belly, vent and tail, and bright red legs, bill and eye-wattle. Parties occur in any well-developed riverine forest or woodland, always in the tree canopies actively feeding and chattering. The call, made by a number of birds together, becomes very excitable and confused, the basic sounds being 'tchee-op, tchee-op . . . trooee, trooee . . . chirru-chirru . . . pitchoo, pitchoo, pitchoo . . .' all interspersed with various grating and chopping sounds plus bill-snapping.   **754**

4 **WHITE HELMETSHRIKE** (Withelmlaksman) *Prionops plumatus.* A fairly common resident, frequenting all regions. Breeds September-December. A conspicuous species, occurring in small flocks which fly from bush to bush at low level resembling large black and white butterflies. The yellow legs and eyes are apparent only on close inspection but the general colouring and behaviour are diagnostic. Individuals in a party periodically set up an excited chattering comprised of 'shgwee' sounds, flute-like notes and bill-snapping. Also has an alarm note 'chow chow'.   **753**

15cm

PLATE 92

Starlings. Family STURNIDAE. Frugivorous and insectivorous birds which sometimes form large flocks, especially when roosting. The blue or glossy starlings are
peculiar to Africa and are conspicuous in the KNP.

1 **BLACKBELLIED GLOSSY STARLING.** (Swartpensglansspreeu) *Lamprotornis
corruscus*. Rare. Occurs only in the vicinity of the Crocodile River. There are no
breeding records but it is probably resident there. Smaller and duller than most
glossy starlings, appearing almost black if not seen in good light. The female is
particularly dull, as is the immature, the latter having greyish not yellow eyes. The
song is a garbled series of mellow trills interspersed with some harsh, grating
notes. **768**

2 **GREATER BLUE-EARED GLOSSY STARLING** (Grootblouoorglansspreeu) *Lamprotornis chalybaeus*. A fairly common resident with a widespread distribution.
Breeds in summer. Appears brightly coloured, even in shade. Differs from (4) in
having royal blue, almost purple flanks and belly and a dark blue ear-patch which
appears black in the field; see illustration. Differs from (3) in being larger, flank
colouring more extensive; cf. that species. The feathers of the folded wing are
peacock-green and the black terminal spots on the secondary feathers are always
in evidence. Becomes very tame at camps where food scraps are offered, otherwise
feeds on fruit and insects. The call is 'weeer-eeer'. **765**

3 **LESSER BLUE-EARED GLOSSY STARLING** (Klein-blouoor-
glansspreeu) *Lamprotornis chloropterus*. Uncommon and localised. Seen only in the Luvuvhu River region of the far north.
Exact status uncertain. Almost exactly similar to (2) but smaller,
flanks (not belly) magenta and less extensive than in (2), the
upper row of wing-spots less obvious. Positive identification
assured when seen with immatures, these having rust-brown
underparts; see margin illustration. Usually seen in small flocks
in broadleafed woodland. On take-off calls 'wirri-girri'; song a
pleasant jumble 'chirp-chirrup-tree-roo-chirp-troo . . .' **766**

4 **CAPE GLOSSY STARLING** (Kleinglansspreeu) *Lamprotornis
nitens*. Common resident, widespread throughout the Park.
Breeds in summer. Similar to (2) and (3) but more blue, less
green on the wings, lacks the blackish ear-patch, flanks same
colour as rest of underparts and only one row of wing-spots
visible in good light. Immature birds look quite dull blue, with
brown wing feathers. Tame and conspicuous in camps, feeding
on fruit, insects and domestic scraps. Song 'trr-treer-treer-cheer'
or 'preeu-cheeoo'. **764**

5 **LONGTAILED GLOSSY STARLING** (Langstertglansspreeu) *Lamprotornis meve-
sii*. Fairly common only in the Luvuvhu and Limpopo River regions. Odd individuals
have been reported further south but such sightings are rare. A resident species,
but no breeding recorded. The only glossy starling in the Park with a *long, graduated
tail.* Is often confused with (6) which also has a dark eye but lacks the long tail.
Occurs in well-developed mopane woodland. The call is a loud 'kow-kow' plus
various whistles. **763**

6 **BURCHELL'S GLOSSY STARLING** (Grootglansspreeu) *Lamprotornis australis*.
Fairly common but found mostly south of the Olifants River. Resident, breeding
through summer. A large, long-legged, dark-eyed glossy starling. The tail is shorter
than that of (5) and is not graduated. The only dark-eyed glossy starling in the
south of the Park. The call is a squeaky 'churrik-urr, churrik-urrik-kerr . . .' Flocks
make a shrill chattering at the roost. **762**

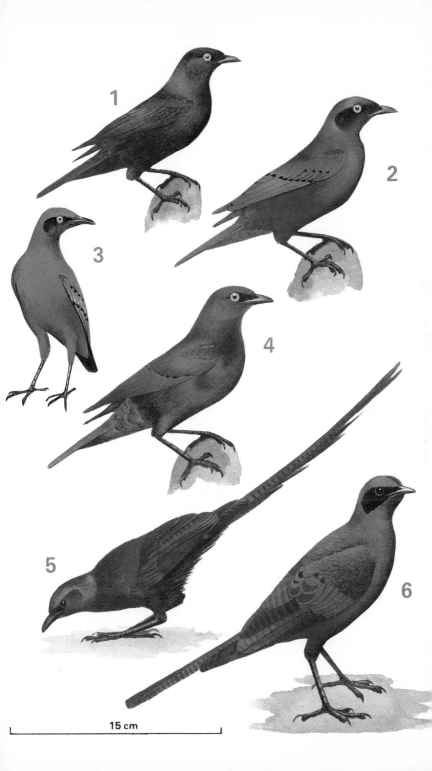

15 cm

PLATE 93

1 **REDWINGED STARLING** (Rooivlerkspreeu) *Onychognathus morio.* An uncommon resident species of patchy distribution. Occurs in rocky localities, especially in the north, east and south and has taken up residence in certain rest camps where it roost and nests in buildings, breeding in summer. A large, glossy black starling, the female with grey head and mantle. In flight the brick-red wings are conspicuous. Normally seen in pairs or flocks in the vicinity of rocky gorges or hills. The call is a melodious 'teeooo' and various other pleasant whistles.   **769**

2 **WATTLED STARLING** (Lelspreeu) *Creatophora cinerea.* Locally very common in summer when breeding, especially in the central and northern regions; when not breeding highly nomadic and often absent from the Park. When not breeding both sexes resemble (a). Breeding males adopt head ornaments which, however, are variable, having either wattles and a normally feathered head or losing all feathering on the head as (b). Various degrees between these extremes may also be seen. The species normally occurs in flocks in open or lightly bushed country. When breeding their stick nests are placed colonially in bushes over a wide area. The call is a rasping, squeaky sound.   **760**

3 **PLUMCOLOURED STARLING** (Witborsspreeu) *Cinnyricinclus leucogaster.* A fairly common intra-Africa migrant present throughout the Park October-March. Breeds October-January. The sexes are entirely different as illustrated. The male is unmistakable at all times, the female not unlike a Groundscraper Thrush (Plate 75) but considerably smaller, shorter tailed and lacking the distinct facial markings of the thrush. Normally seen feeding in fruit trees such as the sycamore fig *Ficus sycamorus,* and frequents camps where these trees grow. In March may occur in flocks prior to departing. Makes a quiet, melodious 'tipu-tee-eeoo'.   **761**

Oxpeckers. Family BUPHAGIDAE. Two African species occur in association with cattle and wild animals, crawling all over them and combing their fur with their bills to feed on ticks and blood-sucking flies. They nest in natural holes in trees, lining the chamber and sealing gaps with animal fur.

4 **YELLOWBILLED OXPECKER** (Geelbekrenostervoël) *Buphagus africanus.* Fairly common and becoming widespread throughout the Park. A resident species, breeding in summer. Slightly larger than (5) with a heavier, red-tipped yellow bill and *pale rump.* Occurs mostly in association with buffaloes and rhinoceroses. The call is a hissing 'kriss' sound.   **771**

5 **REDBILLED OXPECKER** (Rooibekrenostervoël) *Buphagus erythrorhynchus.* Common and widespread throughout the Park. A resident, breeding in summer. Smaller than (4) and with a red bill, yellow eye-wattles and lacking a pale rump. The immature has a blackish bill with yellow gape. Occurs in association with a variety of wild animals, notably impalas and giraffes. Flocks roost at night in dead trees that stand in water or in reeds. The voice is 'zik, zik' plus a twittering sound in flight.   **772**

PLATE 94

Sunbirds. Family NECTARINIIDAE. Small nectar-eating and insectivorous birds with slender, curved, flower-probing bills. Superficially similar to the American hummingbirds but entirely unrelated to them. Sunbird males are usually brightly coloured, often with green or bluish upperparts with a metallic sheen, while most females are plainly coloured in dull greys and browns. Unlike hummingbirds they can hover only briefly, and obtain nectar by clinging to or standing on a flower head, either inserting their bills and long tubular tongues into the open end or piercing the base of the petals or corolla tube. Most sunbirds also eat soft bodied insects and spiders. They build oval, hanging nests with an entrance at one side near the top, often with a small canopy. Many species have attractive warbling songs, usually uttered by the males.

1 WHITEBELLIED SUNBIRD (Witpenssuikerbekkie) *Nectarinia talatala*. Common and widespread throughout the Park. A resident species, breeding July-December. The male, which appears quite blue on its head, mantle and breast, is the only sunbird in the KNP with white underparts. It has the habit of singing for long periods from a tree top, and is then conspicuous. The female, though dull in colour, is whiter below than most other sunbird females. The song of the male is 'chu-ee, chu-ee, chu-ee-trrrrr' frequently repeated. **787**

2 COLLARED SUNBIRD (Kortbeksuikerbekkie) *Anthreptes collaris*. A fairly common and widespread resident species in suitable habitat. Breeds mainly September-January. Occurs in lush riparian vegetation and in rest camps in association with flowering thickets and matted creepers since it is especially attracted to the rambling *Maeurua* and *Bauhinia* species. An unobtrusive little bird, normally remaining in the higher reaches of the food plant where it feeds quietly, and is therefore easily overlooked. Only the male has the collar, while the female is entirely yellow below. The diagnostic feature of this sunbird, apart from very small size and yellow underparts, is the *very short beak;* cf. (3) with which it is often confused. The usual call is 'teree-teree', the first phrase ascending, the second descending. **793**

3 YELLOWBELLIED SUNBIRD (Geelpenssuikerbekkie) *Nectarinia venusta*. Rare generally; uncommon in the far north where it is probably resident in small numbers. Most likely to be confused with (2) but is *larger, longer billed,* males with a greater extent of purple on the breast, females brown above, less yellow below. Seen usually only in the Luvuvhu River region; a few scattered sightings elsewhere. The call is 'seeu-see-see'; also has a melodious rippling song. **786**

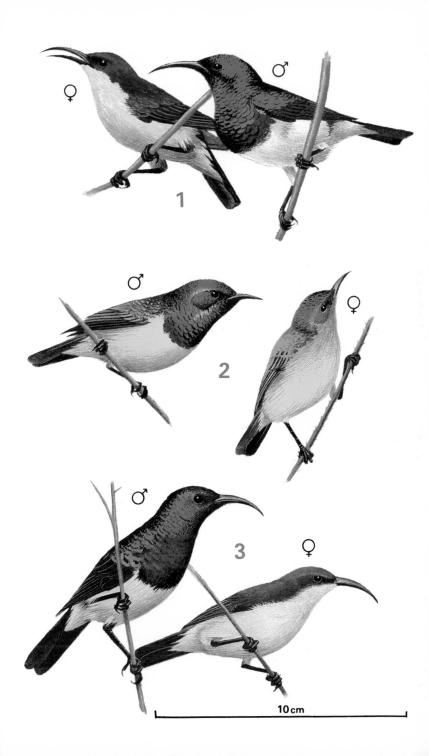

10 cm

PLATE 95

1 SCARLETCHESTED SUNBIRD (Rooikeelsuikerbekkie) *Nectarinia senegalensis.* A fairly common resident, occurring throughout the Park, most commonly in the south. Breeds September-December. The adult male, velvety-black with scarlet breast, is unmistakable. Immatures and female, as illustrated, are less strikingly coloured but large size separates them from all but the next species. The female Scarletchested is darker than the female Black Sunbird, especially on the under-parts, and lacks the pale moustachial streak. Often quite numerous in camps where flowering creepers grow. An active, lively species; the male spends much time chasing females and other males. The male often calls from the top of a tree 'cheep, chip, chop' continually repeated. Also utters a high-pitched chattering sound and, during flight, a sharp 'chit'. **791**

2 BLACK SUNBIRD (Swartsuikerbekkie) *Nectarinia amethystina.* Uncommon but resident, and widespread in its distribution. Appears to be more common in the south-west of the Park, and breeding has been recorded near Pretoriuskop in October. Similar in size and general appearance to the previous sunbird, but males lack the scarlet breast of that species. The green crown patch and mauve throat are visible only in conditions of good light while the mauve shoulder patch and rump may be seen only at close range. Young birds resemble the female but have darker throats and tend to be more yellowish below, showing traces of a mauve throat patch in the sub-adult stage. The Black Sunbird occurs in camps, along watercourses and around well-wooded koppies where it feeds on flowering creepers, bushes and aloes. Also feeds on spiders and small flying insects hawked in the air. Utters a sharp 'zit' in flight and, at rest, a stuttering 'chichichichi'. In addition, males have a pleasant though subdued warbling song given from the depths of a bush. **792**

♂J

♀

1

♂

♀ 2

♂

10cm

PLATE 96

1 MARICO SUNBIRD (Maricosuikerbekkie) *Nectarinia mariquensis*. Fairly common, and the most numerous sunbird throughout the Park. Breeds October-December. The male is a striking little bird with its brilliant bluish-green colouring and may often be seen feeding on aloes and other flowering plants in camps. When several are attracted to a food source, males spend much time chasing one another as well as females. Is sometimes mistaken for the next species but is larger with a distinctly *longer, well-curved bill*. It has a brief but loud warbling song but the call most often heard is a sharp 'chip-chip' or a rapid series of these sounds.   **779**

2 PURPLEBANDED SUNBIRD (Purperbandsuikerbekkie) *Nectarinia bifasciata*. Rare (probably non-breeding) visitor to the eastern regions over the length of the Park, seen mostly in winter with a few summer sightings. Similar in colouring to (1) but *much smaller and shorter-billed*. Has a typical sibilant, chittering sunbird song; the call is 'tsikititik'.   **780**

BLUETHROATED SUNBIRD (Bloukeelsuikerbekkie) *Anthreptes reichenowi*. Rare, exact status uncertain. Has been positively recorded at Lower Sabie. Male unmistakable; female could be confused with female Collared Sunbird but upperparts are dull olive-green, not iridescent green. The call is 'tik-tik'. Mostly feeds unobtrusively in tree canopies.   **794**

White-eyes. Family ZOSTEROPIDAE. Very small, greenish-yellow birds with conspicuous white eye-rings. Feed on insects, fruit and, to a lesser extent, nectar. Usually occur in small flocks.

3 YELLOW WHITE-EYE (Geelglasogie) *Zosterops senegalensis*. Uncommon. Known to occur in the Luvuvhu-Limpopo River region where it breeds in summer. Very small, yellow bird with white eye-wattle; more yellow, less green than next species. An active leaf-gleaner occurring in small flocks in the canopies of trees in densely forested riverine bush. Has a thin, twittering contact call and a melodious warbling song similar to that of the next species.   **797**

4 CAPE WHITE-EYE (Kaapse Glasogie) *Zosterops pallidus*. Generally uncommon, but resident. Regular at Pretoriuskop and Skukuza camps, and at Pafuri. No breeding has been recorded. A very small, greenish-yellow bird with distinctive eye-rings. Prefers large trees, especially in a riparian habitat, where small parties clamber about quietly seeking aphids and other small insects in the outer foliage. Is also attracted to fruit, especially wild figs. Normally the contact call is heard, a melancholy 'phe' uttered by several in a party, but in the breeding season has a pretty, sustained, rambling song given loudly from a tree-top. Also a subdued warbling sub-song, sung from the depths of a bush.   **796**

PLATE 97

Sparrows, weavers, bishop-birds, widowbirds, whydahs and allies. Family PLO-CEIDAE. Hard-billed, mostly granivorous birds. Construct ball-type nests of grasses or sticks attached to reeds or branches. Some sparrows use holes in trees. The whydahs, widowfinches and Cuckoo Finch are brood parasites, laying their eggs in other birds' nests, especially waxbills. All, except sparrows and buffalo weavers, undergo seasonal plumage changes, the males moulting their vivid breeding colours and assuming plumage similar to that of the females.

1 YELLOWTHROATED SPARROW (Geelvlekmossie) *Petronia superciliaris.* A fairly common resident species throughout the Park. Breeds in summer. The only sparrow with a bold white eyebrow. The yellow throat-spot is not always obvious and the species can be confused with the Streakyheaded Canary (Plate 106), which lacks the pale wing-bar of this sparrow. Commonly seen about rest camps, otherwise frequents tall trees in broadleafed woodland and riverine forests. On the ground walks, does not hop like other sparrows. The call is a rapid 'chree-chree-chreechree'.   **805**

2 GREYHEADED SPARROW (Gryskopmossie) *Passer griseus.* A common and widespread resident species, breeding in summer. The plain grey head is diagnostic, the bill being black when breeding and horn-coloured at other times. Occurs commonly about rest camps and picnic sites, feeding on the ground, otherwise frequents large trees. The voice is a monosyllabic 'cheep'.   **804**

3 HOUSE SPARROW (Huismossie) *Passer domesticus.* Common at all rest camps and staff quarters. Breeds at any time. The male with its grey cap and black 'bib' is unmistakable; the female is very much paler in colour and lacks bold markings. Occurs only in and around human settlements. The call is 'chee-ip' or 'chissip'.   **801**

4 REDBILLED BUFFALO WEAVER (Buffelwewer) *Bubalornis niger.* Fairly common and widespread throughout the Park, breeding in summer, nomadic at other times. A fairly large, blackish weaver with a reddish bill and white wing markings. When breeding may be seen attending bulky stick nests in large trees, especially baobabs. Makes a variety of chattering noises at the nest plus a continuous falsetto churring in flight and when feeding.   **798**

5 REDBILLED QUELEA (Rooibekkwelea) *Quelea quelea.* Common to abundant locally and seasonally. A resident species, the numbers greatly augmented during summers of high rainfall. Breeding occurs, under suitable conditions, January-March. The male is variable when breeding, as illustrated, at other times resembles the female. When breeding, hundreds of thousands of small, weaver-type nests are placed in bushes over a large area and attract a variety of predators. Flocks make a concerted twittering.   **821**

6 WHITEBROWED SPARROW-WEAVER (Koringvoël) *Plocepasser mahali.* Rare. Exact status uncertain. Seen several times in the north-western regions and at Letaba camp. A fairly large, sparrow-like bird with black crown, bold white eyebrow plus chestnut upperparts and a black and white wing pattern; in flight shows a broad white rump. The breast may be plain white or spotted. The call is 'cheeoo-preeoo-chop-chop, cheeoo-trroo-cheeoo-preeoo-chop-chip . . .'   **799**

6

208

10cm

2 Br

1

♂ 3 ♀

♀

♂ 4

5 ♂

♀

PLATE 98

1 YELLOW WEAVER (Geelwewer) *Ploceus subaureus.* Irregular and unpredictable. A breeding summer visitor along the Sabie River, abundant some years and absent in others. When present, may be seen in large numbers at Skukuza and Lower Sabie camps where they colonise trees and river reeds, and reach a breeding peak in February. Has been seen as early as August. A small, very yellow weaver with little difference between the sexes in breeding plumage. Highly colonial and noisy in their colonies. (For nest illustration see pages following Plate 99.) Makes a harsh 'zik' and a soft swizzling sound. **817**

2 SPECTACLED WEAVER (Brilwewer) *Ploceus ocularis.* Uncommon, but a resident species in suitable localities throughout the Park. Breeds in summer. Both sexes have the black eye-line but the female lacks the male's black 'bib', otherwise identical. Occurs along well-wooded rivers, notably the Luvuvhu, Sabie and Crocodile, where their characteristic nests may be seen hanging from small trees (see illustration following Plate 99). Not a social species, usually occurring in pairs. The normal call is a descending 'tee tee tee tee tee tee'. **810**

3 BROWNTHROATED WEAVER (Bruinkeelwewer) *Ploceus xanthopterus.* Rare. Exact status uncertain. There have been a few sightings of this weaver in the Letaba region during summer. A small weaver, the male distinguished in breeding plumage by the brown throat and black bill. The female can be confused with other female weavers, but has a pinkish bill and white belly. A social species. Occurring usually in reedbeds or nearby. (See nest illustration following Plate 99.) **818**

4 GOLDEN WEAVER (Goudwewer) *Ploceus xanthops.* Uncommon and localised, having been recorded only at the confluence of the Olifants and Timbavati Rivers and on the Luvuvhu and Limpopo Rivers. Breeds in these localities but may be a summer visitor only. The largest of the yellow weavers and having a heavy, sharply pointed bill, the sexes similar. Very similar in colouring to (1) but has a yellow, not red eye. Fairly gregarious when not breeding, when it occurs in small parties, but nests are found either solitarily or in loose, scattered groups. (See illustration following Plate 99.) Makes a harsh chirp and a sustained swizzling 'cheecheechee . . .' **816**

5 THICKBILLED WEAVER (Dikbekwewer) *Amblyospiza albifrons.* Uncommon but widespread. Breeds in summer but disperses after breeding and may leave the Park. A large brown weaver, the male appearing almost black with white forehead and wing-spots, the female distinctly streaked on the underparts. Frequents reedbeds when breeding, the neat, oval nests slung between reed stems in small, loose colonies (see illustration following Plate 99). Normally a silent species but makes a chattering sound when in the vicinity of the nest. **807**

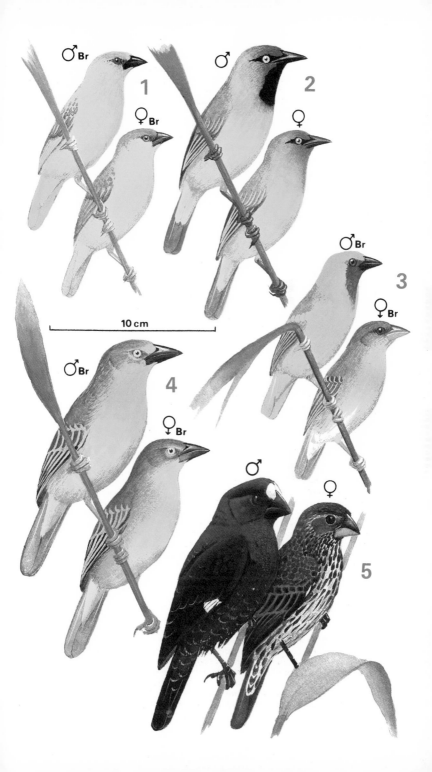

PLATE 99

1 MASKED WEAVER (Swartkeelgeelvink) *Ploceus velatus*. A fairly common, widespread resident species. Breeds throughout the summer. The male in breeding plumage may be separated from (2) by red eyes and from both (2) and (3) by the mask which extends *only over the forehead* and forms a point on the breast. In non-breeding plumage it resembles the female but is more yellow on the underparts. The female, when breeding, has a pale yellow wash over the entire underparts, and has reddish eyes. This species is a colonial breeder, sometimes a small cluster of nests only, but more often a large number suspended from trees or in reedbeds. (See illustration overleaf.) The normal call is 'chip, chip', but breeding males make a prolonged swizzling sound and actively chase females while nest-building. **814**

2 LESSER MASKED WEAVER (Kleingeelvink) *Ploceus intermedius*. Fairly common and widespread throughout the Park; common and conspicuous at breeding colonies during summer. Similar to, but slightly smaller than (1). Males differ from both (1) and (3) in having pale yellow eyes (not red) and in having the black mask extending back over the head to a point *behind the eyes*. On the breast the black area is rounded not pointed. Non-breeding males resemble females; female plumage changes little throughout the year. A colonial breeder, many dozens of nests being suspended from reeds or trees. (See overleaf for illustration of nest.) Males make a swizzling noise when breeding and the collective sound may be considerable at an active colony. **815**

3 SPOTTEDBACKED WEAVER (Bontrugwewer) *Ploceus cucullatus*. Common to very common locally and widespread throughout the Park. As with other colonial breeding weavers they are much in evidence at camps, rivers and dams during September-March, nomadic at other times. Breeding male has a heavily spotted back as illustrated, the top of the head is *yellow to the base of the bill*. The eyes are orange-red and the black of the breast terminates in an elongated point. Non-breeding males resemble non-breeding females, the throat and breast being lemon yellow, the rest of the underparts white as illustrated. Examples of the black-headed race *P.c. nigriceps* are occasionally seen in the Park; see (b). Nests are placed in trees overhanging water or in reedbeds, usually many dozens together. (See overleaf for illustration of nest.) In the breeding season males hang beneath their nests and swivel from side to side, fluttering their wings and swizzling harshly to attract females. **811**

4 REDHEADED WEAVER (Rooikopwewer) *Anaplectes rubriceps*. Uncommon but widespread and resident. Nest-building commences in August in the south, at which time the male assumes nuptial plumage, and breeding appears to be completed by November. In the far north the cycle is October-February. Nomadic when not breeding, foraging in bird parties. Breeding males are unmistakable, but otherwise resemble females, both being recognised by their orange coloured beaks, lemon-yellow throats and breast and clear white underparts; cf. (3). Nests are either solitary or in small colonies of three to six, and are constructed of woven twigs and leaves, not grasses, thus they are brown in colour from the start: see illustration overleaf. This species utters a continuous squeaky chatter at the nest. **819**

♂Br   ♀N-Br   **1**

♂Br   ♀   **2**

b   ♂Br   ♂N-Br   **3**

♂Br   ♀   **4**

WEAVER BIRDS' NESTS

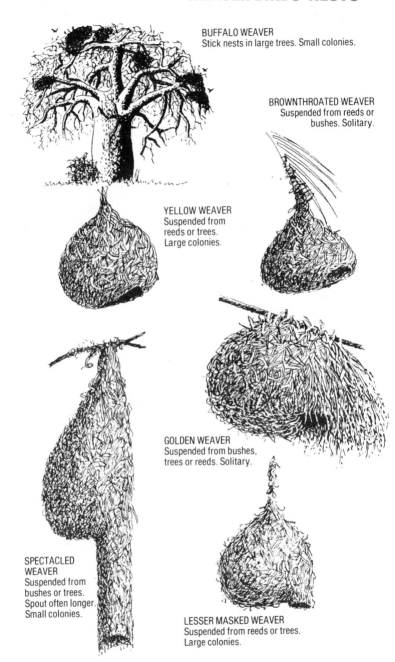

BUFFALO WEAVER
Stick nests in large trees. Small colonies.

BROWNTHROATED WEAVER
Suspended from reeds or
bushes. Solitary.

YELLOW WEAVER
Suspended from
reeds or trees.
Large colonies.

GOLDEN WEAVER
Suspended from bushes,
trees or reeds. Solitary.

**SPECTACLED
WEAVER**
Suspended from
bushes or trees.
Spout often longer.
Small colonies.

LESSER MASKED WEAVER
Suspended from reeds or trees.
Large colonies.

FOUND IN THE KNP

THICKBILLED
WEAVER
Roosting nest.

Same nest
modified for
breeding.

Suspended in reeds
or bushes.
Solitary.

MASKED WEAVER
Suspended from
reeds or trees.
Large colonies.

REDHEADED
WEAVER
Built of sticks and
hung from trees.
Solitary.

SPOTTEDBACKED
WEAVER
Suspended from bushes
and trees over water.
Spout may be longer
or absent. Large
colonies.

PLATE 100

Widow birds and bishop birds. Reed- and grass-loving weavers of the family Ploceidae. Differ from other Ploceidae in that males are predominantly black in the breeding season, some with long tails, and have the habit of puffing out their plumage in display. Non-breeding males and females are plainly coloured and very similar to each other. Their ball-type nests of grass are suspended between reeds or placed low down in grass or sedge, according to species. The populations of most species are subject to occasional irruptions, perhaps associated with wet years.

1 **REDSHOULDERED WIDOW** (Kortstertflap) *Euplectes axillaris.* An uncommon, summer-breeding visitor to the southern half of the Park. A nest with eggs has been found in December. Associates with coarse vegetation of dams and vleis; the male being the only completely black bird with a red shoulder. The female is inconspicuous but carries the red shoulder patch at all times. A husky 'tseek, wirra, wirra, wirra, wirra' is made by displaying males.   **828**

2 **REDCOLLARED WIDOW** (Rooikeelflap) *Euplectes ardens.* An uncommon, breeding visitor to the extreme southern and south-western sections of the Park in summer. Has also been seen at Orpen Dam and near Punda Maria. Breeding has been recorded in December. The male is conspicuous in its haunts when breeding, flying over its territory with its long tail spread. Occurs in waterside sedge and on well-grassed hillsides with bush. The male in display utters a weak 'kizz-zizz-zizz-zizz'. **831**

3 **WHITEWINGED WIDOW** (Witvlerkflap) *Euplectes albonotatus.* Uncommon, but occurs throughout the Park. Most records are for summer, when it breeds, with one for June at Olifants Gorge. The male is conspicuous when breeding, flying about and displaying its white wing-patches, usually in groups with others of both sexes. At rest, the only all-black bird with a yellow shoulder-patch with the exception of the Black Cuckooshrike (Plate 71) which, however, has entirely different habits and habitat preferences. Occurs in reedbeds and in the rank grass and weeds associated with damp situations. The call is a cheerful twittering sound.   **829**

4 **RED BISHOP** (Rooivink) *Euplectes orix.* An uncommon, summer-breeding visitor that occurs throughout the Park; more plentiful in some years than others. The male with its red and black plumage is unmistakable both in repose and in display, when the entire plumage is fluffed; see illustration. Occurs usually in small colonies, breeding in reedbeds of rivers, dams and pans. In display, males utter a wheezy, spluttering 'zik, zik, zik . . .zayzayzayzay'.   **824**

5 **GOLDEN BISHOP** (Goudgeelvink) *Euplectes afer.* Rare. A few scattered records exist for points throughout the Park during summer. The male is unmistakable. In display, flies about its territory with plumage fully fluffed, zigzagging about like a large bumble-bee. Occurs in rank vegetation near damp localities. Males utter various squeaking and buzzing sounds while pursuing one another in the breeding territories.   **826**

10cm

PLATE 101

Whydahs, widowfinches, and Cuckoo Finch. These are the parasitic members of the family Ploceidae. Male whydahs in breeding plumage may be confused with males of the long-tailed widow species, but differ from them in being smaller in body, with white or buff-coloured underparts and tails with stiffer, less floppy plumes. In non-breeding plumage they resemble the confusingly similar females and, at times, may also be seen in transient plumage with traces of the breeding pattern still visible. Young birds are often quite plain in colour. The closely related widowfinches (Plate 102) can probably be identified with certainty only when the male is in breeding plumage, the three species that occur in the Park being distinguished by bill and leg colour. This group parasitises waxbills and small finches. The Cuckoo Finch appears weaver-like and parasitises small warblers.

1 **PINTAILED WHYDAH** (Koningrooibekkie) *Vidua macroura*. Fairly common throughout the Park. A summer-breeding resident. The male in breeding plumage is conspicuous and easily identified, usually being accompanied by several females. In non-breeding plumage, the bill remains a brighter red than that of the female. Young birds, as illustrated, have very plain colouring. The adult male is a very pugnacious bird and spends much time chasing other small birds or hovering in courtship flight over the females, while describing a circle in the vertical plane. Parasitises the Common Waxbill (Plate 104). The male in courtship flight utters a continual 'tseet, tseet, tseet...' Also has a harsh, wispy song 'peetzy-peetzy-peetzy'. **860**

2 **PARADISE WHYDAH** (Gewone Paradysvink) *Vidua paradisea*. Fairly common throughout the Park. Most records are for summer, but winter sightings have been made in the far north. The male (a), with its beautiful tail plumes in breeding plumage, is unmistakable. Resembles the female when not breeding and may be seen in the transitional plumage (b). Young birds resemble the young of (1), the bill horn-coloured. Occurs in all regions, even in the central and northern mopane bush which is not favoured by many species. Males fly about in swift, undulating flight and in purposeful manner at some height. As with other whydahs, the females are inconspicuous at all times but may sometimes be seen feeding on the ground with males. Parasitises the Melba Finch (Plate 103) and probably others. Not a very vocal species but utters a sharp 'chit' and sings a short song of sparrow-like notes. **862**

3 **SHAFT-TAILED WHYDAH** (Pylstertrooibekkie) *Vidua regia*. Recorded only August-March. Seasonally common in the Nwambiya sandveld of the north-east and immediately south, on the eastern border. Uncommon elsewhere in the north and central region, and unrecorded in the southern region. The male is unmistakable, the four tail feathers thin but stiff with bulbous ends. The female has its head less distinctly marked than other whydah females, but is difficult to identify unless accompanied by males. Young birds resemble the female but lack white on the underparts, and are more generally russet-brown. Often occurs in flocks of both sexes with immature birds and frequents thorn scrub and open ground, the males acting in a lively, aggressive manner and disturbing other small birds when feeding. Parasitises the Violeteared Waxbill (Plate 104) and possibly others as yet unidentified. **861**

10cm

PLATE 102

1 **STEELBLUE WIDOWFINCH** (Staalblouvinkie) *Vidua chalybeata*. An uncommon but fairly widespread resident species. Recorded throughout the year and most commonly in the central and northern regions; rather scarce in the south. Both male and female can be distinguished from the next two species only by bill and leg colour. The male is conspicuous during the breeding season, spending much time singing from the top of a bush. Parasitises the Redbilled Firefinch (Plate 105). Has a short song, containing many notes of the Redbilled Firefinch.   **867**

2 **BLACK WIDOWFINCH** (Gewone Blouvinkie) *Vidua funerea*. An uncommon but widespread resident species. Recorded throughout the year, most commonly in the central and northern regions. Both sexes differ from the previous and next species in bill colour, otherwise behave in a very similar manner. Parasitises the Bluebilled Firefinch (Plate 105). Has a chattering little song, incorporating many notes of its host species, sung by the male during the breeding season.   **864**

PURPLE WIDOWFINCH (Witpootblouvinkie) *Vidua purpurascens*. Rare. A few records exist for this species over the length of the Park, most from the far north. Exact status uncertain. Exactly similar to (1) and (2) but bill and legs, in both sexes, are white. Parasitises Jameson's Firefinch (Plate 105) and should therefore be more common and widespread. Mimics the song of its host species.   **865**

3 **CUCKOO FINCH** (Koekoekvink) *Anomalospiza imberbis*. Rare. Two sightings have been made in summer, both in the Olifants River/Bangu Gorge region. Status uncertain. Both sexes have the appearance of weavers in breeding or non-breeding plumage; cf. species on Plate 99. The stout, conical bill and smaller, generally thickset appearance of the Cuckoo Finch serve to distinguish it from weavers but certain identification is difficult at all times. Usually occurs in flocks in open grassland near water. Parasitises prinias and cisticolas (Plates 83-85). Makes various weaver-like chattering and swizzling sounds. The male has a squeaky song 'tsileu, tsileu, tsileu . . .'   **820**

Mannikins, finches, twinspots and waxbills. Family ESTRILDIDAE. Treated by some authorities as a sub-family of the family Ploceidae. Very small, colourful seed-eating birds, which occur in dry thornveld or in riverbeds, often in flocks, and feed on small seeds obtained directly from grasses and weeds or from the ground.

4 **REDBACKED MANNIKIN** (Rooirugfret) *Spermestes bicolor*. Rare resident, but recorded at points throughout the Park. Breeds September-May. Nearly always occurs in flocks, the adults with their black heads and mantles and reddish-brown backs being conspicuous both at rest and in flight. Most flocks contain some immature birds. Is found in grassy regions, especially near rivers. The call is a clear whistle uttered in flight by most adults in a flock.   **858**

5 **BRONZE MANNIKIN** (Gewone Fret) *Spermestes cucullatus*. Fairly common in the north and south of the Park, uncommon elsewhere. Resident. Slightly smaller and less colourful than the previous species, otherwise of very similar habits. Compare the immature with that of the Pintailed Whydah (Plate 101). Always occurs in small flocks, feeding on tall grass stems or on the ground and favouring dry riverbeds. The call is a husky 'chik, chik, chikka'. Song 'chi-chu, chi-chu, che-ri-hit-chu'.   **857**

10cm

PLATE 103

1 QUAIL FINCH (Gewone Kwartelvinkie) *Ortygospiza atricollis*. Uncommon through-out the Park. There are no breeding records. A very small terrestrial finch of shy disposition, flushing immediately when approached. Partial to areas of open ground, especially near water, and may sometimes be seen coming to drink at small pools. Appear to move frequently to new locations, their characteristic calls being heard as they pass overhead; a melancholy, metallic 'tink-tink'.   **852**

2 GREEN TWINSPOT (Groenrobbin) *Mandingoa nitidula*. Rare, exact status un-known. Has been seen at Skukuza and at two points in the far north. Very small, mostly green bird with black underparts spotted white, red face in male, yellow face in female. In the KNP occurs in small flocks in broadleafed forest fringes and in secondary growth in riverine forests, emerging to feed on open ground. Of extremely shy disposition. A small 'tseet' is heard as individuals fly away.   **835**

3 CUTTHROAT FINCH (Bandkeelvink) *Amadina fasciata*. Uncommon resident. Has been recorded at scattered localities throughout the Park. Breeding has been recorded in the abandoned nests of the Redheaded Weaver (Plate 99). The male is unmistakable; the female with its scaly-looking plumage is less easily identified but is usually seen with the male or as part of a small flock. Frequents the drier bushveld regions and often associates with other small seed-eaters. The call is a high-pitched 'eee-eee-eee' in flight.   **855**

4 MELBA FINCH (Gewone Melba) *Pytilia melba*. Fairly common and resident, found throughout the Park in suitable habitat. Breeds October-March. Both sexes distinc-tive; red bill always present. Occurs in pairs in dry thornbush, especially along dry watercourses, where it feeds on the ground, often with other waxbills. The normal call is 'wick'; also has a sweet but quiet rambling song.   **834**

5 REDTHROATED TWINSPOT (Rooikeelrobbin) *Hypargos niveoguttatus*. Rare and very localised. Recorded only in the Nyandu bush of the Nwambiya sandveld, where it is probably resident. The male is unmistakable when good views are obtained, but this highly active species usually darts off when disturbed. It often pauses to perch briefly before entering a thicket, however, and affords the observer a brief view. Unless the white spots of the underparts are seen, can be mistaken for a firefinch (Plate 105). The female has a yellowish throat and orange-red breast. The call is a grasshopper-like trill 'trree-rree'.   **839**

6 PINKTHROATED TWINSPOT (Rooskeelrobbin) *Hypargos margaritatus*. Rare. Re-corded only in the Nyandu bush of the Nwambiya sandveld and in the extreme south-east. Very similar to (5) but pink not red, the female pale grey on face and breast, washed cinnamon. Like (5) feeds on open ground but darts off into a thicket when disturbed. The call is a weak, ringing trill 'tit-it-it-it-it-' or 'trrr-it'.   **838**

10cm

PLATE 104

1 ORANGEBREASTED WAXBILL (Rooiassie) *Sporaeginthus subflavus*. Rare. Has been seen August-February over the length of the Park. Probably a seasonal, non-breeding visitor. A very small waxbill with yellow underparts and orange upper and under tail coverts, the orange breast-patch of the male variable in extent. Occurs in small flocks in waterside reeds and grasses. Very active little birds, with the habit of swivelling from side to side while perched on a grass or reed stem. Utters a quiet, tinkling sound in flight. **854**

2 BLACKCHEEKED WAXBILL (Swartwangsysie) *Estrilda erythronotos*. Rare, exact status uncertain. Recorded both in the far north and the south February-November. Distinctive when well viewed but easily overlooked. May be seen in small flocks or together with other waxbills, frequenting dry thornveld. The contact call between members of a flock is a mournful, descending 'fwooee'. **847**

3 BLUE WAXBILL (Gewone Blousysie) *Uraeginthus angolensis*. Very common to abundant throughout the Park. The most frequently seen waxbill in all regions, breeding throughout the summer. The only small, pale blue bird in the Park, males with a greater extent of blue than the females. Occurs in pairs or flocks, often with allied species, and feeds on the ground in clearings or tracks, mostly in thornveld. When disturbed flies off to the nearest bush uttering its characteristic call 'weety-weet' or 'weet-weet', heard almost continually in some regions. **844**

4 COMMON WAXBILL (Rooibeksysie) *Estrilda astrild*. Fairly common and wide-spread throughout the Park in suitable localities. Resident, but breeding records are lacking. The red face and beak are conspicuous if good views are obtained. Usually occurs in flocks, at times as many as several dozen individuals which frequent reeds and sedges in riverbeds, marshy areas and adjacent open lands. Flocks are constantly on the move, individuals streaming off one after another from place to place. Has the habit of flirting its tail in a sideways movement when perched. The flock maintains a constant reedy twittering. Individuals call 'chewi-chee, chewi-chee'. **846**

5 VIOLETEARED WAXBILL (Koningblousysie) *Uraeginthus granatinus*. Occurs as a rare summer vagrant in the central and southern regions, and as a fairly common resident in the Nyandu bush of the Nwambiya sandveld. There are no breeding records. The unique colours of both sexes, plus the longish tails, distinguish this species immediately. Usually in pairs, often associating with (3) and frequenting dry, sandy country. The most commonly heard call is a repeated 'tiu-woowee', but also has a weak tinkling song. **845**

10cm

PLATE 105

Firefinches. This group of very small seed-eating birds is represented in the Park by three species, all very similar. Observation and identification is usually very difficult because of their small size and wariness. Firefinches feed on the ground in small clearings or on dusty tracks in thornveld and take refuge in bushes when disturbed.

1 REDBILLED FIREFINCH (Rooibekrobbin) *Lagonosticta senegala.* Common and widespread. A resident species which prefers dense thorn scrub near watercourses. The least ruddy of the three firefinches, the female having only the upper tail coverts red. The only firefinch with a pinkish bill, pale at the base, and pink legs. Has more white breast spots than either (2) or (3). Usually found in pairs or small groups and often associates with Blue Waxbills (Plate 104). The call is a slightly nasal 'fweet, fweet'. **842**

2 BLUEBILLED FIREFINCH (Kaapse Robbin) *Lagonosticta rubricata.* Common and widespread. A resident species found in tangled thickets, especially on riverbanks. Both sexes have a distinct *grey-brown cap* and mantle, blackish bills, which are pink at the base of the lower mandible, and grey legs. The male has a black belly. The characteristic call is a bell-like trilling 'trrrrrr-wink-wink', plus a stuttering alarm call. **840**

3 JAMESON'S FIREFINCH (Jamesonse Robbin) *Lagonosticta rhodopareia.* Fairly common resident north of the Sabie River, uncommon in the south. The most ruddy of the firefinches, having little contrast between upper and lower parts. Has no distinct mantle and cap like (2), although the bill and leg colouring is similar. Shares the same habitat as (2) and has a similar call-note. **841**

4 SWEE WAXBILL (Suidelike Swie) *Estrilda melanotis.* Rare and localised. Recorded only in the south-west between Pretoriuskop and the Crocodile River, notably July-August. A distinctive waxbill, unlikely to be confused with any other, the red rump in both sexes showing boldly when the birds fly. Occurs in small flocks, frequenting wooded streams in hilly country. Settles on grass heads to take the seeds, in addition to small insects. When flushed flies off calling 'swee, swee'. **850**

10cm

PLATE 106

Canaries and buntings. Family FRINGILLIDAE. Seed-eating birds with fairly stout, conical bills and, in many cases, good singing repertoires.

1 YELLOWEYED CANARY (Geeloogkanarie) *Serinus mozambicus*. A very common resident throughout the Park. Breeding has been recorded December-February. The dark facial markings are diagnostic. In flight displays a yellow rump, this and (4) being the only yellow-rumped canaries in the region. Occurs usually in flocks in mixed bushveld, frequenting both trees and grass. Contact call 'tseeoo'. Also has an attractive song uttered from treetops during the breeding season. **869**

2 BULLY CANARY (Dikbekkanarie) *Serinus sulphuratus*. Rare. Exact status uncertain. A few records exist for the east and north of the Park. Larger, stockier and *heavier-billed* than (1) or (3). Likely to be seen in large riverine trees where it feeds on hard seeds; also forages on the ground. Singly or in small flocks. The song is an unhurried jumble of husky trills and warbles. **877**

3 CAPE CANARY (Kaapse Kanarie) *Serinus canicollis*. Rare. Exact status uncertain. Has been seen on two occasions in the Letaba-Olifants region. The grey mantle is the identifying feature of this canary. An unobtrusive species unless heard singing, spending much time in the upper branches of large trees, usually in small flocks. Has a prolonged, sweet song; the normal call 'sweet'. **872**

4 BLACKTHROATED CANARY (Bergkanarie) *Serinus atrogularis*. Rare. Probably a casual visitor. Recorded in the far north and south during September-December. A nondescript little bird which, however, displays a bright yellow rump in flight; cf. (1). The black throat may be vestigial or entirely absent. Occurs in small flocks and usually feeds on grass-heads. Has a melodious 'swee' call and a very good song given from a treetop. **870**

5 STREAKYHEADED CANARY (Streepkopkanarie) *Serinus gularis*. Uncommon, but probably resident. Has been recorded at points all over the Park in both summer and winter. The streaks on the crown of the head are not easily seen, but a diagnostic feature is the bold white eyebrow, shared with the similarly coloured Yellowthroated Sparrow (Plate 97). Normal call a chirruping 'see-e-ee'; also has an attractive but short song. **881**

6 LEMONBREASTED CANARY (Geelborskanarie) *Serinus citrinipectus*. Fairly common, localised resident. So far recorded only in the far north. Told by small size, male with buffy flanks and belly, female with entirely buffy underparts, yellow rump; cf. Yelloweyed Canary (1). Has a pretty song with a sparrow-like tone. Small flocks occur in woodland where they are attracted to seeding grasses. Nomadic when not breeding. **871**

PLATE 107

1 LARKLIKE BUNTING (Vaalstreepkoppie) *Emberiza impetuani.* Normally absent in the Park but sudden large-scale irruptions occur in years of low rainfall, at which times it becomes locally abundant. A small, nondescript bunting lacking diagnostic features. Occurs in nomadic flocks which feed on seeding grasses or congregate at water. Walks on the ground (does not hop), and flushes reluctantly. On take-off and in flight makes a nasal 'chut'; the song is a rapidly delivered 'trrrooo-cheeoo-cheep-trree' repeated frequently. **887**

2 ROCK BUNTING (Klipstreepkoppie) *Emberiza tahapisi.* A common and widespread resident species, numbers being greater in summer, at which time it breeds. A distinctive inhabitant of rocky or stony regions, spending much of its time on the ground. The sexes are similar, the female being a dull version of the male. The male has a short but distinctive song 'tee-trrr, chirri-chee'. **886**

3 GOLDENBREASTED BUNTING (Rooirugstreepkoppie) *Emberiza flaviventris.* Common throughout the Park, breeding November-January. The combination of yellow underparts and black head with white stripes is unique. In the female the head and mantle colours are less strong. Occurs in a variety of bushveld habitats, even in very dry areas, and spends much time on the ground. Calls 'sker-cheeew, sker-cheeew, pitchu-pitchu-pitchu...', the last phrase uttered about six times. **884**

4 CAPE BUNTING (Rooivlerkstreepkoppie) *Emberiza capensis.* Rare. Has been recorded a few times June-October in the east and north. Probably a non-breeding vagrant. Might be confused with (2) but is dusky off-white on the underparts and is larger. Usually occurs in hilly, rocky regions. The call is a loud 'wheeooowhee', plus a short, variable song. **885**

10 cm

APPENDIX

This list comprises species in need of further verification or those regarded as accidental vagrants.

ANGOLA PITTA (Angolapitta) *Pitta angolensis*. Rare vagrant. **491**

AUGUR BUZZARD (Witborsjakkalsvoël) *Buteo augur*. Old records only; no new sightings. **153**

BALD IBIS (Kalkoenibis) *Geronticus calvus*. Rare vagrant. **92**

BARTAILED GODWIT (Bandstertgriet) *Limosa lapponica*. Rare vagrant. **288**

BLACK SAW-WING SWALLOW (Swartsaagvlerkswael) *Psalidoprocne holomelas*. Rare vagrant. **536**

BLACKCHESTED PRINIA (Swartbandlangstertjie) *Prinia flavicans*. Rare vagrant. **685**

BLACKWINGED PRATINCOLE (Swartvlerksprinkaanvoël) *Glareola nordmanni*. Rare vagrant. **305**

CAPE BATIS (Kaapse Bosbontrokkie) *Batis capensis*. Rare vagrant. **700**

CAPE SHOVELLER (Kaapse Slopeend) *Anas smithii*. Rare vagrant. **112**

CAPE WEAVER (Kaapse Wewer) *Ploceus capensis*. Verification needed. **813**

COLLARED PALM THRUSH (Palmmôrelyster) *Cichladusa arquata*. Rare vagrant. **603**

DUNLIN (Bontstrandloper) *Calidris alpina*. Rare passage migrant. **273**

FOREST WEAVER (Bosmusikant) *Ploceus bicolor*. Verification needed. **808**

GOLDEN PIPIT (Goudkoester) *Tmetothylacus tenellus*. Rare intra-Africa migrant. **726**

GOLDENBACKED PYTILIA (Geelrugmelba) *Pytilia afra*. Verification needed. **833**

GRASSBIRD (Grasvoël) *Sphenoeacus afer*. Status uncertain; one record only. **661**

GREY WAGTAIL (Gryskwikkie) *Motacilla cinerea*. Rare Palaearctic visitor. **715**

GREY WAXBILL (Gryssysie) *Estrilda perreini*. Rare vagrant. **848**

GROUND WOODPECKER (Grondspeg) *Geocolaptes olivaceus*. Rare vagrant. **480**

KALAHARI ROBIN (Kalahariwipstert) *Erythropygia paena*. Rare vagrant. **615**

KNYSNA LOURIE (Knysnaloerie) *Tauraco corythaix*. Rare vagrant. **370**

LONGTAILED WIDOW (Langstertflap) *Euplectes progne*. Rare vagrant. **832**

PALMNUT VULTURE (Witaasvoël) *Gypohierax angolensis*. Rare vagrant. **147**

PECTORAL SANDPIPER (Geelpootstrandloper) *Calidris melanotos*. Rare passage migrant. **279**

PIED BABBLER (Witkatlagter) *Turdoides bicolor*. Rare vagrant. **563**

PURPLE GALLINULE (Grootkoningriethaan) *Porphyrio porphyrio*. Rare vagrant. **223**

REDEYED BULBUL (Rooioogtiptol) *Pycnonotus nigricans*. Verification needed. **567**

REDFRONTED TINKER BARBET (Rooiblestinker) *Pogoniulus pusillus*. Rare vagrant. **469**

REDNECKED PHALAROPE (Rooihalsfraiingpoot) *Phalaropus lobatus*. Rare passage migrant. **292**

REDSHANK (Rooipootruiter) *Tringa totanus*. Rare vagrant. **268**

REDWINGED WARBLER (Rooivlerksanger) *Heliolais erythroptera*. Verification needed. **682**

ROSYFACED LOVEBIRD (Rooiwangparkiet) *Agapornis roseicollis*. Aviary escapees. **367**

SOOTY TERN (Roetsterretjie) *Sterna fuscata*. Accidental cyclone-blown vagrant. **332**

SPOTTED CREEPER (Boomkruiper) *Salpornis spilonotus*. Rare vagrant. One old record. **559**

SQUARETAILED DRONGO (Kleinbyvanger) *Dicrurus ludwigii*. Verification needed. **542**

Glossary of Terms Used

Accipiter: specifically, sparrowhawks and goshawks. Long-tailed, short-winged raptors with long, unfeathered legs and long toes; they specialise in catching small birds in swift pursuit from a standing start.

Afrotropical Region that region of Africa south of the Palaearctic region; the Tropic of Cancer roughly forms its northern limit.

Aggregation: a gathering of birds brought about by some common interest, such as a temporary food availability, after which individuals disperse separately.

Altitudinal Migrant: birds which move seasonally from one altitude to another.

Bush: refers to any terrain with bushes or trees of moderate height, as opposed to the more luxuriant growth of true forest.

Conspecific: being of the same species.

Cover: in ornithological terms, shelter provided by vegetation.

Crepuscular: active at dusk. When applied to most crepuscular birds, usually infers that they are active in the half-light hours, *dawn* and dusk.

Dam: a man-made water-catchment area.

Dispersal: refers to a more or less random centrifugal movement away from the breeding locality, but does not amount to true migration.

Display: a term used to denote actions that have become specialised in the course of evolution. Examples are threat display, submissive display, greeting display, social displays, etc.

Egg-dumping: the habit among secondary females in such social species as guinea-fowls, the Ostrich and others of laying their eggs in the nest of another, usually the dominant female. Can also refer to egg-laying at random in places other than nests by immature or unmated hens.

Ethiopian Region: Africa south of the Palaearctic Region; now being increasingly replaced by the term AFROTROPICAL REGION.

Falcon: small, swift-flying raptors with pointed wings; they specialise in catching flying birds by means of a fast descent from above, known as a 'stoop'.

Flats: level grassland.

Fledgling: a young bird that has recently acquired its first feathers.

Flock: a group of birds that moves as a more or less cohesive unit.

Gamebird: a somewhat outdated term used by hunters. Refers to ducks, geese, pheasants, partridges, francolins, guineafowls, quails and others. In the past bustards were also included in this category.

Graduated Tail: a tail in which the central feathers are the longest and all others progressively shorter, the outermost being the shortest.

Immature: a young bird, independent of its parents but not yet having acquired adult plumage. In raptors, birds may retain immature plumage for several years.

Intra-Africa Migrant: birds that migrate regularly within the African continent.

Juvenile: in respect of birds, usually refers to a young bird still wearing its first plumage, but is often loosely applied.

Kloof: a cleft or valley, usually with steeply inclined or rocky sides, often well wooded.

Koppie: a small hill, often with a rocky summit.

Local Movement: refers to mass movements, which are not necessarily regular, by birds within a comparatively small area.

Migration: the regular movement of birds between two alternative regions inhabited by them at different times of the year, one region in which they breed and the other region used by them in the opposite season.

Mopane: vernacular name for a bush or tree of the species *Colophospermum mopane.* In some regions, remains as a smallish bush, in other regions may grow to a height of about 12 metres. The leaves are a rounded heart shape, and reddish when young.

Morph: a permanent but alternative plumage colour.

Palaearctic Region: the northern hemisphere, incorporating North Africa, Europe, Scandinavia and Asia.

Pan (or floodpan) denotes a natural depression which fills with water as the result of heavy local rains or river spillage.

Parkland: regions with trees of moderate height and well-developed canopies so spaced as not to interlock; usually without any secondary growth but with well-grassed soil.

Passerine: birds that habitually sing or call and that have 'normal' feet with three toes facing forward and one backward. Also known as perching birds. Excludes all birds with webbed, semi-webbed, lobed or zygodactylous feet.

Range Expansion: a gradual or abrupt process tending to enlarge a species' breeding range.

Raptor: a bird of prey: one which hunts and kills other animals for food. Includes the vultures.

Recurved: bending upwards.

Riparian: of or on riverbanks.

Speculum: a patch of iridescent colour on the wings of certain birds, especially ducks.

Tail-streamer: elongated tail-feathers, usually the central ones.

Understory: secondary growth found in well-wooded or forested regions, usually consists of young trees, small bushes and annual plants.

Veld: a term used loosely in reference to various types of terrain, thus grassveld, bushveld, etc.

Watercourse: refers to rivers that flow only during good rains and are dry the rest of the year.

Waterhole: refers to any natural or man-made water point used by animals for drinking.

Woodland: regions with trees of moderate height and well-developed canopies which are so spaced as not to interlock; may cover flattish ground or hillsides, with or without well-developed secondary growth or ground cover.

Zygodactyl: feet which, in certain non-passerine birds, have two toes directed forward and two backward. Is seen in cuckoos, barbets, woodpeckers, honeyguides and others.

Index to Scientific Names

236

Index to Afrikaans Names

Index to English Names